LIFE IN THE 1870s

LIFE IN THE 1870s

seen through advertisements in The Times

Edited & with an Introduction by R. H. Langbridge

Times Books

First published in volume
form in 1974 by Times Books,
the book publishing imprint of
Times Newspapers Limited,
New Printing House Square,
London WC1X 8EZ

ISBN 0 7230 0114 6

Designed by Ted Trott
Printed in Great Britain by
Tinling (1973) Ltd., Prescot, Merseyside
(a member of the Oxley Printing Group Ltd.)

CONTENTS

INTRODUCTION

Perhaps the most widely accepted view of the Victorian era is that it represented an unbroken sixty-four years of progress, prosperity and peace, a time when man achieved a comfortable compromise with God and Mammon and self-help brought its just reward. This over-optimistic picture scarcely squares with the facts.

First, it should be emphasised that the Victorians witnessed tremendous changes in almost every sphere of life: politics, industry, communications, the army, education, medicine, housing, and living standards generally. Second, although many were able to combine a limited Christianity with the pursuit of self-interest, a growing number of intellectuals and reformers were beset by perplexity and doubt as a result of the writings of Darwin and other scientists, who had aroused grave misgivings about the truth of the Bible. Moreover, just as the 1970s differ from the 1960s or 1950s, so it was in Victorian times, with each decade having its own problems and characteristics.

The fact that historians, novelists, playwrights and film producers have since presented such conflicting views of the period has added to the general confusion.

One source of background material that has been little used for research is the advertising of the contemporary press. And in this respect, where better to study the way people lived, worked and amused themselves than in the columns of *The Times*? Here, in immense detail, are to be found the myriad facts that, taken together, make up the mosaic of Victorian life.

By providing facsimile advertisements for many types of goods and services, selected at intervals during the 1870s, together with a certain amount of background information, we have tried to provide a more accurate and more entertaining picture of the decade than can be obtained by any comparable means.

In the 1870s, advertisements in *The Times* were not yet classified under sectional headings but, nevertheless, the categories were grouped together, often in the same position on the same page each day, so that regular readers had little difficulty in finding them.

The subjects of these announcements have scarcely changed in a hundred years: theatres, concerts, exhibitions, property, business opportunities, food, drink, clothes, furnishings, hotels and board residence, situations wanted and vacant, books and magazines, schools, musical instruments, apartments (the word 'flat' was not yet in common use), travel, patent medicines, and many household requirements ranging from coal to washing. Among the few categories absent, from today's papers is 'Horses and Carriages'.

For actual content, the 'Personal' column has probably changed least. There were the same cries for help, instructions for furtive correspondence and clandestine meetings, details about missing pets and articles lost and found, and the rewards offered.

Occasionally, these announcements provide clues to history as, for example, the many messages in French that appeared towards the end of 1870. These were from refugees separated from families and friends during the Franco-Prussian war, a conflict in which British sympathies lay with the Prussians rather than with the French.

In 1870 Queen Victoria was fifty years old and had been a widow for fifteen years. Edward, Prince of Wales, was twenty-nine. Gladstone, who had led the Liberals to victory in 1868, was Prime Minister until 1874, when Disraeli brought the Conservatives back to power.

Income tax in 1870 was fourpence

in the pound for incomes above £150 a year. Later in the decade the top figure was sixpence, and the lowest, twopence in the pound. The Bank rate, too, fluctuated considerably. In 1870 alone it changed at least nine times, veering between two-and-a-half and six per cent.

For the first year or two of the decade trade and industry continued to expand at a tremendous rate. Exports of coal, iron, steel and machinery were the highest in the world. Shipbuilding, too, grew proportionately to carry the huge increase in foreign trade. All the new ships were built of iron and powered by steam. To emphasise this point, shipping companies usually began their advertisements with the word 'steam' – 'Steam to Colombo', or 'Melbourne by new screw steamship'. A few combined sail and steam. Unfortunately, these boom conditions did not last, mainly because of foreign competition. To make matters worse British agriculture not only experienced several bad harvests in quick succession but also began to feel the effects of cheaply-produced wheat from Canada, the United States and Australia, and of chilled beef from the Argentine. However, this accumulation of troubles did have a bright side; it reduced the price of certain foodstuffs. This, in addition to the higher wages now earned by skilled workers, brought about a new demand for meat, tea, coffee, sugar and other items previously beyond the purchasing power of working-class families.

The population of the United Kingdom at the 1871 census was 27,431,000, as compared with 20,183,000 in 1841. Emigration figures to the United States, Canada, Australia, New Zealand and other places totalled 202,511 in 1870 and 238,345 in 1877.

According to the *British Almanac* for 1871 there were some 2,000,000 horses in Britain, of which 13,000 were employed in London to draw omnibuses and cabs. The total number of horse-drawn vehicles to enter the City of London each morning was 60,000.

In London the human death rate per thousand was 24.4 during the period 1863–70, but improved to 22.7 for the years 1871–77. These totals are roughly double those of the present day. The considerable improvement in public health figures in London was undoubtedly due to the completely new systems for sewage and water supplies put in hand during the 1860s. Outside London the figures were 30 per thousand in Glasgow, 26 in Manchester and Edinburgh, and 24 in Liverpool.

As a guide to the main causes of death during the period we quote the official statistics for 1877, which listed ailments in this order: consumption, bronchitis, atrophy and debility, old age, convulsions, heart disease, pneumonia, diarrhoea, typhus, scarlatina, whooping cough, cancer. The actual figures for consumption, heart disease and cancer were 118,003, 46,499, and 18,000 respectively.

Although smallpox does not figure among the top twelve killing diseases, one notes that during the same year there were no fewer than 846 patients at one time in Metropolitan hospitals.

Overeating rarely kills, but it can result in many distressing and uncomfortable symptoms. Judging from the advertisements included under 'Medicinal and Dental', gluttony was widespread. Many of the patent medicines on the market were intended to relieve indigestion, acidity, flatulence, heartburn, headache, bile, giddiness, spasms and liver complaints. When one considers the huge meals eaten by the middle and upper classes, it seems hardly surprising.

Although Britain was not involved in any major war during the 1870s, there were various minor engagements in different parts of the world. Major-General Sir Garnet Wolseley (he was knighted in 1870 after suppressing the Red River rebellion in Canada), known as 'the master of the small war', dealt with the troubles in Ashanti and Zululand with the economy and dispatch that eventually led to his appointment as Commander-in-Chief of the Army.

Among army reforms, put through in the face of fierce opposition, were the abolition of the purchase system of commissions and of flogging, and the introduction of new conditions of enlistment.

The decade was noteworthy for many much-needed reforms, including competitive examinations for entering the Civil Service; the Metropolitan Water Act for providing a continuous supply of filtered water; the Education Act, which provided for state elementary schools where those provided by voluntary bodies were insufficient or non-existent; the Ballot Act, whereby voting was done in secret and thus bribery and intimidation avoided; the Factory Act, limiting the working week to 56½ hours; and the Merchant Shipping Act, which laid down new regulations regarding the working conditions of seamen and the seaworthiness of ships.

The growth of industry in London and other cities resulted in a demand for new housing for both workers and the prosperous middle class. In addition, local civic pride demanded town halls, churches, libraries, picture galleries and other new buildings.

A survey of architectural improvements in the *British Almanac* spoke highly of the new Eddystone Lighthouse, the Cathedral at Edinburgh, York's Fine Art Exhibition Hall, the Reform Club in Liverpool, the County Hospital at Chesterfield and the Town Hall at Great Yarmouth, among others. The writer spoke of the revival in Queen Anne red brick in London, and of 'the elaborate and showy decorations of buildings known under the title of Restaurants . . . by no means free from vulgarity and ostentation'. His criticism here was directed at the Criterion, Holborn, and Gaiety restaurants, all of which had contributed largely to the new fashion enabling a man and his family to enjoy a well-prepared and inexpensive meal outside the home.

East of Temple Bar was still mainly male territory, although after-theatre dinners in Fleet Street became popular towards the end of the decade. A cut from the joint with vegetables could cost as little as 8d. at lunchtime, with a penny tip for the waiter. Better places might charge up to 2s. 6d. In the evening, a three-course dinner seldom cost more than 3s. 6d.

Routledge's Guide to London informs visitors that West End apartments may be obtained from 10s. a week for a single room, use of sitting room, and attendance.

The same authority quotes terms of 1s. to 5s. for bed and breakfast at small hotels, coffee houses and taverns. Meals were obtainable from just 1s.

As will be seen from the advertisements for 'Hotels and Board Residence', full board at a good hotel, with one's own suite of rooms, cost about £3 a week. Board residence terms varied from 25s. to 42s. a week according to the locality. A suite of furnished rooms at a good address in the West End cost about 42s. a week, while unfurnished apartments were between £40 and £70 a year. Similar prices were charged for office accommodation.

As examples of other everyday prices, popular daily newspapers cost a penny, but *The Times* and *Morning Post* were each threepence. Postage was one penny for a letter and a halfpenny for a postcard. It is interesting to note that there were twelve deliveries daily within a three-mile radius of the London Post Office, and eleven deliveries in other areas.

Telegrams cost 1s. for the first twenty words and another 3d. for every additional five words.

Fares for travelling about London were as follows: by omnibus, the average was just under 3d.; by Metropolitan Railway, the fare from Moorgate to say, Praed Street, was 6d., 4d. or 3d., according to whether you travelled first, second or third class; cab fares (four-wheeled cabriolet or two-wheeled hansom) were 1s. for up to two miles and 6d. for each additional mile or part of a mile. By river steamer the fare was 6d. from Chelsea to London Bridge and 1d. for short stages.

Fares to different parts of the country by railway were reduced by the middle of the decade as a result of competition between the various independent companies. The standard rate then became 1d. a mile third class, and 1½d. a mile first class.

Many examples of the cost of travelling by steamer are to be found under 'Travel Overseas'. A first class rail and steamer return ticket to Paris cost £2.8s.; third class was exactly half this amount.

Return fare to New York, with saloon accommodation, cost 25 guineas. A first class suite to New Orleans was £23, steerage £9. To Melbourne, it cost from £50 for first class accommodation, and from £25 by second class.

The agent for the 900-ton *Shooting Star*, bound for Colombo, reassures its passengers that it will not carry manure. This would be particularly good news for those sailing through the newly-opened Suez Canal during the hot season.

Free passage to Queensland was available to emigrating agricultural labourers and domestic servants.

At home, domestic servants of all types, from butler to housemaid and footman to page, were in steady demand, as will be seen under 'Situations'. Everyone wanted 'a good plain cook'. Wages were around £25 to £30 a year, and all found. Some were expected to bake bread, cure hams and make good butter. Housemaids had to be neat and respectable, good needlewomen, and able to wait well at table. For this they were paid £18 a year, beer money, and all found.

Male servants had to be sober, industrious and respectable, in addition to being able to wait at table and clean plate well.

Respectability, above all, was an essential qualification. 'Only those of undeniable respectability', 'Must be highly respectable', are examples of phrases that recur constantly in advertisements. One is also struck by the number of advertisers for office staff who demand references *and* security. Presumably dishonest book-keepers and clerks were not uncommon. Even so, it could be a trifle hard on the applicant, as, for example:

> SECRETARY. Duties light
> and gentlemanly. Salary £150
> rising to £250. *Security £250.*

Although only a small proportion of advertisers quote salaries, there are enough to give a good idea of contemporary rates of pay: Junior clerk, 15s. weekly; Clerk (24) with unexceptional (*sic*) references, £80 p.a.; Book-keeper, £130 to commence; Lawyer's clerk, £120 and prospects. And what of the 'experienced accountant' who offered 'to post books and audit accounts for 5s. weekly'? Surely a desperate attempt to add to a small salary by some spare-time work?

Almost the only job available to a respectable young woman was that of governess. Salaries ranged from about £20 p.a., with all found, to £100 or more for 'finishing' governesses with special qualifications.

According to the *British Almanac*, the new salary scale for London School Board teachers was as follows: headmaster (average) £203; headmistress, £130.10s.; assistant master, £105; assistant mistress, £78. We are told that these salaries were 'far in excess of that obtained in the majority of the elementary schools of the Kingdom before the passing of the Act of 1870'.

Schools for young gentlemen and young ladies were extensively advertised in *The Times*. Inclusive terms were mostly between 25 and 75 guineas a year, although a surprising number were prepared to reduce their fees.

A school fifteen miles from London

offered 'reciprocal terms' (free education?) to the daughters of grocers or drapers. A few establishments stated 'no holydays unless required'.

One announcement with faintly sinister undertones refers to a clergyman of thirty years' experience who claims: 'unmanageable and backward boys made perfectly tractable and gentlemanly in one year'. He goes on to refer to his 'peculiarly persuasive system and high moral and religious training that elevates children of peculiar tempers and dispositions to the level of others'. Unlike some advertisers, there is no mention here of 'corporal punishment dispensed with'.

An important status symbol of Victorian times was a horse and carriage. For any aspiring middle class family it was essential for paying calls and shopping. The cost could be quite considerable: anything between £65 and £300 for a carriage, another £50 or £70 for a horse, not to mention stabling, feed, and a coachman's wages and uniform. However, facilities were available for spreading payments over three years and livery stables abounded where one could hire by the hour, day or month.

Higher up the social scale a household would own several horse-drawn vehicles selected from the variety obtainable: brougham, phaeton, barouche, landau, victoria and waggonette among them.

A number of announcements under 'Food and Drink' give prices, from which it is possible to get an idea of the cost of living. For instance, best English meat was obtainable for less than a shilling a pound. Tinned Australian mutton, with little waste, was 8d. per lb. Turkeys and ducks cost 1s. per lb.; geese, 9d.; rabbits, 8d.; hares, 7½d.; and prime chickens, 2s. 3d. each. Tinned curried fowl was 4s. or 7s. 6d.; tinned rabbit, 3s. or 5s. 6d.

At the beginning of the seventies rather more coffee than tea was imported, but the consumption of tea quickly passed that of coffee, with cocoa a poor third. Cheap teas (often adulterated) were available at 2s. 3d. per lb., coffee at 1s. 6d., and cocoa at 1s. Potatoes by the sack cost about 1d. per lb., and bread was about 8d. for a loaf weighing 4 lbs. Butter was 1s. 2d. per lb., and milk about 2d. a pint.

The price of spirits, per dozen bottles, was: whisky, 36s.; brandy, 33s.; gin, 29s. Champagne was from 36s. per dozen; claret from 14s.; hock from 24s.; sherry and port from 24s.; burgundy from 15s. Bass Pale Ale was 3s. 6d. per dozen pints.

Coal could be bought at 24s. per ton, but Victorians were fussy about their coal and chose from a dozen or more named varieties, the dearest of which, Best Wall's-end, was 35s. per ton. Other favourites were Silkstone (31s.), Derby Brights (28s.) and Parkgate House (26s.). Coke cost 20s. per 12 sacks, delivered to your door.

An entry in the Rev. Francis Kilvert's *Diary, 1870–79*, provides a revealing glimpse of money standards: 'The Gore's of Whitty Mill are very well-off, make at least £200 a year.' But what was considered well off by a country parson was seen in a different light by the editor of *The Ladies' Treasury*. In answer to a correspondent, she wrote: 'Although I have gladly santioned your marriage upon so small an income as £200 a year . . . I warn you that your daily life will be one of make-shifts and contrivances even for comfort . . . .'

No doubt £200 was enough to support a young married couple, but as few Victorians practised birth control, families grew year by year, which must have thrown a heavy strain on household budgets. Eventually, it would mean moving to a bigger house with more bedrooms and more servants. And according to Mrs Beeton, one needed at least one servant on £200 p.a., two on £300, and five on £1,000.

Confirmation that large houses were in demand can be found in the 'property' advertisements, which also show that prices were geared to the

Many leisure activities were centred on the home: musical evenings, magic lantern shows, charades, conjuring and card games being among the most popular.

Out of doors, croquet, tennis and archery were indulged in by both sexes, and horse-riding, bicycling and 'botanizing' expeditions had their supporters.

low salaries of the period. As examples: Hampton Court. 8 bedrooms. Freehold £1,900, rent £90. Queen's Gate. 10 bedrooms £4,000, rent £350 furnished. Barnet. 3 bedrooms. Freehold 300 gns., rent £65.

The price of clothing provides further interesting comparisons: fur seal jackets, £9. 9s.; men's overcoats, 25s.; men's boots, 21s.; ladies' kid elastic boots, 16s.; knickerbocker suits for boys, 21s.; ball dresses, 35s.

Furnishing prices were in keeping: complete drawing room suites, 60 gns.; bedroom suites, 12 gns.; Brussels carpets from 2s. per yard; Witney blankets, 4s. 11d. per pair; chintz, 10½d. per yard. Pianos by all the best-known makers ranged in price from 25 gns. upwards.

In retrospect, the 1870s appear to have been unusually rich in literary talent. Although Dickens died in the first year of the decade, soon after his final Readings in London, his books continued to enjoy tremendous popularity in cheap editions. Other 'giants' included Tennyson, George Eliot, Wilkie Collins, Trollope, Swinburne, Darwin, Rossetti, John Stuart Mill, Carlyle, Meridith, Stevenson and Charles Reade.

It was also a prolific time for magazines: scholarly quarterlies and monthlies, medium-brow publications of which *Cornhill*, *Macmillan's* and *All the Year Round* were representative, dozens of popular periodicals for women, children and specialist readers, and a large number that were religious or semi-religious in tone.

There were theatres and music halls in many of the cities and large towns, while in London there was cheap entertainment in plenty: many theatres, concert halls, exhibitions of all kinds at the Crystal Palace, Alexandra Palace, Egyptian Hall and St James's Hall, music halls in the West End, City and suburbs, roller-skating, picture galleries, panoramas of famous battles, nigger minstrel shows, public readings by authors and lectures by scientists and, of course, the Zoological Gardens.

At a distance of a hundred years life in the 1870s seems untroubled, blissfully quiet and leisurely, free from the many pressures we face today. But hard facts present a different story. Certainly, the pace was leisurely; horse-drawn traffic, few telephones or typewriters, slow service in shops because few goods were packaged. Quiet could be found in the country but rarely in towns, where the shouting of bus conductors, draymen and hawkers, and the blare of street musicians, mingled with the clatter of iron-shod wheels and horses' hooves on stone-flagged roads. Comfort, too, was relative, with gas lighting in only the better-class houses and offices, oil lamps and candles for the majority. Only the very rich possessed bathrooms, and all cooking and heating was by coal.

Travel on the railways and by omnibus was dirty, cold and uncomfortable. Most roads were in poor condition, muddy in wet weather, dusty in dry. Strikes and riots were not unknown, especially in industrial areas. Hygiene was primitive, particularly in food shops. And if these were the conditions for the upper and middle classes, what was it like for the poor?

R. H. LANGBRIDGE

Personal, Lost & Found

NEDDIE.—WRITE again at once, to the petite Mère, unless you wish to kill the little mother.

NOV. 14th, 1869.—Would that you were here, or that I could go to you. All is the same, and I am weary of it.

IF Mr. WESTON, late of the Sussex Hotel, Southsea, will kindly forward his present ADDRESS to X. Y., post-office Broad-street, City, he will be conferring a great favour.

CARINA.—COME HOME, as soon as you can, and never be induced to go farther than you have been, as was once intended. Every thought, every breath, is for you.

ACCIDENT to a LADY at PORTLAND-ROAD STATION.—If the persons who saw a lady fall between the train and the platform at the above station on Saturday evening, the 14th inst., will COMMUNICATE with Mr. H. W. Christmas, Solicitor, St John's-chambers, 22, Walbrook, they will be rendering the lady a great service.

THE HOLDERS of the FIRST MORTGAGE BONDS of the NEW YORK and OSWEGO MIDLAND RAILROAD COMPANY are requested to SEND their NAMES, address, and the number and amounts of their bonds, to Messrs. Alexander and Green, Solicitors for the Trustees, Equitable-building, 120, Broadway, New York City, United States of America.

ANONYMOUS POSTAL-CARDS.—FIFTY POUNDS REWARD.—Whereas, several leading West-end firms complain to me respecting certain postal cards received by them, containing malicious innuendoes, &c., and purporting to emanate from my office:—The above reward will be paid by me for such INFORMATION as shall lead to the conviction of the writer of said spurious and infamous productions.—POLLAKY, 13, Paddington-green.

ANNA.—Thousand THANKS for your kind PRESENT and for your PHOTOGRAPH sent in March. May I send mine ?—Yours, P. M., London.

J. B. B., a lad, 18 years of age, who arrived 18th Dec., per Dover Castle, from Melbourne, has not since been heard of. INFORMATION as to his present whereabouts will be REWARDED by Mr. POLLAKY, Private Inquiry office, 13, Paddington-green.

TWENTY POUNDS REWARD for INFORMATION leading to conviction of the person who wrote the FORGED LETTER in the name of Lord ST. LEONARD'S, ordering jewellery, copied in The Times of the 27th ult., and the forged letter in his name, ordering of Messrs. Fortnum, Mason, and Co., five hampers of expensive articles for five members of Lord St. Leonard's family residing in different parts of the country. Apply at Bayle Farm, Thames Ditton.

DOG FOUND, about three weeks since, in the neighbourhood of South Kensington—a small White Female Dog, with a brown ear and spot on the side. The owner can have it by paying expenses. Apply at 255, Hampstead-road, N.W.

METROPOLITAN POLICE OFFICE.—FOUND, on the 3d December, in the Lowther Arcade, Strand, a FRENCH WATCH, in ebony half-hunting case, enamelled figures raised on face, monogram on back in silver, L. B. C., silver fastening to hang on a lady's belt. Application to be made at Bow-street Police Station.

MIRA. All is safe. (14. 12. 70.)—POLLAKY.

RUSSELL-SQUARE.—Making very favourable progress. The worst over. Expect success.

PLACHECKA, enfants, famille, et amie se portent très bien.

THE PINK TIE.—Sunday, 26th June. Keep loyal to the death. I am true to the core, darling.

MANAGEMENT.—Been much out of town. Not one gone wrong. Have advertised before. Did you not see it? Please acknowledge sight of this to J. C. Club.

PARIS.—Vingt francs à quiconque pourra faire savoir au journal La Presse, à Paris, que Mesdames OCTAVIE et EMMA HALBRON, ainsi que Monsieur et Madame MATHILDE NEUMANN, Faubourg Poisonniere 59, et tous leurs enfants, se portent bien et reçoivent lettres par ballon.

PRIERE à quiconque lira ces lignes de faire savoir à Mr. LAFONT, Rue de Greffulhe, 7, Paris, que Mme. Lafont et sa fille sont en bonne santé, à Brighton, Grenville-place, 41, et ne manquent de rien.—MARIE.

PRIERE à quiconque lira ces lignes de faire parvenir à Monsieur HENRI BURGUIERES, Banque Franco-Egyptienne, No. 39, Boulevard Haussmann, que sa mère est à l'Hôtel Gibbon, Lausanne. Santé bonne. Point de nouvelles depuis le 28 Octobre. Ecrivez par ballon à Mons. Gilbert, 14, Pembridge-gardens, London.

POUR PARIS.—Monsieur GAILDRAUD, 43, Rue du Bac. Votre femme est à Bruxelles, avec sa famille, et la famille La Personne. Tout va bien. N.B. Quiconque aura la bonté de communiquer l'avis ci-dessus obligera beaucoup.

MONSIEUR BIOLLAY, 74, Boulevard Malesherbes, quitté Boulogne pour Bruxelles, 24, Place Louvain. Maman toujours Dieppe. Bonnes santés.—HELENE. N.B. Quiconque aura la bonté de communiquer l'avis ci-dessus obligera beaucoup.

VINGT FRANCS à quiconque pourra faire savoir à Madame GONDOLO, 53, Boulevart Strasbourg, Paris, que son mari et fils sont à Londres, 3, East India-avenue. Sans nouvelles.

LOST, last week, TWO BUNCHES of KEYS (one labelled). If taken to 12, Henrietta-street, Cavendish-square, a REWARD will be given if desired.

LOST, on Sunday last, between 2 and 3 p.m., in the Addison-road, Kensington, a GRAY SCOTCH TERRIER, with large tulip ears. Answers to the name of Buz. Had on collar, engraved Capt. W. H. Adams, 234 R. W. Fusiliers. Any one taking the dog to 10, Cromwell-road, Earl's-court-road, Kensington, shall receive ONE POUND REWARD.

PLAIN GOLD BRACELET, with heart, LOST, on Saturday, Dec. 10. ONE GUINEA REWARD will be paid if taken to Mr. Belton, stationer, St. George's-place, Knightsbridge.

FIVE POUND NOTE.—LOST, on Tuesday evening, between Burlaige's library, Queen's-road, Bayswater, and Porchester-terrace, a FIVE POUND NOTE, with the name Fenning written on the back. Whoever will take the same to the above address shall be liberally REWARDED.

FIVE POUNDS REWARD.—LOST, when returning from Birmingham Show, a FOX TERRIER BITCH, colour white, with tan on one ear, which is slightly torn: has a light-coloured nose, weighs about 17lbs., and answers to the name of Trinket. Apply at 50, Canning-street, Liverpool.

TWO GUINEAS REWARD.—LOST, last Monday, at St. James's-hall, a large DOUBLE OPERA GLASS (Black), with the name of the owner, J. W. D., and of the donor, T. B., both in full. The above reward will be paid at Chappell's, 50, New Bond-street.

TWO GUINEAS REWARD.—LOST, on Thursday evening, Oct. 27th, in Fulham-road, near Maud-grove, a small DANDIE DINMONT TERRIER DOG, back, back of head, ears, and tail very dark brown, face and breast light sandy colour, legs same colour, but darker, rather long hair on face; had on a plated collar and bell. Answers to the name of Tiney. Whoever will take the same to Mr. Jessup, Hollywood-mews, Hollywood-road, West Brompton, shall receive the above reward.

R—D to B—S.—Thanks, dearest. Delighted. All right. 6.8.10.11 will suit—not 7—prefer 6. Your own R—.

ANNA.—Thousand THANKS for your kind PRESENT and for your PHOTOGRAPH sent in March. May I send mine?—Yours, P. M., London.

RESURGAM.—The individual is now in New York. Telegraph immediately to chief of police in that city.—C. NICHOLLS, Devereux-court, Temple, Private Inquiry-office. Established 1851.

J. B. B., a lad, 18 years of age, who arrived on the 18th Dec. per Dover Castle from Melbourne, and has not since been heard of. INFORMATION as to his present whereabouts will be REWARDED by Mr. Pollaky, Private Inquiry-office, 13, Paddington-green.

C. C.C.C.—Do not despair, my Marguerite. Only have patience. I hope we shall meet on the 3d. at P. Be cautious, and attend to all the advice I gave you. Do write to the London address, if you possibly can, and tell me what has happened that prevents your writing. If I wrote in l. j.. it would betray us.—Thine for ever, B.B.B.B.

AMERICA.—From Lodge-road.—I trust you are well on your return home. For my address apply at the Queen's Arms, William-street, High-street, St. John's-wood. The above address will always find me.

DEAR JOE.—Why do you not come home? You were not well when you left town on Friday. You are ill somewhere, and we are in great distress. Can I come to you? or if you want money let me know. You have only to ask for anything you want, and nothing to fear.—Your Sister, M. S. R.

TRAVERS W., to JOE R.—If you do not like to communicate with home, and you want money or advice, why not communicate with me, Henry W., or Tom R.? You know either of us would help you.

TEN POUNDS REWARD.—MISSING, a YOUNG GENTLEMAN, age 26, height 5 feet 6 inches, fair and pale complexion, broad forehead, very white teeth, light hair, short whiskers, beard and moustache of a darker colour, very slightly-built frame; wearing brown overcoat with velvet collar, dark serge surtout bound with broad braid, dark mixed trousers, black lavender striped tie, boots with elastic sides and false buttons, linen marked in full, gold wrist studs engraved "J. R.," silver watch, maker's name "West,' Ludgate-street, thin gold Albert chain. Had a third-class quarterly ticket between New-cross and London. Left his business in Walbrook on Friday, December 17th, between 2 and 3 o'clock, evidently unwell, and was seen at Charing-cross Station shortly after. Information to be given to the nearest Police Station.

R. ACKNOWLEDGES, with sincere thanks, the RECEIPT of BANK NOTE (83379), £50, from a kind friend.

BILL LOST.—Reward £5.—A BILL, dated Manchester, for £694 19s. 5d., drawn by Messrs. Mendel upon and accepted by Messrs. Kraeutler and Miéville, which became due on the 4th December, 1869, and was payable at the London and Westminster Bank, having been MISLAID, or Lost in the city of London, any person who will take the same to Mr. J. W. Vickers, Cowper's-court, Cornhill, shall receive the above REWARD. The bill, having been already paid, is of no value.

ONE POUND REWARD.—LOST, on Monday, the 13th of December, a WHITE POMERANIAN DOG, with a foxy face and bushy tail. Name "Tip." Whoever will take it to 61, Springfield-road, Marlborough-road, St. John's-wood, shall receive the above reward.

A RETRIEVER DOG, black, with the exception of white mark on breast, one tooth broken in lower jaw. Strayed at Camberwell on the night of Thursday, Dec. 30. A REWARD of ONE GUINEA on his being returned to the Lime Works, Surrey-canal, Camberwell. No further reward will be offered.

ISLE of SKYE TERRIER.—LOST, in the Marylebone-road, near Baker-street (from a gentleman's trap that met with an accident), a small SANDY COLOUR ISLE of SKYE TERRIER. Had on a bell attached with a blue riband. Whoever will restore it to the coachman, 21, Cleveland-mews, Lancaster-gate, shall receive TEN SHILLINGS REWARD.

FOUND, a FIVE-POUND BANK of ENGLAND NOTE. On giving particulars the owner may have it by applying at 96, Fleet-street.

PLEASE arrange for more time than of late.—A. K. K.

CURIOUS CIRCUMSTANCE. Many, many thanks.—BOO BOO.

CONQUEROR has seen last two advertisements, and on the word of a gentleman promises to do as his dear friend wishes. Begs that he may be further assured as to being the one intended by a newspaper direct, about the ages of both, or in any other manner, and an answer to this in the usual way.—Yours also for ever, CONQUEROR.

SPILLER.—If the LEGAL PERSONAL REPRESENTATIVE of HENRY REYNELL SPILLER, who was in practice in London as a Solicitor in 1759, will APPLY to Frederick Bradley Solicitor, 75, Mark-lane, E.C., he will hear of something to his advantage.

TRAMWAY ACCIDENT to ELDERLY LADY in CAMBERWELL-ROAD.—If the GENTLEMAN who saw an elderly lady fall out of a tram-car in the Camberwell-road, about 11.30, on the morning of 14th September last, and afterwards enquired at Mr. Field's, Furrier, Camberwell-road, regarding her, will COMMUNICATE with Mr. H. W. Christmas, Solicitor, St. John's-chambers, No. 22, Walbrook, he will be rendering the lady a service.

LOST, a GOLD GLOVE BUTTON-HOOK. Any one taking it to Messrs. Ortner and Houle, St. James's-street, London, may receive THREE POUNDS REWARD.

LOST, a PROMISSORY NOTE for £82 6s. 8d., payable this month. Not indorsed and not negotiable. Whoever takes this note to Evans and Co., 28, Nicholas-lane, Lombard-street, shall receive TWENTY SHILLINGS REWARD.

LOST, a MS., entitled "Hamlet Improved," by Colonel Colomb, F.S.A. It was sent to the Court Theatre by post. The finder will be REWARDED on application to the Junior United Service Club, London, S.W.

IF CHARLES DICKIE, late of Deptford, Kent (son of Thomas Ebenezer Dickie) will APPLY to Mr. James Sprott, of Shrewsbury, Solicitor, he will hear of something to his advantage.

BILLYBOY.—Wy hebben alles Klaar gemaakt. Wees gerust en laat my alles hebben want ik ben gebroken. Jimmey. Schryf my. Uncle of Corbyn.

LEFT her HOME, in the Borough-road, on Sunday evening, December 28th, 1873, a YOUNG LADY, 15 years of age, looks older, 5 feet 4 in height, dark, reddish brown hair, worn down her back and cut short on the forehead, dark brown eyes, rather full mouth, and wart on right side of nose, near the eye; wore a light drab dress, skirt scolloped, semi-tight jacket trimmed with black fur, sometimes worn with cape to match, and high, dark green, felt hat, turned up one side, with black bow and small feather; had high comb in hair, with small balls on top, and jet and cameo brooch and earrings. INFORMATION of her whereabouts will be rewarded by Mr. Pollaky, 13, Paddington-green.

BERTIE.—Out of London when your letter came. Write and make another appointment.

SILURES.—The assurance is given that E.C. reached her destination on Friday, Oct. 17th.

CLAPHAM.—WRITE here. Have left W. through death. Wish to see you very much.

BÉBÉ.—I saw a doctor. One thing alone can make me well, but meanwhile it will help me if each day brings a letter to tell that she is better, and able to keep all her promises strictly. I go to S. for two days. Do let us meet on my way back.

MESSRS. CAMPBELL, NICHOLL, and Co., or their Representatives, are requested to APPLY to Messrs. Grindlay and Co., 55, Parliament-street, London, with regard to a remittance received from India.

A Valuable SAPPHIRE RING.—A lady, giving the name of Clucas, won the above at a charitable raffle in Rome, February, 1878, and will oblige by COMMUNICATING with the Duchess of Marino, Palazzo Colonna, Rome. The ring will be sold for the charity if not claimed soon.

BANK of ENGLAND.—Unclaimed Dividend.—Application having been made to the Governors of the Bank of England to direct the payment of one dividend on the sum of £1,797 12s. 2d. Consolidated £3 per Cent. Annuities, heretofore standing in the names of EDITHA AGNES SERGISON, of Cuckfield, Sussex, Spinster, and JOHN PETER FEARON, of 21, Great George-street, Westminster, Esquire, and which dividend was paid over to the Commissioners for the Reduction of the National Debt in consequence of having remained unclaimed since the 5th July, 1869;—Notice is hereby given that, on the expiration of three months from this date (October 23d, 1879), the said Dividend will be Paid to Editha Agnes Sergison, Spinster, who has claimed the same, unless some other claimant shall sooner appear and make out his claim thereto.

Entertainments

THEATRE ROYAL, COVENT-GARDEN. — Under the sole Management of Mr. A. Harris.—THIS EVENING (Saturday), January 1, will be performed an entirely new and grand Spectacular Pantomime, written by Henry J. Byron, entitled THE YELLOW DWARF; or, Harlequin Cupid And The King Of The Gold Mines. The scenery by Messrs. Hawes Craven, Julian Hicks, Dayes, and Caney; also by Messrs. W. Telbin and W. Telbin, jun. Principal characters by Mesdames Julia Mathews, Nelly Power, Esta, Love and Craven, Mrs. Aynsley Cook, and Misses Nelly and Maria Harris; Messrs. J. D. Stoyle, Aynsley Cook, H. Payne, F. Payne, and W. H. Payne. Première danseuse, Mdlle. Blanche Ricois. The Divertissement and dances arranged by M. Desplaces. Costumes designed by Matt Morgan, and executed by MM. Hennier and Gustave Moring, Mrs. James, and Madame Wallet. The jewellery by M. Leblanc Granger. The appointments by Mr. Labhart. The music composed and selected by Mr. Betjeman. Morning Performances every Wednesday and Saturday, at 2 o'clock. The Box-office is open daily from 10 till 5, under the direction of Mr. Edward Hall, to whom post-office orders are to be made payable.

THEATRE ROYAL, HAYMARKET.—Great success of the new comedy of New Men and Old Acres, of which a Morning Paper, of the 27th of October last, states the following:—"A great success. Whether we regard the delicacy of satire, neatness of construction, healthiness of tone, or polish in writing, there are few plays now before the London public which are so thoroughly satisfactory as New Men And Old Acres."—Revival of Planche's fairy extravaganza The Fair One With The Golden Locks, with new scenery, &c.—THIS EVENING, January 1, 1870, to commence at 7 o'clock, A CO-OPERATIVE MOVEMENT. After which, at 7.40, NEW MEN AND OLD ACRES; Mr. Buckstone, Mr. Chippendale, Mr. Howe, Mr. Rogers, Mr. Braid, Mr. Buckstone, jun.; Miss Robertson, Mrs. Chippendale, Miss C. Hill, and Mrs. E. Fitzwilliam. To conclude with THE FAIR ONE WITH THE GOLDEN LOCKS. King Lachrymoso, Mr. A. Wood; Graceful, the King's Minstrel and Favourite, Miss Fanny Wright; Queen Lucidora (the Fair One with the Golden Locks), Miss Fanny Gwynne; Papillotina, Miss Francis; Viscount Very-So-So, Miss Murray. Box-office open daily from 10 to 5, under the direction of Mr. George Turpin.

LYCEUM THEATRE.—Under the direction of Mr. Allerton.—THIS EVENING, at a quarter past 7 o'clock, ELIZABETH, QUEEN OF ENGLAND. "The signing of the warrant for Mary Stuart's execution, and the impressive death of Elizabeth in the last act, may be cited as undeniable proofs of the ability of the actress, while in the passages illustrating her coquettish love for Essex Mrs. Lauder shows a lightness of touch which belongs to the region of high comedy."—Daily Telegraph. To conclude with, at a quarter past 10, BAMBOOZLING. Box-office open from 11 till 5 daily. Doors open at a quarter to 7; commence at a quarter-past. Acting manager, Mr. John Huy.

ST. JAMES'S THEATRE.—66th night of SHE STOOPS TO CONQUER, at 7: Misses Herbert, Henrade, Larkin, Turner; Messrs. Hill, Mark Smith, Shore, Young, and Lionel Brough. At 9.15, LA BELLE SAUVAGE: Mrs. John Wood, Misses Everard, Lovell, Armstrong, Ramsay, Carrie Wright, and entire corps de ballet: Messrs. Mark Smith, Young, Grainger, and Lionel Brough. Scene 1. Immigration; Scene 2. Examination; Scene 3. Intimidation; Scene 4. Recreation; Scene 5. Preservation. To conclude with A HAPPY PAIR: Miss Herbert; Mr. William Farren. Box-office, 10 to 5.

THEATRE ROYAL, ADELPHI.—Sole Proprietor and Manager, Mr. Benjamin Webster.—Great Attraction.—The two great dramas of the Season. At 7 o'clock, The Long Strike. At 9, Lost At Sea. Grand effects.—Fifth week of Dion Boucicault's celebrated drama of The Long Strike, with entire new scenery by Messrs. F. Lloyds, Maugham, and assistants.—29th appearance of Mr. Benjn. Webster and Miss Furtado in The Long Strike.—THIS EVENING, at 7, Dion Boucicault's celebrated drama, in three acts, entitled THE LONG STRIKE, in which Mr. Benjamin Webster and Miss Furtado will make their 29th appearance this season. Messrs. Arthur Stirling, G. Belmore, J. Atkins, W. Rignold, C. H. Stephenson, C. J. Smith. At 9, LOST AT SEA, grand effects: Messrs. G. Belmore, A. Stirling, Atkins, W. Rignold, C. H. Stephenson; Miss L. Grey, Miss Furtado (fourth time). Miss Eliza Johnstone, Mrs. Leigh Murray. Box-office open from 10 till 5. No fees for booking.

ROYAL PRINCESS'S THEATRE.—Lessee and Manager, Mr. Benjamin Webster.—After Dark and The Streets of London, Dion Boucicault's two celebrated dramas.—TO-NIGHT, at 7, AFTER DARK, in which Mr. Vining will sustain his original character of Old Tom, for the sixth time this season, Messrs. R. Phillips, Ashley, J. G. Taylor, J. D. Beveridge, D. Leeson, Eburne, Romer, Misses R. Leclercq, E. Barnett, &c. At 9.30, THE STREETS OF LONDON, concluding with the celebrated fire scene: Badger (his original character), Mr. Vining, Messrs. R. Phillips, Ashley, Stuart, J. D. Beveridge, D. Leeson, Eburne, Mesdames A. Mellon, E. Barnett, Addie, M. Brewer, &c. Box-office open daily from 10 till 5.

OLYMPIC THEATRE.—LITTLE EM'LY. Mr. G. F. Rowe, every evening, as Micawber.

A Charming Young Lady requests the pleasure of your company at the OLYMPIC. Do not disappoint her, but go and see LITTLE EMILY, and with her other old friends of the names of Peggotty, Copperfield, and Micawber, and that celebrated rascal, Mr. Uriah Heep. You will stay some hours with them, for they have a remarkable knack of making themselves agreeable to visitors. "Canterbury Cathedral" and "The Wreck" are two scenes to be seen and talked of, and not readily forgotten.—Punch.

ST. JAMES'S THEATRE.

ST. JAMES'S THEATRE.—Mrs. JOHN WOOD as H.R.H. the Princess POCAHONTAS, in the grand Indian burlesque, LA BELLE SAUVAGE. "A brilliant success."—Morning Paper. "An immense success."—Standard.

ST. JAMES'S THEATRE.—New Songs and Dances for the New Year.—Flutter Song, Dutchman's Wee Dog, Britannia's Bend, Mammoth Sunflower, the Velocipede. "A decided success."—Telegraph. "Most legitimate success."—Daily News.

ASTLEY'S.—E. T. Smith's Grand Pantomime, JACK AND THE BEANSTALK. Everything has been done to make this pantomime amusing and instructive. To describe the beautiful scenery, 300 superb dresses, valuable properties, gorgeous and superb decorations, in an advertisement is impossible; come and judge for yourself. Public favourites engaged:—Caroline Parkes, Mesdames Fosbroke, Howard, Wright, Clair, Seymour, Ashton, Forster, and Miss Erskine; Master Percy Roselle, Messrs. Yarnold, Coles, Dudley, &c. The harlequinade by Stonette (clown), Lacey (harlequin), Beckenham (pantaloon), Madame Rowella (columbine). The grand and effective ballet scene by Rutland. The artistic transformation scene by Brew. Others by Potts and Co. Fathers of families are informed the reduced prices of admission at this theatre are a great desideratum, being half of the west-end theatres. Over in time for late trains, and close to the Metropolitan, South-Eastern, and South-Western Railways. Book your places by telegraph, post, and post-office orders. Address to Mr. Drysdale, box-office.

ROYAL AMPHITHEATRE and CIRCUS, HOLBORN. Announcement Extraordinary.—Notwithstanding the immense expense attendant on the recent engagements, the proprietors have determined to leave no stone unturned, nor to be daunted by any question of outlay in procuring for their patrons, not only the best talent, but also the most wonderful combination of talent existing. To this end they have entered into arrangements with the MATTHEWS BROTHERS' TROUPE of C. C. C. CHRISTY MINSTRELS, who will make their first appearance at this establishment on Monday, January 3d. The reputation these gentlemen have achieved, both in London and the provinces, renders further eulogy unnecessary. The troupe has, however, been recently strengthened, and includes the Great Harry Matthews, Prince of Comedians; W. Matthews, the irresistible "bones," and the finest choir of tenors, baritones, and bassos ever brought together. It is, moreover, the only troupe that has been honoured by a command to appear before the Prince and Princess of Wales. This arrangement will in no way interfere with the "scenes in the circle," which will form Parts I. and III. of the entertainment.

THE ORIGINAL CHRISTY MINSTRELS, who first came to England in 1857 and introduced the entertainment of which they were the founders and originators in this country,

APPEAR at the ST. JAMES'S-HALL ONLY, where they have been permanently located for many years. They never perform elsewhere.

ST. JAMES'S GREAT HALL.—The CHRISTY'S CHRISTMAS FESTIVAL has again proved the greatest success of the season. On Boxing-day more than 9,000 persons paid for admission to the two performances given on that day. Even with this enormous return the traffic, both in Regent-street and Piccadilly, was completely stopped for a time by the thousands of persons turned away.

THE GREAT SIGHT of LONDON at this festive season is the ST. JAMES'S GREAT HALL, as fitted and decorated for the CHRISTY'S HOLYDAY PERFORMANCES. Splendid proscenium and scenery, floral decorations, rich drapery, flags, &c. Beyond all these, the enormous assemblages brought together each night, filling this vast structure in every available nook from area to topmost gallery.

ST. JAMES'S GREAT HALL.—TO-NIGHT, at 8, the CHRISTY MINSTRELS' GRAND CHRISTMAS and NEW-YEAR'S FESTIVAL, which has already attracted upwards of 39,000 persons to this Hall in the series of day and evening performances given since Boxing-day.

DORE GALLERY.—GUSTAVE DORE, 35, New Bond-street.—EXHIBITION of PICTURES, including "Triumph of Christianity," "Rossini," "Titania," "Francesca de Rimini," at New Gallery. OPEN 10 to 5. Gas at dusk. Admission 1s.

ELIJAH WALTON'S ALPINE and EGYPTIAN PICTURES.—The WINTER EXHIBITION now OPEN, at the Pall-mall Gallery, 48, Pall-mall (Mr. W. M. Thompson's). Admission 1s. Open daily from 10 till dusk.

THE LAST GRAND WORK by A. BIERSTADT, MOUNT HOOD, now ON VIEW, for a short time, at T. McLEAN'S new gallery, 7, Haymarket. Admission by presentation of address card.

MR. MORBY'S COLLECTION of PICTURES. Henriette Browne; Holman Hunt; Tadema; Rosa Bonheur; Frith, R.A.; F. Goodall, R.A.; Frere; Ruiperez; Nicol, A.R.A.; Ansdell, A.R.A.; Birket Foster; W. Hunt; F. Tayler.—24, Cornhill.

NOW ON VIEW, Sir EDWIN LANDSEER'S NEW WORK, "The Forest" a Series of 20 line engravings, illustrative of deer stalking. Henry Graves and Co., 6, Pall-mall.

NOW OPEN, for a very short time, Mr. W. W. WARREN'S unique COLLECTION of OIL SKETCHES, painted with the spirit of nature, and taken in Rome, Naples, Venice, Corsica, Sardinia, Normandy, Brittany, England, Ireland, &c., at the German Gallery, 168, New Bond-street, next door to the Clarendon Hotel. Open from 10 to 4. Admission 2s. 6d.

BY COMMAND of Her MAJESTY.—Now ready, HIGHLANDERS of SCOTLAND; comprising 31 Illustrations of the Highlanders and Followings of Scotland during the Reign of Queen Victoria, from Drawings made by KENNETH MACLEAY, Esq., R.S.A. (by command of Her Majesty); with copious Letterpress Description of the several Clans. 2 vols. imperial folio, handsomely bound, 18 guineas. Subscribers' copies are now ready for delivery. Mr. Mitchell, publisher to Her Majesty, 33, Old Bond-street, W.

CHOICE CHROMOLITHOGRAPHS and COLOURED PHOTOGRAPHS.—Largest collection of LANDSCAPE and FIGURE SUBJECTS ON VIEW at W. M. THOMPSON'S, 20, Cockspur-street, Trafalgar-sq., S.W. See priced catalogues.

CRYSTAL PALACE NEW YEAR'S GUINEA SEASON TICKETS, dating from 1st of January, 1870, for 12 months, NOW READY at all the entrances to the Palace, at Exeter-hall, and at all agents.

It was prominently noticed at the meeting of shareholders of the Company on Thursday, that upwards of £36,000 was expended last year for concerts, operas, flower shows, firework displays, and other great fêtes, to which all season ticket holders had free entry. A continuance of this liberal policy was emphatically declared to be that best calculated to advance the interests of all connected with the Crystal Palace Company.

The high character and variety of the exceedingly numerous fêtes held at the Palace make it no idle boast, that the season tickets are, as so often described, "the best guinea's worth in the world."

As a more favourable opportunity for entry than the present cannot be found, it is confidently anticipated that from the preceding enunciation of the policy of the management, a very considerable accession to the already large number of season ticketholders must commence with the new year.

Tickets for children under 12 half-price.

Note.—Visitors desirous of purchasing season tickets at the Palace entrances this day will oblige by coming prepared with card or written name and address.

CRYSTAL PALACE GUINEA SEASON TICKET. The best New Year's Gift.

MR. CHARLES DICKENS'S FINAL READINGS.—Mr. CHARLES DICKENS will RESUME his interrupted SERIES of FAREWELL READINGS, at the St. James's-hall, London, on Tuesday evening, Jan. 11, and conclude the same on Tuesday, March 15. The readings will be only 12 in number, and none will take place out of London. There will be Two Morning Readings, one on Friday, January 14th, when Mr. Dickens will read his Christmas Carol; and one on Friday, January 21st, when he will read his Boots at the Holly Tree Inn, and Sikes and Nancy (from Oliver Twist). The Evening Readings will proceed as follows:—Tuesday, January 11th, David Copperfield, and the Trial from Pickwick; Tuesday, January 18th, Doctor Marigold, and Mr. Bob Sawyer's Party (from Pickwick); Tuesday, January 25th, Nicholas Nickleby (at Mr. Squeers's School), and Mr. Chops, the Dwarf; Tuesday, February 1st, Boots at the Holly Tree Inn, Sikes and Nancy (from Oliver Twist), and Mrs. Gamp. The morning readings will commence at 3 o'clock, and the evening readings at 8 o'clock. Prices of admission—sofa stalls, 7s.; stalls, 5s.; balcony, 3s.; admission, 1s. Tickets may be obtained at Chappell and Co.'s, 50, New Bond-street.

NOW ON VIEW, Sir EDWIN LANDSEER'S NEW WORK, "The Forest," a Series of 20 line engravings, illustrative of deer stalking. Henry Graves and Co., 6, Pall-mall.

THE NATIONAL PICTURE of the QUEEN (in Robes of State), size of life, and painted by command, in commemoration of Her Majesty's gift to Mr. Peabody, will be EXHIBITED in March. Orders for the engraving received by Messrs Dickinson, publishers to Her Majesty, 114, New Bond-street.

SIMPSON'S INDIA, &c.—The remaining DRAWINGS of this celebrated series ON VIEW and for SALE at greatly reduced prices, at the Pall-mall Gallery, 48, Pall-mall (Mr W. M. Thompson's). Priced list of subjects on application.

NOW OPEN, for a very short time, Mr. W. W. WARREN'S unique COLLECTION of OIL SKETCHES, painted with the spirit of nature, and taken in Rome, Naples, Venice, Corsica, Sardinia, Normandy, Brittany, England, Ireland, &c., at the German Gallery, 168, New Bond-street, next door to the Clarendon Hotel. Open from 10 to 4. Admission 2s. 6d.

ROYAL HORTICULTURAL SOCIETY, South Kensington, W.—FIRST EXHIBITION of FLOWERS, in 1870, on Wednesday, January 19th. Band of Royal Horse Guards from 2. Admission 2s. 6d., or by tickets purchased before the day by Fellow's order, 1s. 6d. There will be exhibitions of flowers, fruit, and vegetables on Wednesdays, February 16th, March 2d and 16th, April 6th and 20th, May 4th and 18th, August 3d and 17th, September 7th and 21st, October 5th, November 2d, December 7th, on all of which occasions the Band of the Royal Horse Guards will play.

CHRISTMAS HOLYDAYS.——ZOOLOGICAL SOCIETY, Regent's-park. Admission 6d. every day (except Sunday) from Dec. 24th to Jan. 6th, 1870, inclusive.

WHITTINGTON CLUB, 37, Arundel-street, Strand.—The NINETEENTH ANNUAL JUVENILE BALL will be held on Tuesday, January 11, 1870. The programme includes, besides dancing, a series of dissolving views, and a giant Christmas tree, with a prize for each juvenile visitor. Tickets, 2s. each, may be obtained by members of the Club for themselves and friends, in the Secretary's office.

BALL at Mr. LAYLAND'S large, elegant Hall, Tuesday, 4th Jan. Tickets 2s. 6d. Long soirée every Tuesday, tickets 1s. 6d.; short soirée every Friday. Band at 8. Classes for ladies and gentlemen on Mondays at 8. Three private waltz lessons 10s. 6d., eight for 21s., with lady.—157, Blackfriars-road.

ARGYLL ROOMS.—Great success of Signor Luigi Mosca's new and charming SHADOW VALSE, with the electric light effects, by Sabin, Brothers. Admission, 1s.; balcony, 2s.—Windmill-street, Piccadilly. Musical director, Signor Curti.

MADAME TUSSAUD'S EXHIBITION.—On view PORTRAIT-MODELS of the EMPEROR and EMPRESS of the FRENCH and PRINCE IMPERIAL, also Marshal Bazaine, Marshal Canrobert, General Trochu, &c. Admission 1s.; children under 10 years of age, 6d.; extra rooms, 6d. Open from 10 a.m. till 10 p.m.

MADAME TUSSAUD'S EXHIBITION.——On view, PORTRAIT-MODELS of the KING and CROWN PRINCE of PRUSSIA and PRINCE LEOPOLD of HOHENZOLLERN, also Count von Bismark and Count von Moltke. Admission 1s.; children under 10 years of age, 6d.; extra rooms, 6d. Open from 10 a.m. till 10 p.m.

VISITORS to LONDON during the HOLYDAYS are requested to observe that omnibuses from all parts of London stop at the EGYPTIAN-HALL, Piccadilly, every 10 minutes.—This central and fashionable hall is the only place in London where POOLE and YOUNG'S NEW and COLOSSAL PANORAMA of the WAR, painted by England's greatest scenic artists, is now being EXHIBITED twice every day, afternoons at 2.30; evenings at 8.

HEADS of FAMILIES will please note that juveniles under 10 are admitted to all parts at half price to what the Press calls that highly instructive, intellectual, beautiful, and truthful entertainment, POOLE and YOUNG'S PANORAMA of the WAR, with the magnificent scenery on the Banks of the Rhine, the Saare, the Seine, the Moselle, &c., at the Egyptian-hall, Piccadilly.

EGYPTIAN-HALL, Piccadilly.—Twice every day at 2.30 and 8 p.m.—Beautiful Paintings, Excellent Music, Reliable Lecture.—POOLE and YOUNG'S PANORAMA of the WAR.- See the opinions of the leading Press. Prices 3s., 2s., and 1s. Juveniles half price. See the beautiful dioramas, not dissolving views, of Paris, Berlin, Metz, Strasbourg, &c., each are 500 square feet of canvas, all new and original paintings, at the Egyptian-hall. 2.30 and 8.

THE WAR.—Eighth Week.—Westbourne-hall, Bayswater.—MONTAGUE'S GRAND DIORAMA of the WAR. The Battles and Sieges of the Campaign; Paris in Peace and War. Every night at 8. Note.—Day Representations every Monday, Wednesday, and Saturday, at 3. Admission, 2s., 1s., and 6d.

ZOOLOGICAL GARDENS, Regent's-park, OPEN DAILY except Sundays. Admission, 1s. On Mondays, 6d. Children under 12, 6d. Among the recent additions are two ant-bears.

MILLAIS.—YES or NO? the exquisite engraving from this celebrated picture, by Samuel Cousins, R.A., is just completed.

SIR JOSHUA REYNOLDS.-The STRAWBERRY GIRL: Mr. Samuel Cousins' beautiful engraving from the celebrated picture by Sir Joshua Reynolds, the property of Sir Richard Wallace, Bart., M.P., now exhibiting at the Bethnal-green Museum.

MESSRS. THOMAS AGNEW and SONS have the honour to announce that the above WORKS, engraved for their firm, may be seen at their Galleries:—London, 5, Waterloo-place, Pall-mall; Liverpool, Exchange Fine Art Gallery; Manchester, No. 14, Exchange-street.

SIR EDWIN LANDSEER, R.A.—EXHIBITION of the complete SERIES of ENGRAVED WORKS of the late Sir E. LANDSEER in the choicest and scarcest states, extending from 1809 to 1872, and including many most rare and interesting works now first collected together.—BURLINGTON GALLERY, 191, Piccadilly. Admission, including catalogue, one shilling.

THE CAVENDISH BALL.—Mr. EDWARD HUMPHREY'S NEXT BALL, at Willis's Rooms, will be held Wednesday, March 4. Dan Godfrey's Band. Tickets to be had only of the Stewards, or Mr. E. Humphrey, Cavendish Rooms, Mortimer-street, W.

ARGYLL ROOMS. Proprietor, R. R. BIGNELL. Treasurer, Mr. W. Price. Immense success of Mons. Charles D'Albert's Princess Marie Galop, and La Fille de Madame Angot Lancers. Conductor, Signor Curti. Solo euphonium, Signor Mosca. Managers, Messrs. R. Friend and F. Gray. Admission 2s.

PRIVATE BALLS, Concerts, Readings, &c.—The QUEEN'S CONCERT ROOMS, Hanover-square, W. Only a few vacant days. (Ladies and gentlemen may find their own wines.) For terms apply to Mr. Hall.—Robert Cocks, Proprietor.

FANCY BALLS and PRIVATE THEATRICALS. – Caution to Customers. -SIMMONS'S, the celebrated Court Costumier, only establishment, 8, King-street, Covent-garden. Magnificent selection of costumes and portable theatres on hire. Country orders attended to. Direct all letters Simmons's, 8, King-street.

THE TICHBORNE TRIAL, painted by NATHAN HUGHES, the Prince of Painters, is now added to his 375 works ON VIEW on Stockwell-green, S.W. Admission and catalogue 4d. It creates intense interest.

DUKE and Duchess of EDINBURGH.—— PORTRAITS of their Royal Highnesses, authorized by H.R.H. the Duke, have just been published by Mr. MITCHELL, Royal Library, 33, Old Bond-street. Proofs, 7s. 6d.; prints, 5s.

CHROMO-LITHOGRAPHS, Oleographs, and Engravings, most suitable for wedding and other presents.—600 of those choice WORKS of ART after celebrated artists, comprising all the most charming and favourite subjects, including views in Italy, Switzerland, Germany, the Rhine, Lake Districts, and figure subjects, at wholesale prices. Parcels forwarded for approbation.—WILLIAMS and Co., 27, Gresham-street, near the Bank of England.

GAINSBOROUGH.—A charming LANDSCAPE, by the great master, to be DISPOSED OF. Enquire of Mr. McNair, Egyptian-hall, Piccadilly.

ME. CHARLES PILLET, Auctioneer, 10, Rue de la Grange Batelière, Paris, will SELL, on Thursday, 5th March, 1874, at the Hotel Drouot, Rooms 8 and 9, the ANCIENT PAINTINGS, composing the valuable collection of Mr. Lemaitre, Trésorier Payeur-Général, at Laon. Catalogues of Me. Charles Pillet.

FINE ARTS.—To Proprietors of Old Baronial Halls and others.—Messrs. Joseph J. Flack and Co. beg to announce to their numerous customers they have now on SALE several hundred OIL PAINTINGS by the old masters, consisting of portraits from the time of Henry VIII., gallery pictures of all kinds, cabinet pictures by the Dutch, Flemish, Italian, and English schools; also modern works by young rising artists, the whole of which are now being offered to the public at less than half their real value for ready money.—JOSEPH J. FLACK and Co., 6 and 11, Hemming's-row, Charing-cross, W.C., back of the National Gallery. Established in 1818

ALEXANDRA PALACE.—BALAKLAVA FETE. —Next Saturday, the 25th anniversary of the Battle will be celebrated at the Alexandra Palace. Banquet of the Survivors of the Charge of the Six Hundred; Promenade Concert of Patriotic Music (Mr. Dan Godfrey), concluding with Jullien's British Army Quadrilles; Mr. W. H. Pennington will recite The Charge of the Light Brigade, dressed in the uniform in which he rode into the Valley of Death, Oct. 25, 1854; Assault at Arms by Men of the Royal Horse Guards Blue; Bands of the Grenadier Guards, the Palace, Drum and Fife Bands, Buglers, Pipers of Scots Guards, &c.; Grand Battle Fireworks by Mr. James Pain, including a huge Representation of Lord Cardigan charging at Balaklava. One shilling day. Note.—Zazo's Balista Flight for the first time on Saturday, at 5.

ALEXANDRA PALACE.—LAST GREAT TROTTING MEETING of the season Monday and Tuesday next. Over 60 entries. The best horses in the kingdom, besides entries from France and Canada.

ROYAL AQUARIUM.—The pleasantest lounge in London. Open 11 till 11. Always something new. Constant amusement. Admission 1s.

THE AQUARIUM DEPARTMENT.—Finest collection of MARINE ANIMALS in Europe, 150 different species. Thousands of living specimens.

ROYAL AQUARIUM.—At intervals, Fleas, Tubbs' Views, Otters and Seals fed three times daily, Obang, Edgar Granville's Entertainment, Farini's Zulus, the new Fine Art Gallery, Reading Room, and Library.

3.15.—Royal Aquarium Orchestra.
3.30.—Nat Emmett's wonderful Goats.
3.45.—Herr Blitz: Plate Spinning Extraordinary.
4.10.—Phillipson's splendid Troupe of Bell Ringers.
4.25.—Leclaire, the King of Conjurors.
4.40.—Gale St. John and Mlle. Celia Dwight.
4.50.—Poluski, Brothers, well-known Musical Clowns.
5.20.—Mons. Nathan, marvellous Chair Manipulator.
5.30.—Special Performance of Farini's Zulus.
6.30.—Recital on Grand Organ by Mr. James Halle.
8.0.—Vocal and Instrumental Concert. Mons. C. Dubois.
9.0.—Special Performance of Farini's Zulus.
9.5.—Second Unsurpassed Variety Entertainment.

THE marvellous SWORD SWALLOWER, THIS DAY.

ROYAL AQUARIUM.—FARINI'S ZULUS. Special performance at 5.40 and 9 o'clock.

THE ONLY GENUINE ZULUS in ENGLAND, and the only ones that ever left their country. Admission 1s.

BRIGHTON GRAND AQUARIUM.—Just arrived, from the upper part of the River Amazon, TWO fine, healthy MERMAIDS (MANATEES), male and female. The only living specimens in Europe. No extra charge.

FIREWORK DISPLAYS, for Festivities and Rejoicings of every kind. Estimates forwarded upon application to C. T. BROCK and Co. (sole Pyrotechnists to the Crystal Palace, &c.), Norwood Junction, S.E., and 109, Cheapside, E.C.

C. T. BROCK and Co.'s CRYSTAL PALACE FIREWORKS. Choice selections, from 1s. to £10 10s. Price lists and contents of cases sent free upon application. Fireworks for export. For shipping terms apply to Norwood Junction, S.E.—No. 109, Cheapside, E.C.

MR. and Mrs. GERMAN REED'S ENTERTAINMENT. St. George's-hall, Langham-place (Managers, Messrs. Alfred Reed and Corney Grain), TO-NIGHT, at 8. Miss Edith Brandon, Miss Lucy Williams; Mr. Corney Grain, Mr. Alfred Bishop, and Mr. Alfred Reed.

BRANDRAM TUESDAY AFTERNOON RECITALS at Willis's Rooms, in January, February, and March. Full particulars advertised every Saturday, or may be had on application at Mr. Mitchell's Royal Library, 33, Old Bond-street.

BRANDRAM SUBSCRIPTION LIST will be CLOSED on Dec. 27, after which date seats will be booked for any single recital. Reserved seats 5s.; unreserved seats, 2s.

MASKELYNE and COOKE.—Egyptian-hall, England's Home of Mystery (under the management of W. Morton). Patronized by the Royal Family. The present programme is most complete and successful, and, in addition to Mr. Maskelyne's original and popular features, the mystery and music of an Electric Organ are interesting attractions; and Mr. Walter Pelham also gives a portion of his clever facial entertainment. Boxes, from 21s.; stalls, from 5s.; admission, 2s. and 1s. The performance is given every evening at 8; and on Tuesday, Thursday, and Saturday, at 3 and 8. Seats can be booked at the box-office and at any opera ticket agents.

SANGER'S GRAND NATIONAL AMPHITHEATRE (late Astley's).—The only entertainment in Great Britain embracing the circus and theatre.—The Excelsior Pantomime, entitled CINDERELLA AND THE LITTLE GLASS SLIPPER; or, Harlequin Ride-A-Cock Horse and The Fairy of the Golden Dreams, written by W. M. Akhurst, produced with all the completeness and grandeur that have characterised this world-famed Amphitheatre under its present liberal management. The grand production pronounced on Boxing-day and night to by far excel anything that has ever been submitted to the public. The whole produced under the personal superintendence of Messrs. P. and G. Sanger. Characters by Messrs. Randall, J. Holloway, Ross, Lynn, P. Miles, Hughes, Holland, Hazlewood, Bradfield, Parry, Loraine, W. Hourey, H. Hourey, W. Holloway, J. Watson, Avolo, J. Crockett; Mesdames Kate Allwood, E. Allwood, E. Randall, Mary Pitt, Julia Stuart, Fanny Daley, Maud Soily, Marie Ellis, and the great Danish Burlesque actress, Mlle. Burdett Riviere. Clown, W. Hourey; Pantaloon, D. Hourey; Harlequin, Loraine; Columbine, Mdlle. Rosalie. Box-office open from 11 till 4.

HENGLER'S GRAND CIRQUE, Argyll-street, Oxford-circus.—Increasing popularity of this unrivalled establishment. Crowded audiences nightly delighted with the charming entertainment. The best of riders, the best of gymnasts, the best of clowns, and well-trained horses. Open at 7, commence at 7.30.

HENGLER'S GRAND CIRQUE, Argyll-street, Oxford-circus.—THIS DAY (Monday) the juvenile spectacle CINDERELLA; or, The Little Glass Slipper. Open at 2 o'clock, commence at 2.30; and Evening at 7, and every day and evening throughout the holydays. Prices:—4s., 3s., 2s., 1s.; children under 10 half-price; private boxes, £1 10s. Box-office open daily from 10 till 4. To prevent disappointment visitors are respectfully urged to secure their seats in advance.—Proprietor, Mr. Charles Hengler.

TRUTH STRANGER THAN FICTION.—TO-NIGHT, the unparalleled adventures of James Annesley and his sweetheart Philippa Chester will be taken from history and played upon the stage of the QUEEN'S THEATRE, Long-acre.

MRS. JOHN WOOD as PHILIPPA, in Charles Reade's New Drama.

CHARLES READE'S new drama, THE WANDERING HEIR, TO-NIGHT, January 5, at the QUEEN'S THEATRE. Box-office open daily from 10 till 5.

ALHAMBRA THEATRE ROYAL.—Manager Mr. John Baum.—DON JUAN (by H. J. Byron), 13th time To-NIGHT, at 8. An original Musical, Pantomimic, Comical Christmas Extravaganza. Music by Offenbach, C. Lecocq, F. Clay, and M. Jacobi. The scenery by A. Callcott and assistants. Principal Characters:—Haidee, Miss Kate Santley; Spalatrar, Miss Ann Sheridan; Donna Anna; Miss M. Barrie; Dudu, Alice Hilton; Zerlina, Lottie Venn; Don Juan, Mdlle. Rose Bell; Leporello, Mr. Harry Paulton; Zambra, W. Worboys; Pedro, J. H. Jarvis; Masetto, J. H. Paul; Carlos, Miss F. Coleman; Guzman, Miss J. Howard; Don Alphonso, Miss E. Hatherley; Don Enricquo, Miss Frederick; Police, Noblemen, Pirates, &c. At 7, THE LOTTERY TICKET.

NATIONAL STANDARD THEATRE, Bishopsgate.—MORNING PERFORMANCE THIS DAY, and every Monday, Thursday, and Saturday, at 12.30, to which children under ten half-price. Box-office open from 11 till 4.

ROYAL PHILHARMONIC THEATRE.—MADAME ANGOT THIS EVENING, at 8.30 (79th time).—Notice.—This eminently successful, original, and acknowledged best version, by H. J. Byron, music by C. Lecocq, with its unrivalled cast of characters, powerful chorus, full and efficient orchestra, new and splendid dresses and appointments, can only be witnessed at the Philharmonic Theatre. Private boxes and fauteuils at all the libraries.

PAVILION THEATRE, Mile-end.—MORNING PERFORMANCE TO-DAY, at 1 o'clock, of the greatest Pantomime, PUSS IN BOOTS, ever produced in the east of London. The press has justly styled it the gem of the Pantomime season, and further adds that all London ought to see the great battle scene, performed by 200 well trained children, headed by Major Mite and General Tom Dot, accompanied by a corps de ballet of 50 ladies, forming a scene of grandeur unsurpassed in London.

WHY GO to the WEST, when the best Pantomime in London is in the East. PAVILION THEATRE. MORNING PERFORMANCE, TO-DAY, and every Monday, at 1 o'clock. Children under 12 half-price.

BARRY SULLIVAN as HAMLET, Richelieu, Richard III., King Lear, Gamester, and Othello, this week.—THEATRE ROYAL, BELFAST.

DRURY-LANE.—TO-NIGHT. Act 1.—The Throne Room in the Palace of Westminster; Exterior of the Boar's Head; the Beach at Southampton; the English Fleet at Anchor. Act 2.—Room in the Palace of Charles VI.; the English Entrenchments within bow shot of Harfleur; the Duke of Glo'ster's Quarters; the Siege of Harfleur; Signs of a Severe Conflict; French Palace at Rouen; Departure of the French Army. Act 3.—Night scene, the Dauphin's Tent within the English Lines; English Position at Agincourt; the Field of Battle; Battle of Agincourt; the Plains after the Victory. Act 4.—Historical Episode; Triumphal Entry of King Henry V. into London. Act 5.—Palace at Troyes; Interior of the Cathedral; Espousal of Henry V. and Princess Katherine.

ADELPHI.—NICHOLAS NICKLEBY, by Charles Dickens, dramatised by Andrew Halliday, THIS EVENING, at 8. Stage Manager, Mr. Charles Harris. Doors open at 6.30 POOR PILLICODDY, at 7. To conclude with JESSAMY'S COURTSHIP. In preparation, to precede Nicholas Nickleby, J. R. Planché's comic drama, Who's Your Friend? Box-office open 10 to 5. No booking fees.

MR. HENRY IRVING, Sole Lessee and Manager.—THIS (Saturday) EVENING, and every evening (Wednesdays excepted), at 8 o'clock, will be presented Shakespeare's comedy of THE MERCHANT OF VENICE: Shylock, Mr. Irving; Antonio, Mr. Forrester; Bassanio, Mr. Barnes; Gratiano, Mr. F. Cooper; Solanio, Mr. Elwood; Salarino, Mr. Pinero; Lorenzo, Mr. Forbes; Duke of Venice, Mr. Beaumont; Prince of Morocco, Mr. Tyars; Launcelot Gobbo, Mr. Johnson; Old Gobbo, Mr. C. Cooper; Tubal, Mr. Carter; Jessica, Miss Alma Murray; Nerissa, Miss Florence Terry; Portia, Miss Ellen Terry. The scenery includes a Street in Venice, a Corridor in Portia's House, and an Italian Garden with Terraces, painted by Mr. Hawes Craven; a Public Place in Venice and a Room in Portia's House, painted by Mr. Walter Hann; a Court of Justice, painted by Mr. H. Cuthbert; and a Public Place in Venice and Shylock's House by a Bridge, painted by Mr. W. Telbin. The incidental music, specially composed by the Musical Director, Mr. Hamilton Clarke, will be executed by a selected choir and full orchestra. The costumes by Auguste and Co. and Mrs. Reid. Box-office of the theatre, under direction of Mr. Harst, open from 10 to 5, where seats may be taken one month in advance. Stage Manager, Mr. H. J. Loveday; Acting Manager, Mr. Bram Stoker.—LYCEUM.

MERCHANT OF VENICE, LYCEUM, TO-NIGHT (Saturday), at 8 o'clock; preceded by DAISY'S ESCAPE.—Lyceum.

GARRICK THEATRE, Whitechapel.——THIS EVENING, at 8.15, the 81st representation of Bazin's comic opera, A CRUISE TO CHINA. Preceded, at 7.15, by VOKINS' VENGEANCE. Mesdames May Bulmer, Viola Dacre, Cita Beauchamp, Agnes Consuelo, and Adelaide Newton; Messrs. Barri, Roche, Brenham, Williams, Carson, Wilton, C. A. White, and full chorus.

GENEVIEVE WARD.——FORGET-ME-NOT.—Provincial tour, with her great Lyceum success. TO-NIGHT, at THEATRE ROYAL, DUNDEE; Edinburgh next week.

GAIETY.—French Plays.—Madame Sarah Bernhardt every night for four weeks—two weeks with M. Coquelin, First appearance in FROU-FROU Four weeks of entire Palais Royal Company. Fifty pieces. Seventh season of eight weeks, beginning May 24.

GAIETY.—FRENCH PLAYS COMPANY, to support M. Coquelin and Madame Sarah Bernhardt:—Madame Helen Petit, MM. Talbot, Berton, Marais, Porel, Amaury, and others from the Odéon and Comédie Française. The whole Palais Royal Company for four weeks; Mlles. Legault, Magnier, Lemercier, Faivre, Raymonde, Georgette-Olivier, &c.; MM. Geoffroy, Hyacinthe, l'Heritier, Daubray, Milher, Montbars, Luguet, Pellerin, Calvin, and about 20 others. General Manager for French Plays, Mr. M. L. Mayer.

VAUDEVILLE THEATRE.—THIS EVENING, at 7.30, HOME FOR HOME, by Richard Lee. After which, at 8 o'clock, revival of James Albery's celebrated comedy, in three acts, TWO ROSES (448th time). Concluding with OUR DOMESTICS. Supported by Messrs. Henry Howe, David James, W. Herbert, L. Fredericks, C. W. Garthorne, J. W. Bradbury, W. Hargreaves, and Thomas Thorne; Mesdames Marie Illington, Kate Bishop, L. Telbin, Cicely Richards, E. Palmer, and Sophie Larkin.

OPERA COMIQUE.—H.M.S. PINAFORE, every evening (466th performance).—The original company, at the Opera Comique Theatre only. Messrs. George Grossmith, jun., Rutland Barrington, Thornton, G. Power, Clifton, Ramsay; Mesdames Elinor Loveday, Everard, Bond, &c.

H.M.S. PINAFORE, every evening.—MORNING PERFORMANCE, TO-DAY and every Saturday, at 2.30. Mr. G. Grossmith's drawing-room sketch, A SILVER WEDDING, at 4.30.—Note.—OPERA COMIQUE THEATRE.

H.M.S. PINAFORE, every evening, by the original company, organised by Mr. D'Oyley Carte for its first production in May, 1878, and as played by them 460 times since with uninterrupted success.—OPERA COMIQUE.

Concerts & Music

SIGNOR MARRAS' SEVENTH APRES-MIDI (16th Season), THIS DAY, January 3d, and every Monday during the season, 1870, at 3 o'clock, for the study of concerted vocal music. Repetition of Rossini's, Gounod's, and Mendelssohn's sacred "Quartetti;" new songs by Stella, "I wait for thee, my only love," and "Separation" (by desire); "Ce nom qui me rappelle tant de rêves charmants" (le premier jour de bonheur), Auber; "Du bist wie eine Blume," Schuman; "Caro, son tua così," Schira; "Pastorale napolitana" (1st time), Marras.—10, Hyde-park-gate, London.

SIGNOR MARRAS' FIRST VISIT to HEREFORD, on Thursday next, Jan. 6th, for the PRACTICE of SOLI and CONCERTED VOCAL MUSIC. Terms for private lessons and further particulars at Mr. Bezant's pianoforte and music warehouse, Hereford.

SIGNOR MARRAS' FIFTH APRES-MIDI in CHELTENHAM, on Saturday next, January 8th (by kind permission of H. Brown, Esq., at Douro villa). Full information respecting the new music to be studied, &c., at Mr. Davies's, Montpelier Library, Cheltenham.

HANOVER-SQUARE ROOMS.——Herr CARL HAUSE'S next CONCERT (fourth in the present series of 17) will take place on Thursday evening, January 6. Instrumentalists—Herr Carl Hause, Herr Josef Ludwig, and Signor Piatti. Vocalists—Mlle. Bauermeister and Mr. Santley. Tickets, 5s. and 2s. each, at the Rooms, and at Herr Hause's residence, 19, Hanover-street.

HALF-MAST HIGH, the last composition by Claribel, will be SUNG by Miss JULIA ELTON, at the first Ballad Concert, St. James's-hall, Wednesday evening, January 5th. Tickets of Boosey and Co., Holles-street.

MR. SANTLEY will SING "A Mother's Smile" and "Farewell" (Farewell by Carl Hause), at the Hanover-square Rooms, on Thursday evening, January 6.

MLLE. ENEQUIST will SING Ganz's highly popular song "The Nightingale's Trill," at Maidstone, January 4.

MISS JULIA ELTON will SING Arthur Sullivan's much admired and highly successful song, "O fair dove, O fond dove," at Brighton, January 6th.

MR. FRANK ELMORE will SING his own popular composition, "Farewell, Fair Ines," at all his concert engagements this winter. Letters respecting terms for oratorios, concerts, and lessons in singing should be addressed to his residence, 1, Leamington-villas, Westbourne-park, W.

MLLE. SOPHIA FLORA HEILBRON (the celebrated Pianiste), age 12 years, acknowledged by the Press to be a musical little wonder, is prepared to RECEIVE ENGAGEMENTS for concerts, pianoforte recitals and soirées. Selections of all great masters. For terms and opinions of the Press apply Heilbron's-villa, No. 13, Cathnor-road, Shepherd's-bush.

CHRISTMAS PARTIES. —— QUADRILLE PIANISTS ENGAGED on the shortest notice; also the best performers on the harp, violin, cornet, &c. Programmes printed and mounted at Robt. W. Ollivier's, 19, Old Bond-street. Pianos on hire at 10s. 6d. per month.

SACRED HARMONIC SOCIETY, Exeter-hall.
Conductor, Sir MICHAEL COSTA.
On Friday, January 14th, Haydn's CREATION. Principal vocalists —Mme. Lemmens-Sherrington, Mr. Vernon Rigby, and Mr. Santley.
Tickets 3s., 5s., and stalls 10s. 6d., now ready, at the Society's office, 6, Exeter-hall.
Note.—On Friday, January 21st, Mendelssohn's Elijah. Principal Vocalists—Mme. Sinico, Mrs. Sidney Smith, Mme. Sainton-Dolby, Miss Julia Elton, Mr. Vernon Rigby, Mr. G. T. Carter, Mr. C. Henry, and Mr. Santley. Tickets as above.

EXETER-HALL.—Saturday Evening Concerts will commence on Saturday next, 8th January, 1870.—Mlle. SINICO will SING aria, "Qui la Voce;" new song, "The Birds were telling one another," Henry Smart; and with Signor Foli, duetto, "La dove prende." Doors open at 7.30. Prices of admission, 1s., 2s., 3s., and reserved seats 5s. Tickets at Cramer and Co.'s, 201, Regent-street, and 43, Moorgate-street, city.

EXETER-HALL.—Saturday Evening Concerts will commence on Saturday next, 8th January, 1870.—Mr. SIMS REEVES will SING "Adelaida," "My own, my guiding star" (G. A. Macfarren), and "Tom Bowling." Concert to commence at 7.30. Tickets at Mr. Austin's ticket office, St. James's-hall, Piccadilly.

EXETER-HALL.—Saturday Evening Concerts will commence on Saturday next, 8th January, 1870.—Signor FOLI will SING "David singing before Saul," "Over the rolling sea," and with Mlle. Sinico duetto, "La dove prende." Prices 1s., 2s., 3s., and reserved seats 5s. Tickets at Mr. Alfred Hays', 4, Royal Exchange.

EXETER-HALL.—Saturday Evening Concerts, Saturday next, 8th January, 1870.—Miss AGNES ZIMMERMAN will PLAY Concerto in D minor for pianoforte, and Stephen Heller's "Reveries d'Artiste" and "Nuits Blanches." Tickets at Messrs. Lamborn Cock and Co.'s, 63, New Bond-street. Concert to commence at 7.30 and terminate at 10. Prices 1s., 2s., 3s., and stalls 5s.

THE CHRISTY MINSTRELS, St. James's-hall. Every evening, at 8; Wednesdays and Saturdays, at 3 and 8. It has long been universally conceded by the public, and also by the leading metropolitan press (without a single exception), that the entertainment given by the Christy Minstrels is beyond question the very best to be found amidst the entire round of London amusements, always presenting fresh features. Programme ever changing, ever new. Fauteuils, 5s.; stalls, 3s.; area, 2s.; gallery, 1s. No fees or extra charges whatever. Tickets and places at Mr. Austin's office, St. James's-hall; Mr. Mitchell's, Bond-street; Keith and Prowse's, Cheapside; and at Hays', Royal Exchange-buildings. Doors open at 2.30 for day; 7.30 for evening. Proprietors, Messrs. G. W. Moore and Frederick Burgess. General Manager, Mr. FREDERICK BURGESS.

COMUS and HERRMANN.—St. James's-hall.—Grand success. The two greatest prestidigitateurs that have ever appeared in London will continue their extraordinary SEANCES of MAGIC at the above hall, TO-DAY (Thursday) and To-morrow (Friday), at 3. Fauteuils, 5s.; stalls, 3s.; area, 2s.; gallery, 1s.

ALHAMBRA PALACE. — Managing Director Mr. F. STRANGE.—Great Success.—PROMENADE CONCERTS, 300 vocal and instrumental performers. Grand orchestra, conducted by Mr. Riviere. Military Bands of the Scotch Fusilier Guards and Royal Horse Artillery (by kind permission of the commanding officers).

ALHAMBRA PALACE. — WAR SONGS of FRANCE and GERMANY, as sung on the battle-fields of France.

ALHAMBRA PALACE.—RULE BRITANNIA, in character, by Miss CAROLA ALEXANDRONCA.

ALHAMBRA PALACE.—Miss MARION WENTWORTH, Mlle. Degrange, Mlle. Hollar, Mlle. Secretain, Mlle. Phillippine, and Julie Siedle; Mr. Geo. Bicknell, Herr Waldmann, and Mr. Jonghmans.
Jullien's British Army Quadrilles, THIS EVENING. Doors open at 7.30; commence at 8. Prices 1s., 2s., and gallery 6d.; dress circle, 5s.; private boxes, 21s., 31s. 6d., and 42s. Box office open from 11 till 7.

SOUTH LONDON PALACE.-GRAND MYTHOLOGICAL BALLET, supported by 100 ladies. The Royal Tycoon Troupe of Japanese; Misses Webb and Wilson, A. F. Forrest and Sons; the performing monkeys; all the star comics, and comic ballet; the Lauri Family. Admission, 3d., 6d., and 1s.

LANGTON WILLIAMS' TARANTELLE.—Miss KATE GORDON will PLAY this highly successful new work at each Pianoforte Recital during her tour in Scotland.

REFUGEES' BENEVOLENT FUND.—The Gentlemen Amateurs known as the WHITE LILIES of the PRAIRIE (who have had the honour of appearing before their Royal Highnesses the Prince and Princess of Wales) will kindly give their ENTERTAINMENT, in Aid of the Refugees' Benevolent Fund, at the Hanover-square Rooms, THIS EVENING (Thursday), Dec. 15th, Doors open at 8. To commence at half-past 8. Tickets numbered stalls, 7s. 6d. ; unreserved seats, 2s. 6d., can be obtained from the Hanover-square Rooms ; from the Committee of Ladies, 15, Bruton-street ; at the offices of the Refugees' Benevolent Fund, 30, King-street, Cheapside ; of Mr. Mitchell, Bond-street ; Messrs. Oller and Co., Bond-street ; Mr. Hays, Royal Exchange-buildings ; Messrs. Keith and Prowse, Cheapside ; and at the stalls of the Refugees' Benevolent Fund, at the Baker-street Bazaar ; or any of "The White Lilies of the Prairie." Subscriptions to the General Fund may be sent to Francis Bennoch, Hon. Sec., 30, King-street, E.C.

MRS. JOHN MACFARREN'S PIANOFORTE and VOCAL RECITAL, at Coalbrookdale, on Tuesday next, when she will play Walter Macfarren's celebrated third "Tarantella," and Jules Brissac's brilliant Scottish Fantasia "Scotia."

ITALIAN LYRIC SCHOOL.—REHEARSAL of FAUST, at St. George's-hall. Entrance in Mortimer-street, on Monday, Dec. 19th, at 8 o'clock. Conductor, Signor Gilardoni.

THE NEW ORGAN at the QUEEN'S CONCERT ROOMS, Hanover-square.—Mr. Robert Cocks, proprietor, begs to announce that Mr. W. T. BEST, Organist of St. George's-hall, Liverpool, will give an opening RECITAL of ORGAN MUSIC upon the new instrument now erected in these rooms, by T. C. Lewis and Co., on Friday evening, Dec. 23d, at 8 o'clock. Tickets, price 2s. 6d. each, may be procured from Mr. Hall, at the rooms ; or from Messrs. Robert Cocks and Co., No. 6, New Burlington-street, W.

THE LONDON ACADEMY of MUSIC, St. George's-hall, Regent-street north.—The ANNUAL PERFORMANCE of HANDEL'S Oratorio, the MESSIAH, by the professional students of the London Academy of Music, will take place on Wednesday, Dec. 21, at 8 o'clock. Conductor, Professor WYLDE, Mus. Doc. Orchestra and chorus of 200 performers. Tickets 5s. and 2s. 6d.

UNDER the PATRONAGE of H.R.H. the Duchess of CAMBRIDGE, H.R.H. the Princess MARY ADELAIDE (Princess Teck).—Miss WALTON (of the Conservatoire, Leipzig) will give her PUPILS' INVITATION CONCERT, Saturday next, Dec. 17th, at 3 o'clock. Programme :—Sonata, Op. 18, Dussek ; song, V. Gabriel ; sonata appassionata, Beethoven ; vocal duet, Rubinstein ; Capriccio, Op. 33, Mendelssohn ; trio, Pinsuti. Part II. Rigoletto, Liszt ; song, Schira ; Scherzo, Op. 20, Chopin ; song, Wecherlin ; fantasia, Kuhe ; coro, Rossini.—27, Harley-street, Cavendish-square, W.

MONDAY POPULAR CONCERTS, St. James's-hall.—Last Concert before Christmas.—On Monday evening next, Dec. 19, the PROGRAMME will include Beethoven's Grand Trio in B flat, op. 97 ; the quartet in E flat, for strings, op. 74, &c. Executants—Mme. Norman-Néruda, MM. Chas. Halle, Straus, L. Ries, Zerbini, and Piatti. Vocalist—Herr Stockhausen. Sofa stalls, 5s. ; balcony, 3s. ; admission, 1s. Programmes and tickets at Chappell and Co.'s, 50, New Bond-street ; and at Austin's, 28, Piccadilly.

HERR STOCKHAUSEN will SING Schubert's "Erl King," and two songs by Schumann, at the Monday Popular Concerts, St. James's-hall, on Monday evening next, Dec. 19.

SATURDAY POPULAR CONCERTS, St. James's-hall.—On Saturday afternoon next, Dec. 17, the programme will include the quartet in C major, op. 59, No. 3 ; the pianoforte trio in B flat, op. 70 ; and the Waldstein sonata, for piano alone ; all by Beethoven. Executants—Mme. Norman-Néruda, Chas. Hallé, L. Ries, Straus, and Piatti. Vocalist, Mr. Sims Reeves. To commence at 3 o'clock. Conductor, Mr. Benedict. Sofa stalls, 5s. ; balcony, 3s. ; admission, 1s. Tickets at Chappell and Co.'s, 50, New Bond-street ; and at Austin's, 28, Piccadilly.

MR. SIMS REEVES, at the Saturday Popular Concerts, St. James's-hall, on Saturday afternoon next, Dec. 17, when he will SING "Adelaide" and the "Lieder-Kreis." Sofa stalls, 5s. ; balcony, 3s. ; admission 1s.

MADAME SAINTON DOLBY begs to announce that she will give a MATINEE MUSICALE, at her residence, No. 71, Glocester-place, Hyde-park, on Tuesday next, the 20th inst., in aid of the Refugees Benevolent Fund. To commence at 4 o'clock precisely. Vocalists—Madame Sainton Dolby and Signor Gardoni ; violin, M. Sainton; pianoforte, M. Delaborde ; violoncello, M. Lasserre. Conductor, Mr. Thouless. Tickets, one guinea each, may be obtained of Madame Sainton Dolby, at her residence ; and at the office of the Ladies' Committee, 15, Bruton-street, Berkeley-square.

WAGNER SOCIETY.—Last CONCERT but one. St. James's-hall, March 13, at 8.30. Orchestra and chorus 120 performers. Conductor, Mr. E. DANNREUTHER. The programme will include the following :—Beethoven, overture, König Stephan, and choral fantasia (solo pianoforte, Mr. W. Bache) ; Berlioz, song, De spectre de la rose ; Wagner, Huldigungsmarsch, chorus of the Messenger of Peace (Rienzi) ; selections from Tannhauser, Die Meistersinger von Nürnberg ; and finale to Act I. from Lohengrin. Tickets 10s. 6d., 7s. 6d., 5s., 3s., 2s., 1s., of Stanley Lucas, Weber, and Co. ; Chappell and Co. ; Mitchell, Ollivier, Lamborn Cock, Bond-street ; Austin, St. James's-hall ; Schott and Co., Cramer and Co., Regent-street ; Keith, Prowse, and Co., Cheapside ; Hays, Royal Exchange ; and Davies, Brothers, 19, Craven-terrace, Lancaster-gate, W.

MONDAY POPULAR CONCERTS, St. James's-hall.—On Monday evening next, March 2, the PROGRAMME will include Beethoven's posthumous quartet in C sharp minor; Bach's sonata in B minor for pianoforte and violin ; Haydn's quartet in G major, Op. 64, No. 4 ; and Schumann's sonata in G minor for pianoforte alone. Executants—MM. Joachim, Dannreuther, L. Ries, Straus, and Piatti. Vocalist, Mr. Bentham. Conductor—Mr. Zerbini. Stalls, 5s. ; balcony, 3s. ; admission, 1s. Programmes and tickets at Chappell and Co.'s, 50, New Bond-street ; and at the Hall, 28, Piccadilly.

BEETHOVEN'S POSTHUMOUS QUARTET in C SHARP MINOR at the Monday Popular Concerts, St. James's-hall, on Monday evening next, March 2. Executants—MM. Joachim, L. Ries, Straus, and Piatti.

SACRED HARMONIC SOCIETY, Exeter-hall. Conductor, Sir MICHAEL COSTA.—Final Series of Concerts in Exeter-hall.—The 48th SEASON will COMMENCE in November. The office, No. 6, Exeter-hall, will be open on Monday next for the receipt of subscriptions and issue of the prospectus.

ROYAL ALBERT-HALL.—FOUR ORATORIO PERFORMANCES.—October 30th, Messiah ; December 18th, Hymn of Praise and Stabat Mater ; January 1st, Messiah ; February 19th, Elijah. Four National Concerts :—St. Andrew's Eve, November 29th ; St. David's Day, March 1st ; St. Patrick's Day, March 17th ; St George's Day, April 23rd. All the principal artistes. Full Band. Mr. William Carter's Choir. Subscription for the eight concerts :—Stalls, £2 2s. ; arena, £1 11s. 6d. ; central balcony, £1 1s. ; side balcony, 15s. All seats numbered, reserved, and transferable.

ROYAL ALBERT-HALL.—Thursday, October 30th, at 8, MESSIAH. Madame Nouver, Miss Beata Francis, Madame Patey, Mr. Edward Lloyd, Mr. H. Winter, Signor Brocolini. Organ, Mr. Bending. Full band. Mr. William Carter's Choir. 7s. 6d., 5s., 4s., 2s. 6d., and 1s. Ladies and gentlemen wishing to join the choir or orchestra are requested to attend at 23, Colville-square, W., on Friday or Saturday, after 7.

MLLE. ANNA BOCK'S EVENING CONCERT, Steinway-hall, Thursday, Oct. 30, at 8 o'clock. Herr Ludwig, violin ; Herr Daubert, violoncello ; vocalist, Mme. Antoinette Sterling. Reserved seats, 10s. 6d. ; unreserved seats, 5s., may be obtained of Messrs. Chappell and Co., 50, New Bond-street ; at Steinway-hall ; and of Mme. Anna Bock, 30, Aldridge-road-villas, Westbourne-park, W.

MRS. JOHN MACFARREN at St. Mary's-hall, St. Mary's-road, Canonbury, will give a PIANOFORTE RECITAL, Oct. 29. Selections from Beethoven, Schubert, Weber, Chopin, Rubinstein, Raff. Vocalist, Miss McKenzie.

MADEMOISELLE JANOTHA begs to annonuc that she will give a PIANOFORTE RECITAL in the St. James's-hall, on Wednesday Afternoon, November 12, 1873, to commence at 3 o'clock. Programme :—Sonata appassionata, in F minor, Op. 57 (Beethoven) ; gavotte, in B minor (Bach) : scherzo, in B minor (Brahms) ; rondo capriccioso (Mendelssohn) ; fantasia, in F minor (Chopin) ; carnaval (Scènes Mignonnes), Op. 9 (Schumann). Sofa stalls, 7s. 6d. ; balcony, 3s. ; admission, one shilling. Tickets may be obtained of Chappell and Co., 50, New Bond-street ; and at Austin's Ticket office, 28, Piccadilly.

MOORE and BURGESS MINSTRELS' Fifteenth Consecutive Year, at the St. James's-hall, in one continuous and unbroken season. This company is the only minstrel organization in existence countenanced by the public and acknowledged by the press, comprising upwards of 40 artists of known excellence. The old and hackneyed trash, formerly associated with this class of entertainment, is totally ignored by the management of this company. New and original songs (written and composed by authors and musicians of the greatest celebrity, among whom may be enumerated C. J. Dunphie, F. Vizetelli, Henry S. Leigh, B. L. Farjeon, E. L. Blanchard, Edward Oxenford, F. E. Weatherly, Elizabeth Philp, U. M. Lutz, John Hobson, Robert Stœpel, and other authors of eminence), will ever form a prominent feature in the musical portion of Messrs. Moore and Burgess's entertainment.

Food & Drink

MARAVILLA COCOA for BREAKFAST.—The Globe says "TAYLOR BROTHERS' MARAVILLA COCOA has achieved a thorough success, and supersedes every other cocoa in the market. Entire solubility, a delicate aroma, and a rare concentration of the purest elements of nutrition, distinguish the Maravilla Cocoa above all others. For homœopaths and invalids we could not recommend a more agreeable or valuable beverage." Sold in packets only by all grocers.

JOHN RICHARD WACE and Co. beg to announce that they are prepared to supply GROCERIES, Italian Goods and Household Stores of every description at the same prices as the Civil Service Co-operative Society, with these additional advantages, that they do not require a subscription, and will deliver the goods by their own carts on the day following the receipt of the order, which must be accompanied by cash. Country orders will receive immediate attention.—Foreign Warehouse, 45 and 46, Baker-st., Portman-sq., W.

CLUN FOREST MUTTON.—This small, old, and excellent MUTTON is again in season. It is remarkable for its tenderness, colour, and fine flavour. LIDSTONE and Co., of No. 110, New Bond-street, respectfully solicit patronage, and guarantee the best produce in the kingdom.

AUSTRALIAN COOKED MUTTON, of very prime quality can be obtained of all grocers and Italian warehousemen, in 6lb. and 4lb. tins. N.B.—1lb. of cooked meat at 8d. equals 1½lb. of uncooked butcher's meat, costing 1s. 3d. See that the label bears the name of W. J. COLEMAN and Co., 13, St. Mary-at-Hill, London.

LIEBIG'S EXTRACT of MEAT, genuine (Gold Medal, Amsterdam Exhibition), made according to Liebig's special instructions, from cattle of English breeds, by R. Tooth, Esq., Sydney. Also Extract of Mutton, invaluable for mutton broth. Sold everywhere in white jars, with patent stoppers.—W. J. COLEMAN and Co., 13, St. Mary-at-hill.

LIEBIG COMPANY'S EXTRACT of MEAT.—Amsterdam Exhibition, 1869, First Prize, being above the Gold Medal. Supplied to the British, French, Prussian, Russian, Italian, Dutch, and other Governments. One pint of fine flavoured beef-tea at 2½d. Most convenient and economic stock. Caution.—Only sort warranted genuine by the inventor, Baron Liebig, whose signature is on every genuine jar. Ask for Liebig Company's Extract, and not for Liebig's Extract of Meat.

DEVONSHIRE-HOUSE, 16, Warwick-street, Belgrave-road, Pimlico.—W. BAKER begs to call the attention of heads of families to his superior BUTTER and POULTRY, direct from Devonshire. Prime chickens 4s. 6d. per couple.

E. LAZENBY and SON'S PICKLES, Sauces, and Condiments.—E. Lazenby and Son, sole proprietors of the celebrated receipts and manufacturers of the pickles, sauces, and condiments so long and favourably distinguished by their name, are compelled to CAUTION the public against the inferior preparations which are put up and labelled in close imitation of their goods, with a view to mislead the public.—90, Wigmore-street, Cavendish-square (late 6, Edwards-street, Portman-square), and 18, Trinity-street, London, S.E.

HARVEY'S SAUCE.—CAUTION. The admirers of this celebrated sauce are particularly requested to observe that each bottle, prepared by E. LAZENBY and SON, bears the label used so many years, signed "Elizabeth Lazenby."

BORWICK'S BAKING POWDER has been awarded two gold medals for its superiority over all other baking powders. Makes Bread, Pastry, and Puddings light and wholesome.

TO CLUBS in TOWN and COUNTRY.

TO HOTELS in TOWN and COUNTRY.

TO large WHOLESALE ESTABLISHMENTS in TOWN and COUNTRY.

TO PRIVATE FAMILIES in TOWN and COUNTRY.

TO the TRADE in the COUNTRY.

PULLEN and SON beg to draw the attention of the above to the facility they have of SUPPLYING fresh from the markets every article of produce in FRUIT and VEGETABLES, of the best, and at lowest possible prices. Contracts given for large entertainments.—Covent-garden and Farringdon Markets.

LEA and PERRINS'

WORCESTERSHIRE SAUCE.

LEA and PERRINS' WORCESTERSHIRE SAUCE, pronounced by connoisseurs to be "the only good sauce." Sold wholesale by CROSSE and BLACKWELL, and retail by grocers and oilmen universally.

BORWICK'S BAKING POWDER.—Gold Medal, Havre Exhib., 1868; Gold Medal, Paris Society of Arts, 1869. For its superiority over all other baking powders.

BORWICK'S BAKING POWDER makes delicious Bread without Yeast.

BORWICK'S BAKING POWDER makes Puddings, Pastry, and Piecrusts with less butter and eggs.

BORWICK'S BAKING POWDER. Sold everywhere, in 1d. and 2d. packets, and in 6d. and 1s. patent boxes. Be sure to ask for and see that you get

BORWICK'S GOLD MEDAL BAKING POWDER.

YEATMAN'S YEAST POWDER makes delicious and wholesome bread in a few minutes. Pastry and puddings without eggs or butter. Used in Her Majesty's kitchen. Recommended by the medical faculty. Sold everywhere. Depot, 119, New Bond-street, W.

FRESH MEAT PRESERVATIVE (PERRY'S PATENT).—This preparation will keep meat, fish, poultry, game, &c., sound for any period and during the greatest changes of temperature, without in the least injuring their flavour or nutritious qualities. This preservative has been successfully tested and used in Australia. Sold in jars, at 3s. 6d. per gallon. Depot, 66, St. John-street, West Smithfield, E.C.

NYE and Co.'s PATENT MINCING and SAUSAGE MACHINES. Mills for Coffee, &c., and Knife Cleaners in great variety; also Masticators to assist digestion, and numerous useful domestic appliances. Lists free.—373, Oxford-st., W.

SMOKERS' PASTILS.—PIESSE and LUBIN'S. "Through all my travels few things astonished me more than seeing the beauties of the Harem smoking the Stamboul. After smoking, a sweet aromatic Lozenge or Pastil is used by them, which is said to impart an odour of flowers to the breath. I have never seen these breath lozenges but once in Europe, and that was at Piesse and Lubin's shop in Bond-street."—Lady W. Montague. Sold in boxes, 2s. —2, New Bond-street, London.

TEA. —— The distinctive feature of MOORE, BROTHERS' system is that they supply families direct who are willing to pay cash at merchants' prices. The saving to families will be considerable. £3 value carriage paid. Price circular free.—Moore, Brothers, merchants, 35, London-bridge, city.

THE CHEAPEST PACKAGE of TEA in ENGLAND.—A Chinese caddy, containing 16lb. of really good black tea, sent carriage free to any railway station or market town in England, on receipt of 40s., by PHILLIPS and Co., tea merchants, No. 8, King William-street, city, E.C.

BREAKFAST.—EPPS'S COCOA.—"By a thorough knowledge of the natural laws which govern the operations of digestion and nutrition, and by a careful application of the fine properties of well-selected cocoa, Mr. Epps has provided our breakfast tables with a delicately flavoured beverage which may save us many heavy doctors' bills."—Civil Service Gazette.

EPPS'S COCOA, prepared by James Epps and Co., homœopathic chymists, London.

BREAKFAST.—EPPS'S COCOA. The agreeable character of this preparation has rendered it a general favourite. Made simply with boiling water or milk. Sold only in tin-lined packets, labelled "James Epps and Co., homœopathic chymists, London," who prepare also Epps's Glycerine Jujubes, for cough, throat, &c.

RARE OLD WINES, for connoisseurs.—Messrs. HEDGES and BUTLER invite attention to their extensive stock of choice old PORT, selected and bottled with the utmost care, and now in the highest state of perfection, embracing all the famed vintages at moderate prices.

Wines for Ordinary Use :—

Claret	14s.	18s.	20s.,	24s.,	30s.,	36s. per doz.
Sherry		24s.,	30s.,	36s.,	42s. per doz.	
Port		24s.,	30s.,	36s.,	42s. per doz.	
Champagne		36s.,	42s.,	48s.,	60s. per doz.	
Hock and Moselle ..		24s.,	30s.,	36s.,	48s. per doz.	
Fine old Pale Brandy		48s.,	60s.,	72s.,	84s. per doz.	

On receipt of a post-office order, or reference, any quantity will be forwarded immediately by Hedges and Butler, 155, Regent-street, London, and 30, King's-road, Brighton (originally established A.D. 1667).

KINLOCH'S CATALAN :—

	Per doz.	
Crown Catalan (Red and White), ...	20s.	Bottles
Diamond ditto	17s.	Included.

We are the sole proprietors and importers of Kinloch's genuine Catalan. The "red" wine, full bodied, delicious, fruity port flavour. The "white," exquisitely delicate, rich, and nutty, equal to Madeira.

Claret (OLanyer's) ..	12s. 6d., 14s. 6d., 18s.	Bottles Included.
Sherry	20s. 0d., 24s. 0d., 30s.	
Virgin Sherry	26s. 0d., 30s. 0d., 34s.	
Old Cognac..	36s. 0d., 42s. 0d., 48s.	
Marsala, finest imported	20s.	

Our own carts deliver daily in London. Six dozens assorted, railway carriage paid. 1s. 6d. per doz. allowed for bottles returned.

C. Kinloch and Co., 14, Barge-yard-chambers, Bucklersbury, London, E.C.

FRENCH WINE COMPANY, 20, Budge-row, Cannon-street, E.C.—FRENCH WINES at wholesale prices. No intermediate between producer and consumer. 5,000 hhds. Vin de Bordeaux, 1868 vintage, produce of the districts Bas, Medoc, Cotes, Blaye, &c., at £5 10s. per hhd., in bond ; 1,000 hhds. of other growths, as per Company's list, from £5 10s. to £100 per hhd., in bond ; Cos d'Estournel, 1867 vintage—100 hhds. of this much approved wine remaining, at £22 10s. per hhd., bond price. Note.—Each hhd. contains 46 galls., and would yield about 23 dozens, in bottles six to the gallon. Duty, &c., per hhd., £2 10s. Beaujolais and Macon, at £8 per hhd. of 46 galls., bond price ; duty, &c., per hhd., £2 10s. Chablis, excellent quality, at £12 per hhd. of 46 galls., bond price ; duty, &c., per hhd., £2 10s. Sparkling Champagne—2,000 dozens, in baskets one doz. each, at 24s. per dozen, duty paid ; usually sold at 36s. to 42s. per doz. ; a trial only needed to ensure approval. Verzenay (dry or sweet), at 46s. per doz. quarts, or two dozen pints. Eau de Vie—100 hhds. at 5s. per gall., in bond ; duty 10s. 5d. per gall., proof. Brandy, in cases—1,000 cases, one doz. each, at 36s. per case, duty paid ; cases and bottles included. The wines and brandies can be tasted at the Company's offices, or where lying in bond. Terms cash. Country orders must be accompanied by remittance or reference in London.

BRANDY, Pure Brandy, direct from Charente—importers, C. DEVEREUX and Co., 26, East India-chambers, Leadenhall-street, London—at 36s., and for premiere qualite 40s. per dozen, either pale or brown. Bottles and case included. Forwarded same day against post-office order or remittance.

BRANDY, the best and cheapest in the world :—Cognac Brandy, 15s. per gall. ; 33s. per doz. Champagne Brandy, 18s. per gall. ; 39s. per doz. This splendid brandy cannot be equalled. Best London Gin, 13s. per gall. ; 29s. per doz. The above prices per dozen include railway carriage and bottles.—GEORGE PHILLIPS and Co., 69, High Holborn, London.

COURVOISIER'S COGNAC, the only brandy supplied to H.M. Napoleon III., is in the opinion of those who have tried it the finest and most delicate imported. Price per dozen, delivered free, 48s., 54s., 60s., 66s., 72s., 84s., 120s., according to age.—PHYTHIAN and SONS, 432, West Strand, London.

LA GRANDE MARQUE BRANDY, bottled at Cognac.—G. A. KNOTT, 38, Crutchedfriars, E.C.

Carte Bleue (five years old), at 48s. per dozen.
Carte Janne (nine years old), at 54s. per dozen.
Carte Rose (11 years old), at 60s. per dozen.
Carte Blanche (18 years old), at 66s. per dozen.

Pure Bodega Sherry, very pale, elegant dinner wine, at 24s. per dozen.

Terms net cash.

KINAHAN'S LL.—Dublin Exhibition, 1865.—This celebrated old IRISH WHISKY gained the Dublin Prize Medal. It is pure, mild, mellow, delicious, and very wholesome. Sold in bottles, 3s. 8d., at the retail houses in London, by the agents in the principal towns in England, or wholesale at 8, Great Windmill-street, W. Observe the red seal, pink label, and cork branded "Kinahan's LL Whisky."

SCOTCH WHISKY.—This article has, as J. and G. COCKBURN'S OLD GLENLIVET MIXTURE, long held the first place in the market. They, therefore, invite comparison, and recommend gentlemen who may not have tasted it to have a few gallons by way of trial, feeling assured that no such quality is offered at the price—18s. per gallon, or 36s. per dozen, cash. All orders must be accompanied with a remittance or known reference.—J. and G. Cockburn, wine and brandy merchants, 135, Princes-street, and 21, South Castle-street, Edinburgh.

ROSE and Co.'s PATENT PRESERVED LIME JUICE, Cordial, Champagne, and Citronade, combining excellent beverages, entirely free of spirit, with highly valuable medicinal properties. Sold by grocers, wine and spirit merchants, &c. L. Rose and Co., Leith, importers and patentees. London, 24, Budge-row, E.C.

ALLSOPP'S PALE and BURTON ALES.—These Ales are now being supplied in the finest condition, in bottles and in casks, by FINDLATER, MACKIE, and Co., 33, Wellington-street, Strand, W.C.

BASS'S PALE ALE, Guinness's Stout, and Scotch Ale, 6s. quarts, 4s. 6d. imperial pints, 3s. 6d. pints, per dozen; pale India ale and stout, 4s. 6d. quarts, 3s. 6d. imperial pints, and 2s. 9d. pints, per dozen.—HENRY WATSON and Co., 16, Clement's-lane, city.

BASS'S PALE ALE (October brewings), in cask and bottle. Younger's Edinburgh Ale. Strong Burton Ale. London and Dublin Stout, &c. Cyder and Perry.—FIELD, WARDELL, and Co., 10, Adam-street, Adelphi, W.C.

CHRISTMAS CONFECTIONERY, Christmas Tree Ornaments, figures, bonbon crackers, somebody's luggage, motto nuts and kisses, magic flowers, French boxes of bonbons, English, German, and French confectionery.—The largest assortment in London, the very best that can be produced, and at prices to suit all, at BAINBRIDGE'S, 408, Strand, near the Adelphi Theatre.

EXTRACT of MEAT SUPERSEDED.—GUICHON'S MUSCULINE, prepared in the form of a sweetmeat from pure meat pulp, combined with fruit and sugar, for debility in consumption, cancer, chronic diarrhœa, dyspepsia, &c. Recommended especially for children. Boxes, 2s., post 2s. 2d.; 22s. dozen free.—Of THOMAS TOMLINSON, chymist, 6, Lower Seymour-street, Portman-square, W., and all chymists.

DEVONSHIRE-HOUSE, 16, Warwick-street, Belgrave-road, Pimlico.—W. BAKER begs to call the attention of heads of families to his superior BUTTER and POULTRY, direct from Devonshire. Prime chickens 4s. 6d. per couple.

POTATOES—the choicest quality York Regents, free from disease. Warranted to keep well. Delivered free to any address in London, at 12s. the sack of 168lbs. net. Fluke kidneys, 13s. 6d. ditto. Country orders carefully attended to. Address CHARLES BEECHING, salesman, Farringdon-market, E.C.

THE SOVEREIGN CASE, for presents, contains two bottles French Brandy, one each of Port, Sherry, Rum, and Whisky, best quality. Forwarded on receipt of post-office order, 20s., payable to S. POWNCEBY, wine merchant, 356, Oxford-street.

THE UNIVERSITY CLARET, at 12s. per dozen (bottles included), as supplied to the leading London clubs, &c.—E. GALLAIS and Co., wine growers in Medoc, 61, Regent-street, Quadrant, W., and 27, Margaret-st., Cavendish-sq., London, W.

GOOD SPANISH SHERRIES, from 18s.; Clarets, from 12s.; Crusted Ports, from 36s.; Champagne, from 30s. per doz.; other Wines in proportion.—WINCKWORTH and PRICE, wine, spirit, and beer merchants, 80, Marylebone-road, N.W.

LA ANDALUZA, Sociedad de Almacenistas, Puerto de Santa Maria, Cadiz Bay. Spanish wines exclusively. For duty-paid price list of 35 different qualities address JOSE PIODELA, 124, Fenchurch-street, E.C. Sample, one dozen cases, 25s. and 54s., sent on receipt of remittance.

1865 VINTAGE CLARETS, at Bordeaux or London.—Mr. T. W. STAPLETON, on his return from Bordeaux, begs to announce he has a splendid selection of VINTAGE WINES (of 27 growths) ready for delivery, in bottle or cask, from £12 to £96 per hhd., or by dozen 14s. to 96s. For price lists or samples apply at 203, Regent-street, W.

TWENTY-TWO Thousand Bottles EPERNAY CHAMPAGNE, first quality, vintage 1865. Full-bodied, fine condition, and dry. 36s. per dozen. Supplied on approval or return (with reference). Address T. W. STAPLETON, 203, Regent-street, corner of Conduit-street. Established over 30 years. In three dozen cases, £5 8s. Introduced in 1833 by The Times' advertisement.

TWO Thousand Magnums or Double Bottles of FLEUR de SILLERY d'AY CHAMPAGNE. Magnificent wine, 1865 vintage, carried first prize at Paris. Dozen case, magnums, 96s., quarts, same wine, at 50s. per dozen. Address T. W. STAPLETON, as above.

SIX Hundred and Twenty-four Hogsheads, 45 gallons each, PURE MEDOC, of 1865 vintage. Excellent sound dinner wine. Duty paid, £1[illegible], or 14s. per dozen; worth £20. In bond, £9. Address T. W. STAPLETON, as above.

NATURAL SHERRY, £10 10s. per quarter-cask, duty paid, being part of the third thousand quarter-casks sold since September 1866. Vintage 1864. Very dry, clean, pretty wine, warranted pure, and from Xeres. Can be tasted, free, at T. W. STAPLETON'S, as above. New parcel now landing.

HOOPER'S BRIGHTON SELTZER, 4s. per dozen. To be obtained of the principal chymists and wine merchants. Wholesale Depot, 7, Pall-mall east, S.W.

TEA (DARJEELING PEKOE).—A small consignment to a private order of the above excellent tea of the best brand. Boxes, containing 21lb. each, price £3 16s. Address F., at J. E. EVANS', Tea Merchant, 134, New Bond-street.

MC CALL'S WEST INDIAN TURTLE, Mock Turtle, Ox Tail, and other SOUPS, in tin, ready for immediate use. Sold by Grocers and Italian Warehousemen. Wholesale by John McCall and Co., 137, Houndsditch, London.

THE SOUP for WINTER.—MULLIGATAWNY, prepared by the Western Meat Preserving Company, in 2lb. tins, ready for use, at all Grocers and Italian Warehouses. Wholesale only from JOHN McCALL and Co., 137, Houndsditch, London.

IMPROVED and ECONOMIC COOKERY.—The LIEBIG COMPANY'S EXTRACT of MEAT as "stock" for beef tea, soups, made dishes, and sauces, gives fine flavour and great strength. Invariably adopted in households when fairly tried. Caution. - Genuine only with Baron Liebig's facsimile across label.

HALFORD'S INDIAN CURRIES.

HALFORD'S CURRIED FOWL, as prepared by him in India for the Governor-General, in tins ready for use. Also Curried Rabbit and Curry Sauce. Sold at the Depôt, 12, Upper St. Martin's-lane, and by all first-class grocers. Wholesale agents, Crosse and Blackwell, Soho-square, London. Fowl, 4s., 7s. 6d.; Rabbit 3s., 5s. 6d.; Sauce, 1s., 1s. 9d.

MESSRS. FELTOE and SONS ask indulgence of the public for a little unavoidable delay in executing orders, arising from their great number daily; they are executed in rotation, but where immediate attention is requested, priority is given.

THE recent Medical Correspondence in The Times demonstrates how injurious to health is artificially made-up Sherry "as Liqueur."

FELTOE and SONS, Sole Importers of the

SPECIALITE SHERRY.

UNUSUALLY FREE FROM ACIDITY,

LONG REQUIRED and LOOKED-FOR WINE.

THIRTY SHILLINGS per DOZEN.

NINE POUNDS per OCTAVE CASK, 6½ Dozens.

EIGHTEEN POUNDS per QUARTER-CASK, 13 Dozens.

OF BRIGHT WINE in CASK,

CARRIAGE PAID to any Railway Station in England or Scotland, and to any port in Ireland.

CASKS, Cases, and Bottles must be either paid for or returned carriage paid.

NECESSARY CAUTION.—The SPECIALITE SHERRY, unusually pure and free from acidity and heat, referred to in the important correspondence between the Rev. Sir Edward Jodrell, Bart., and the distinguished Analyst to the Pharmaceutical Society of Great Britain, Professor Redwood, can only be obtained from the sole Importers (and their appointed agents), Messrs. FELTOE and SONS, 26, Conduit-street, Regent-street, London, and Nos. 16 and 18, Tib-lane, Manchester. This long required wine was exhibited by special permission of the Council of the British Medical Association in their Museum, 1872, as a dietetic

---

FELTOE and SONS. Established 59 years.

BY APPOINTMENT to the QUEEN.

H.R.H the Prince of WALES.

NO. 26, CONDUIT-STREET, Regent-street, London.

NOS. 16 and 18, TIB-LANE, Manchester.

THE CASH SYSTEM ONLY.

SPIERS and POND, Wine and Spirit Merchants, Central Depot, 38, New Bridge-street, Ludgate, E.C., where their comprehensive WINE LIST may be obtained, post free, on application.

SPIERS and POND recommend for General Family Use

Sherry, Letter C in the list, a good sound wine	24s. a dozen.
Port, Letter C in the list, a capital wine	30s. a dozen.
Claret, Letter B in the list, pure Medoc	15s. a dozen.
Burgundy, Letter B in the list, in excellent condition ..	15s. a dozen.
Champagne (S. and P.'s Carte d'Or)	48s. a dozen.

Packing cases, 1s. 6d. a dozen. No charge for bottles.

Brandy, Letters A and B, pale or brown, fine Old Cognac	21s. a gallon	Jars extra.
Whiskey, Scotch or Irish, Letter A	18s. a gallon.	
Gin, best London Distilled, Letter C or D ..	15s. a gallon.	
Rum, Old Jamaica, Letter E	18s. a gallon.	

SPIERS and POND, Wine and Spirit Merchants, Central Depot, 38, New Bridge-street, Ludgate, E.C.

MAYFAIR SHERRY, 36s.—C. WARD and SON, No. 1, Chapel-street west, Mayfair, W.

FOSTER'S MOUNTAIN PORT, own vintages, finest Red Wine, rich grape flavour, 15s., 18s., 21s. per dozen; old bottled, 30s. ditto.—Thos. Foster and Co., 45, Cheapside, London.

OLD MARSALA WINE, guaranteed the finest imported, free from acidity or heat. Much superior to cheap Sherry 23s. per dozen; selected dry Tarragona, 20s. per dozen. Terms cash. Three dozen rail paid.—W. D. WATSON, Wine Merchant, 373, Oxford-street, and 56, Berwick-street, W.

AUSTRALIAN WINES.—Muscat of Alexandria, Rich or Dry.—This delicious amber Wine is guaranteed strictly unfortified, and without any addition whatever it retains all the fragrance and flavour of the fully ripe grape from which it is expressed. Received direct from the vineyard by P. B. BURGOYNE, the Australian Vineyards Association, Adelaide, and 50, Old Broad-street, London, E.C. Entrance Bank of New Zealand.

HEDGES and BUTLER solicit attention to their excellent DINNER SHERRY, at 24s. and 30s. per dozen:—

Superior Sherry, pale, gold, or brown		36s.	42s.	48s.		54s.
Port of various ages	24s.	30s.	36s.	42s.	48s.	66s.
Claret .. .. 14s.	18s.	21s.	30s.	36s.	48s. to	66s.
Champagne		36s.	42s.	48s.	60s.	66s.
Hock and Moselle		24s.	30s.	36s.	48s. to	120s.
Old Pale Brandy		44s.	48s.	60s.	72s.	84s.

No. 155, Regent-street, London, and 30, King's-road, Brighton.

VIN de BORDEAUX (1868), 16s. and 20s. per dozen.

Macon and Beaune	30s. and 36s. per dozen.
Epernay Champagne	36s. and 42s. per dozen.
Pale Sherry	24s. and 30s. per dozen.
Port (from the wood)	30s. and 36s. per dozen.

JAMES CAMPBELL, after many years' experience, confidently recommends these wines. Hennessy's old pale brandy, vintage 1858, 64s. per dozen; Glenlivat whisky, seven years old, 40s. per dozen. Address James Campbell, Wine Merchant, 158, Regent-street, London.

T. W. STAPLETON and Co.'s WINE TARIFF. By Custom-house report the largest importers in England (not supplying the trade), duty paid in 1873 being 65,086 gallons. Address No. 203, Regent-street, corner of Conduit-street, W. Established 1833.

1868 Clarets—pure Bordeaux, 14s. per dozen, or £12 per hhd., duty paid; will improve by keeping. With 27 others up to the first growths.

1868 Epernay Champagne, magnificent in quality, brilliant in condition, ripe for drinking, 36s. per dozen. Also the pale, delicate, and dry Creme de Bouzy, at 42s. per dozen quarts; 24s. pints.

1868 L'Empereur Champagne—premiere qualité—a superb dry wine, the cream of the vintage; quarts, 62s.; pints, 34s.

1860 Vintage Port, mature and fit for immediate use, 34s. per dozen, or £5 for three dozen. Old crusted ports, 36s. to 84s.

1864 Natural Sherry. This elegant, pure, dry Xeres, by the quarter cask, only £10 10s.; or the Star brand, by the dozen 24s., or £6 6s. per octave; £12 12s. per quarter cask.

1861 Manzanillas, very delicate, and not too dry, at 30s.; and the driest and finest that can be shipped, 36s. per dozen. Specially recommended for invalids, being free from acidity.

T. W. Stapleton and Co. invite attention to their choice selection of Old Brandies, Whiskies, and other spirits.

EXSHAW'S BRANDY, same as shipped to India. No. 1, 72s. per dozen; F.O.C., 64s. per dozen. Imported by Messrs. GEO. BATTCOCK and SON, Carlton street, Regent-street, London.

COURVOISIER'S CHAMPAGNE BRANDY, the only brandy supplied to His late Majesty Napoleon III., the finest and most delicate imported. Price per dozen, delivered free, 48s., 54s., 60s., 66s., 72s., 84s., 120s., according to age.—PHYTHIAN and SONS, 432, West Strand, London.

CAMPBELL'S OLD GLENLIVAT WHISKY, seven years old, 20s. per gallon, 40s. per dozen. The finest of Scotch Whiskies, in quality unrivalled. Address James Campbell, Wine Merchant, 158, Regent-street, London.

FALKNER'S REAL MALT WHISKEY has been esteemed in Ireland for the last century as the finest Irish Whiskey being pure as distilled and refined by age only. Seven years old, 20s. per gallon; 10 years old, 22s. per gallon. London depot No. 40, Charing-cross. Established in Dublin A.D. 1780.

KINAHAN'S LL WHISKY.—This celebrated and most delicious, old, mellow spirit is the very cream of Irish whiskies, is unrivalled, perfectly pure and more wholesome than the finest Cognac brandy. Note red seal, pink label, and cork branded "Kinahan's LL Whisky." Wholesale, 20, Great Titchfield-st., Oxford-street, W.

STAR BRAND XERES SHERRY—excellent, soft, delicate sherry, not sweet. Three dozen cases, £3 12s.; quarter-casks, £12 12s., duty paid (over 13 dozen).—At T. W. STAPLETON'S, as above. Can be tasted free.

MANZANILLA.—This extremely delicate, highly-flavoured SHERRY, vintage 1861, direct from the vineyard in Andalusia, at £15 10s. quarter-cask, or three dozen for £4 10s.—At T. W. STAPLETON'S. Can be tasted free. Usually charged, per dozen, 36s. Highly recommended by the faculty.

1860 PURE VINTAGE PORT. Magnificent condition, ripe for immediate use, from cask, if desired. Octaves, £10; quarter-casks, £20; or three dozen for £5. Over 400 pipes of this fine pure wine have been sold by T. W. STAPLETON since 1865. Address, 203, Regent-street, corner of Conduit-street.

HENRY DOLAMORE'S choice old MADEIRA, at the old-fashioned price and quality of 1850:—No. 1, old dry, 30s.; No. 2, extra superior, 36s.; No. 3, old reserve gold, 48s.; No. 4, seven years in bottle, 60s. Champagne, speciality, 27s. 6d. per dozen case.—16, Baker-street, W.

OLD MARSALA WINE, guaranteed the finest imported, free from acidity or heat, and much superior to low-priced Sherry. See Dr. Druitt's Report on Wines. One guinea per dozen. Choice old Rousillon, 24s. per dozen. Terms cash. Three dozen rail carriage paid.—W. D. WATSON, wine merchant, 72 and 73, Great Russell-street, corner of Bloomsbury-square, W.C. Established 1841.

NEUCHATEL (SWISS) CHAMPAGNE; Bouvier, Frères (Prize Medals, 1862 and 1867). Quarts, 42s.; pints, 24s. per dozen net. Clarets and all light wines, ports, sherries, brandies, and liqueurs of the best shippers, at lowest rates. Price list, &c., on application.—J. and R. McCRACKEN, wine merchants, &c., 38, Queen-street, Cannon-street, E.C.

COCKBURN'S GREEN GINGER WINE, the superior quality of which needs no comment. Each bottle is now secured with Betts' Patent Capsule to prevent fraud. Forwarded in cases of one, two, three, four, or six dozen and upwards to all parts of the kingdom at 20s. per dozen.—J. and G. COCKBURN, wine and brandy merchants, 135, Princes-street, and 21, South Castle-street, Edinburgh.

THE NATURAL WINES of FRANCE.—J. CAMPBELL recommends his VIN de BORDEAUX, at 20s.; St. Julien, at 22s.; and other clarets, from 26s. to 48s.; Vin de Grave, at 30s.; Chablis, at 26s.; and champagne, at 42s. per dozen. With regard to J. C.'s general stock of wines and spirits, he particularly recommends an excellent dry, pale sherry, at 36s. per dozen, also his old Glenlivat whisky, at 20s.; old Irish whisky, at 20s.; and Hennessey's old pale brandy, at 32s. per gallon. Remittances or town references should be addressed James Campbell, 158, Regent-street.

COOPER, COOPER, and Co. SELL the finest TEA the world produces, a perfect luxury, at only a fraction of the cost of other luxuries.

THE crop of really fine TEA grown in China this year is estimated to be only one-fifth of the total quantity consumed in this country. It follows that four people out of five have to drink Tea other than fine. COOPER, COOPER, and Co. therefore, recommend families to secure a good stock of fine Tea while it is to be had. They sell the best black Tea imported into England at 3s. a pound, full of flavour, full of strength; in fact, a perfect luxury.

COOPER, COOPER, and Co. are now SELLING BLACK TEAS of special excellence, at 2s. and 2s. 6d. a pound. Samples post free on application.—50, King William-street, London-bridge, E.C.; 63, Bishopsgate-street within, E.C.; 268, Regent-circus, W.; and 35, Strand, W.C.

SCHWEITZER'S COCOATINA, Anti-Dyspeptic Cocoa or Chocolate Powder. Guaranteed pure soluble cocoa, with the excess of fat extracted. Pronounced by the Faculty the most nutritious, perfectly digestible beverage for breakfast, luncheon, or supper. Keeps in all climates. Suits all palates. Requires no cooking. Four times the strength of cocoas thickened with starch, &c. In air-tight tins only, at 1s. 6d., 3s., 5s. 6d., &c., by all Chemists and Grocers. Sole Propriators, H. Schweitzer and Co., 10, Adam-street, London, W.C. Cocoatina is the best coacoa for export to India, the Colonies, &c.

SCHWEITZER'S COCOATINA à la VANILLE is the most delicate, digestible, cheapest Vanilla Chocolate, and may be taken when richer chocolate is prohibited. Sole Proprietors, H. Schweitzer and Co., 10, Adam-street, London, W.C.

SADLER'S DOUBLE SUPER MUSTARD, sold in oblong tins.

SADLER'S MUSTARD, sold in 6lb. tins.

SADLER'S MUSTARD, sold in 4lb. tins.

SADLER'S MUSTARD, sold in 1lb. tins.

SADLER'S MUSTARD, sold in ½lb. tins.

SADLER'S MUSTARD, sold in casks.

SPARKLING ST. GALMIER.—"Everybody is in Paris diluting his vin ordinaire with a slightly aerated and very palatable mineral water, called Eau de St. Galmier."—Augustus Sala, "Paris After the War."

SPARKLING ST. GALMIER.—50 champagne quarts, 22s.; 100 champagne pints, 32s. 1s. per dozen charged for bottles, and allowed for when returned.

CAUTION.—Each bottle must bear the address,

E. GALLAIS and Co., 27, Margaret-street, Regent-street, London. All kinds of Mineral Waters sold at reduced prices.

PATENT MALTED NURSERY BISCUITS. Wheaten flour contains from 60 to 70 per cent. of starch. The digestive organs of very young infants are not strong enough to enable them to extract any suitable nourishment from starchy preparations, such as biscuit powder, corn-flour, arrowroot, or tops and bottoms. By the process of malting the greater part of this starch is changed into flesh-forming material, and any food prepared in this manner becomes at once nourishing and digestible.

PATENT MALTED NURSERY BISCUITS.—in shilling packets and in half-crown tins.

PATENT MALTED NURSERY BISCUITS.—On receipt of 5s., two half-crown tins

PATENT MALTED NURSERY BISCUITS.—Will be delivered, carriage free,

PATENT MALTED NURSERY BISCUITS.—Within a radius of 10 miles of town.

W. HILL and SON, Purveyors to Her Majesty the Queen.

W. HILL and SON, Wholesale and Retail.

W. HILL and SON, 60, Bishopsgate-street, London, E.C

W. HILL and SON, 3, Albert-mansions, Victoria-street, London. S.W.

THE HALF-GUINEA CHRISTMAS PRESENT contains one good Hen Turkey, 1lb. Cambridge Sausages, and 1lb. Devonshire Butter, hamper included. Orders, pre-paid, to GILSON and Co., 4, Lyall-place, Chesham-street, Belgravia, S.W.

CHRISTMAS TURKEYS, 11d. per lb.—The LONDON FOOD STORES (Limited), 316, Oxford-street (formerly the Oxford-circus Skating Rink), are now SELLING best hand-fed TURKEYS at the above price; birds over 12lbs., 1s.; geese, 9d.; ducks, 1s.; hares 7½d.; rabbits, 8d.; best English meat, 8½d. per lb.; fowls, 2s. 3d. to 3s. 6d. each; game, fish, &c., at equally low prices. No tickets required. Terms, cash before delivery. Deposit accounts opened. Postal order forms 6d. per dozen. The remaining 7½ per Cent. Preference Shares of £2 each are now being allotted, the interest on which is well secured by the rents receivable from subletting the premises. The Directors have themselves subscribed for over £2,000. Price lists and prospectuses on application.

CHRISTMAS PRESENTS.

RULE'S BEST NATIVES ONLY.

OYSTERS, packed in barrels, 15s. and 30s., and sent to all parts of the Kingdom direct from the beds daily.—HENRY RULE'S Oysteria, 35, Maiden-lane, Strand, London, W.C. Established 1798.

CHRISTMAS PRESENTS.—RIDGWAY and Co.'s TEAS, in 7lb., 10lb., 14lb., 20lb. tins, or 20lb., 50lb., 100lb. chests. Also in ¼lb., ½lb., and 1lb. packets, in specially prepared air and waterproof paper, for distribution. Price lists and samples free on application.—4 and 5, King William-street, City, London, E.C.

Property

NO. 1, HYDE-PARK-GATE.—To be SOLD, with immediate possession, this noble MANSION, overlooking the park, with or without large and very superior stabling close by. Its position is unrivalled, and it contains entrance and inner halls, noble dining, drawing, and other reception rooms, smoking or billiard room in tower, 14 bed and dressing rooms, bath room, kitchen expensively fitted with cooking apparatus, lift, &c., and the usual offices. Apply to Mr. Philip D. Tuckett, surveyor, &c., 10a, Old Broad-street, E.C.

NEAR HAMPTON-COURT.—Capital FREEHOLD detached RESIDENCE, known as Langfords, charmingly situate on high gravelly soil, near the church, at New Hampton, to be SOLD or LET, with immediate possession, containing four large reception rooms, eight capital bed rooms, dressing room, kitchen, scullery, wine and coal cellars, china closet, two water closets, &c.; large croquet lawn an good garden, in all about three-quarters of an acre. Rent £90. Freehold £1,900. May be viewed at any time. Apply to Mr. W. Austin, estate agent, New Hampton.

OXFORDSHIRE.—To be LET, on LEASE, for seven, 14, or 21 years, a FAMILY MANSION, partially Furnished, with large gardens, and beautifully-timbered grounds running down to the Thames; from 60 to 70 acres of meadow and arable land. Good covert and partridge shooting. Five miles from Reading, two from Pangbourne Station. Any intending occupier can have more or less land, as required. For further particulars apply to Mr. R. Oades, land agent, Egham; Mr. Holmes, upholsterer, St. Mary's-butts, Reading; Mr. G. Lovejoy, London-street, Reading; or H. E. Brown, Esq., solicitor, 11, Pall-mall east, London.

QUEEN'S-GATE, Hyde-park.—To be LET or SOLD (No. 43, Elvaston-place), a most convenient HOUSE, close to the park, Horticultural and Kensington gardens, Metropolitan Railway Station, &c. Rent £230. Price £3,600. Apply at the house.

RANELAGH-MEWS, Westbourne-square.—To Builders and others.—To be LET, capital, large PREMISES; comprising three large workshops, stabling, living rooms, &c. For terms and cards to view apply to Wood, Langridge, and Co., estate agents 65, New Bond-street. (517 H.)

RUSSELL-SQUARE.—Corner House.—To be LET, unfurnished, a capital RESIDENCE, with offices or billiard room at back, and good side entrance as well as front. Especially suitable for a professional man's residence and offices. Rent only £150. Premium for lease and fixtures, £425. Cards to view of Mr. Greenwood, 152, Southampton-row.

RUSSELL-ROAD, Kensington.—To be LET, unfurnished, for three or five years, a HOUSE, containing three reception rooms, five bed rooms, bath room, with hot and cold water, closets, and well-arranged domestic offices. The furniture, which is entirely new, with carpets and glasses, may be taken at a valuation. A sacrifice will be made in consequence of the proprietor leaving England in a few weeks. Apply to F. W. Durrant, 1, Holland-place, Kensington.

SOMERSET, near Taunton.—About 100 acres of excellent LAND, with good Residence and Farm Buildings, to be SOLD. Apply to Mr. William Easton, land surveyor, Hammet-street, Taunton.

SURREY.—To be LET, furnished or unfurnished, with immediate possession, The GRANGE, West Molesey. Distance from Waterloo Station 14 miles. Terms moderate. For further particulars apply to W. B. A., 19, Green-park, Bath.

SOUTH WALES.—A clergyman wishes to LET his commodious HOUSE, Furnished, with every convenience; 20 minutes by rail from Tenby; climate adapted to delicate persons, good society and neighbourhood. Immediate possession. Rent £60 a year. Apply to Mr. Beal, estate and auction offices, 209, Piccadilly, London, W. (Fo. 326.)

SUSSEX.—Messrs. Hyde and Hall are instructed to LET, unfurnished, an excellent FAMILY MANSION, in the baronial style, seated in a finely-timbered park, with neat pleasure grounds, well-stocked gardens, and with or without the home farm, comprising about 180 acres of well cultivated land. It is most desirably situate in a healthy and attractive locality, 36 miles from London, and about two from a first-class station and good market town. Further particulars may be obtained, and photographs inspected, at the estate and auction offices, 31, New Bond-street, W.

STREATHAM-HILL, four minutes from the Station. To be LET, for six months, from the end of January, elegantly Furnished, a superior HOUSE, standing in its own ground, delightfully situated contains eight bed rooms, bath room, drawing and dining rooms, library, breakfast room, two kitchens, butler's pantry, larder, beer and wine cellars. The whole in perfect order, having been built and furnished within the last two years, at great cost. Stabling for three horses, with loose box and coach-house for three carriages, servants' room over. The servants, pair of horses, the carriage to open or close, hooded mail phaeton, saddles, bridles, &c., will be left if desired. For terms apply to Mr. R. Stapleton, auctioneer, No. 37, Broad-street-buildings, E.C.

WALHAM-GREEN.—HOUSE, with garden, to be LET on LEASE. Rent £80 per annum. Inquire for particulars at Messrs. Crace's, 33, Wigmore-street, W.

WILTON-PLACE, Belgrave-square.—ONE of the larger of these HOUSES, in the best part, well Furnished, to be LET, for a term of not less than seven years. Apply to Mr. Godwin, 15, Motcomb-street, S.W.

WATFORD.—To be LET, unfurnished, with immediate possession, a charming detached VILLA RESIDENCE, containing five bed rooms, large fitted bath room and water-closet, dining and drawing rooms, with French casements, library, kitchen, and convenient domestic offices, with about three-quarters of an acre of garden; situate within half a mile of the railway station. Rent £80 per annum. Apply to Messrs. Humbert and Cox, land agents, &c., No. 8?, St. James's-street, S.W., and Watford, Herts. (Fo. 269.)

WOODFORD.—To be LET, on LEASE, the capital FAMILY MANSION, known as The Rookery, adjoining the George-lane Station, containing four reception rooms, 10 bed rooms, bath room, and complete domestic offices, with stabling and outbuildings; also capital pleasure and kitchen gardens, the whole containing an area of 2a. 0r. 20p. Further particulars, with orders to view, may be obtained of T. Spreckley, Esq., 13, Cannon-street, E.C.; or of Messrs. Beadel, 25, Gresham-street, London, E.C.

SYDENHAM, Norwood, Forest-hill, Croydon, Dulwich, Tulse-hill, Streatham, &c.—Particulars of Houses for Disposal can be inserted free in Mr. W. B. SNELLING'S next SOUTHERN REGISTER.—Estate offices, 163, Fenchurch-street, E.C.

SYDENHAM-PARK.——£100.——A commodious HOUSE, with unusually good gardens, full of old, productive fruit trees and shrubs. Seven bed, dining, and drawing rooms, good offices. Newly repaired.—Mr. W. B. Snelling, 163, Fenchurch-st. (835.)

CATFORD-BRIDGE (Cannon-street Line).—£32, £45.—TWO not new, pretty, newly-decorated VILLAS; four or six bed, three good sitting rooms; nice gardens, summer house. High position; seven minutes' from station.—Mr. Snelling, 163, Fenchurch-st.

SOUTHFIELD, Bromley-road, near Ladywell Station (from Cannon-street).—This capital HOUSE, of seven bed rooms, three sitting rooms, offices; good gardens. Rent £75; hitherto £58.—Mr. W. B. Snelling, 163, Fenchurch-street, E.C. (530.)

SOUTH BELGRAVIA (£70), 25 minutes' by Thames or omnibus, shorter by rail.—Newly-decorated, cheap, roomy HOUSE, very healthy, on gravel; six or seven bed, bath, three reception rooms, offices, &c.—Mr. Snelling, 163, Fenchurch-street, E.C.

FOREST-HILL, near Honor Oak (the highest part, and with most lovely views).—A detached FAMILY HOUSE, known as Oaklands. Rent £150. Pretty, well-grown pleasure grounds, stabling, carriage house, &c. Nine bed, three reception rooms.—Mr. W. B. Snelling, estate agent, 163, Fenchurch-street. (866.)

UPPER SYDENHAM (The Grove).—A charming, detached HOUSE, in large fruit and flower gardens, in perfect condition, unfurnished. Six bed and dressing, dining and drawing rooms, domestic offices. Choice situation, near church, station, Crystal Palace, and shops.—Mr. W.B. Snelling, 163, Fenchurch-street, E.C. (836, 865.)

ENFIELD.—Suitable for an Indian Family.—A large, roomy old-fashioned HOUSE, furnished £180, unfurnished £150. Eight bed, three reception, school rooms; excellent gardens.—Mr. W. B. Snelling, 163, Fenchurch-street. (2 .)

BRIGHTON, 19, Brunswick-terrace, corner of the square.—The LEASE and FURNITURE (making 20 beds) of this handsome RESIDENCE for DISPOSAL, on moderate terms. Excellent stabling.—Mr. W. B. Snelling, 163 Fenchurch-street, E.C.

TOWN HOUSES for SALE.—Messrs. Wilson, Brothers are instructed to SELL the CROWN LEASE, at a nominal ground-rent, of a capital FAMILY MANSION and STABLING, close to Berkeley-square, price, including furniture, only 10,500 guineas; a first-class Family Residence in Hertford-street, newly decorated; a Residence and Stabling for four horses in Eaton-square, ground-rent £10, price £8,000; a Mansion and Stabling for seven horses in Upper Brook-street; a Freehold House in Stratton-street, price 8,000 guineas; a first-class Residence in Queen-street, Mayfair, price £7,500, ground-rent £8; a spacious Family Residence and Stabling in Hyde-park-square, price 6,000 guineas; a medium-sized House in Lowndes-street, lease 60 years, price £5,000; a Residence and Stabling in Prince's-gardens, price £8,500; a Residence at Rutland-gate (facing Hyde-park), lease 18 years, price for lease and furniture, 5,000 guineas. For particulars and cards to view apply to Messrs. Wilson, Brothers, 17, South Audley-street, Grosvenor-sq., W.

PARLIAMENTARY SEASON.—Messrs. Wilson, Brothers are instructed to LET, well FURNISHED MANSIONS and RESIDENCES, in Mayfair, Grosvenor-street, Belgrave square, Grosvenor-place, Grosvenor-crescent, Eaton-place, Eaton-square, Lowndes-square, Mansfield-street, Portland-place, Portman-square, Upper Grosvenor-street, Wilton-crescent, Princes-gardens, Hyde-park gardens and square, Lancaster-gate, Beaufort-gardens, and Queen's-gate-terrace. For particulars and cards to view apply at their offices, No. 17, South Audley-street, Grosvenor-square.

HANTS.—A charming RESIDENCE, surrounded by 11 acres of beautiful grounds, situate in a romantic position, on an eminence, and commanding extensive views of an undulating, well-timbered country. The abode is replete with every convenience for a family, and contains eight bed and dressing rooms, drawing and dining rooms, library, all requisite offices, and stabling. It will be Sold or Let, Furnished.—Wilson, Brothers, 17, South Audley-street, Grosvenor-square, W.

TO be SOLD, 8, CORNWALL-GARDENS, Queen's-gate, W. (Folio 8-164), unexpired LEASE over 90 years, situate within five minutes' walk of the Kensington and Horticultural Gardens, and of the Metropolitan Railway (Glocester-road Station). Price £4,000, or would be let, furnished, for £350, from or after January 1st, to the end of the Parliamentary season. Contains two drawing rooms and boudoir, two dining rooms and third room, two staircases, 10 bed and dressing rooms, and very good offices. Has been occupied five years and has just been newly decorated. For further particulars and cards to view apply to Mr. Geo. Gouldsmith, 2, Pont-street, Belgrave-square; or to Mr. J. Elsworth, 3, Trevor-terrace, Knightsbridge.

DEAN-STREET, Park-lane (Fo. 6-141).—Mr. Geo. Gouldsmith has to LET, on LEASE, for about 17 years, at a moderate rent, without premium, a desirable FAMILY RESIDENCE; containing 12 bed and dressing rooms, suite of drawing rooms, three rooms on the ground floor, and complete offices. Apply at his offices, 2, Pont-street, Belgrave-square, S.W.

ECCLESTON-SQUARE (Fo. 6-106).—Mr. Geo. Gouldsmith is instructed to LET or SELL a desirable FAMILY RESIDENCE, containing nine bed rooms, usual reception rooms, and offices. Price only £4,000 for long lease, at a ground-rent of £33 per annum. The Furniture may be Purchased at a valuation. Apply at his offices, 2, Pont-street, Belgrave-square, S.W.

EBURY-STREET, Pimlico (Fo. 8-130).—Capital RESIDENCE and valuable plot of BUILDING GROUND, extending over an area of 10,000 feet, well suited for the erection of business premises, warehouses, stabling, or a public hall; also a second Residence, in Graham-street.—Mr. Geo. Gouldsmith is instructed to LET or SELL the above eligible property, either in one or two lots. Particulars and cards to view at his offices, 2, Pont-street, Belgrave-square, S.W.

GROSVENOR-GARDENS (Fo. C. 128).—Mr. Geo. Gouldsmith is favoured with instructions to LET or SELL a spacious FAMILY MANSION, in this fashionable situation, containing 13 bed and dressing rooms, two drawing rooms, boudoir, dining room, library and third room, complete domestic offices; large coach-house, four-stall stable, and four rooms above. The original Lease to be Sold at a low ground rent. Apply at his offices, 2, Pont-street, Belgrave-square, S.W.

JAMES-STREET, Buckingham-gate (Fo. 8-170).—Mr. Geo. Gouldsmith has to LET, from 1st January to the end of March, or for the full season, a RESIDENCE. Contains eight or nine bed rooms, good reception rooms, and offices. Rent for the first three months, eight guineas per week. Apply at his offices, 2, Pont-street, Belgrave-square, S.W.

ONSLOW-GARDENS (Fo. E. 292).—Mr. Geo. Gouldsmith is instructed to SELL a spacious FAMILY MANSION; containing 10 bed rooms, bath room, five reception rooms, capital offices, and good stabling in the rear. Lease about 70 years; ground-rent only £6 per annum. Price £7,000; or to be Let, Furnished, for six months or longer. Apply at his offices, 2, Pont-street, Belgrave-square, S.W.

PIMLICO.—Capital Investment (Fo. 8-174).—Mr. Geo. Gouldsmith is instructed to SELL a well-built HOUSE, in Stanley-street, recently put into repair, and let for five years, at £55 per annum; held for upwards of 60 years, at £[illegible]. Premium 550 guineas. Apply at his offices, 2, Pont-street, Belgrave-square, S.W.

THURLOE-SQUARE, South Kensington (Fo. C. 158).—Mr. Geo. Gouldsmith is favoured with instructions to LET, on LEASE, several HOUSES, in this favourite square, close to the South Kensington Station of the Metropolitan District Railway, at rentals varying from £50 to £200 per annum; the use of fixtures included. Apply at his offices, 2, Pont-street, Belgrave-square, S.W.

UPPER GROSVENOR-STREET (Fo. 9-78).—Mr. Geo. Gouldsmith is favoured with instructions to SELL a desirable FAMILY MANSION, within a few doors of Park-lane. It contains nine bed rooms, two handsome drawing rooms, and conservatory, dining room, morning room, and library, complete offices. Price £ ,500. Immediate possession. Apply at his offices, 2, Pont-street, Belgrave-square, S.W.

WARWICK-SQUARE (Fo. 7-173).—To be LET, on LEASE, or for Sale, a capital RESIDENCE, containing 10 bed rooms, bath with hot and cold water supply, double drawing rooms, dining room, library, and third room, complete domestic offices. Lease over 70 years. Ground rent £26 per annum. Price £4,200. For cards to view apply at Mr. Geo. Gouldsmith's offices, 2, Pont-street, Belgrave-square, S.W.

CHEAP HOUSE, Charles-street, Grosvenor-square. Three floors permanently let, leaving ground floor for occupation. Rent £15 . Price £500 for lease and furniture. Rare opportunity. Apply to Mr. Walther, 27a, Old Bond-street.

COUNTRY HOUSE to be LET, Furnished, in a very pretty and healthy situation, in a good hunting country, a short distance from a railway station, and about an hour from London. For particulars and terms apply at J. H. Smee and Co.'s office, Moorgate Terminus, Finsbury.

COUNTRY, detached BIJOU RESIDENCE, suitable for a gentleman's small family, to be SOLD or LET. Freehold 300 guineas, subject to mortgage. Rent £65 for a term. Charmingly situate at Lyonsdown, Barnet, five minutes' from station. Drawing and dining room, three bed rooms, one small room and closet, large lawn, flower and kitchen gardens, fowl and out houses. Very compact, retired, not overlooked, well built, and in perfect order.—A. B., The Engineering Company, 91, Gracechurch-street.

ADELAIDE-ROAD, South Hampstead.—A very convenient, pleasantly-situate, semi-detached FAMILY RESIDENCE, with nine bed and dressing rooms, bath (with hot and cold supply), three water-closets, and three reception rooms, good domestic offices, and garden back and front, to be LET. Rent £85. Cards to view of Mr. Walter Holcombe, Auctioneer, 62, Haverstock-hill, N.W.

ACTON, Middlesex.—A detached VILLA, in the neighbourhood of Horn-lane, to be LET, on LEASE, comprising drawing, dining, and morning room, with entrance-hall and staircase on the ground floor, with eight bed and dressing rooms over, and with convenient domestic offices in the basement. Side entrance, with garden. For further particulars inquire by letter, prepaid, to Mr. Parsons, 14, Argyll-street, Regent-street, W., London.

BRYNMOR-HOUSE, Llanfairfechan, North Wales.—To be LET, a well FURNISHED HOUSE, from September 1st, for any time, as a whole or in apartments. Near the beach. Address Mrs. H. Bradley-Jones, Fern-bank, Llanarmon, Mold, North Wales.

BAYSWATER.—Clanricarde-gardens.—ONE of these choice RESIDENCES to be LET. Contains nine bed rooms, bath room (hot and cold), large drawing and dining rooms, library, and good servants' offices. Rent £170. Apply 11, Clanricarde-gardens, Bayswater-road, W.

BAYSWATER (best position).—To be LET, a first-class, semi-detached FAMILY RESIDENCE, containing handsome drawing room, large dining room, library, conservatory, eight bed rooms, kitchens, and domestic offices. Newly decorated. Good gardens. Rent £105. Apply on premises, 50, Norfolk-terrace, Westbourne-grove.

BUCKLAND-CRESCENT, near the Swiss Cottage.—To be LET, for three months or longer, a handsomely FURNISHED HOUSE, containing drawing, dining, and smoking rooms, five bed rooms, two dressing rooms, and bath room, three water-closets, and good domestic offices; good garden, semi-grand piano, gas. Terms £4 4s. per week. Stabling to be had near. Apply to Mr. Higgins, 12, Finchley-road, St. John's-wood.

BARNET (1,217).—Furnished.—To be LET, for a year, close to the station, a detached FAMILY RESIDENCE; four bed rooms, bath room, three spacious reception rooms, good garden, containing about a quarter of an acre. Rent moderate.—Prickett, Venables, and Co., 62, Chancery-lane, W.C.; Highgate, N.; and Barnet, Herts.

BERKSHIRE (4,752).—To be LET or SOLD, all that fine FREEHOLD RESIDENTIAL ESTATE, known as Prospect-hill-park, with commodious mansion, stabling, glasshouses, and farmstead, splendidly timbered park, highly productive gardens, arable and pasture lands, 252 acres in all.—J. Omer Cooper and Son, Land Agents, Reading.

A Detached HOUSE WANTED, to RENT, from Ladyday, within a few miles of London, near the church and rail, containing three sitting and seven bed rooms; good garden. Rent from £80 to £100. Address A. B., Mr. Morris's, news agent, Camberwell-green.

AN unfurnished COTTAGE RESIDENCE WANTED, on or near the banks of the Thames, on South-Western Line (Teddington, Hampton Court, or Hampton preferred). Rent about £36 per annum. Must be within 20 miles of Waterloo. Address N. Z., care of Mr. G. Street, 30, Cornhill, E.C.

A HOUSE WANTED, to RENT, or the Upper Part and Basement of a large House, containing two or three good reception rooms, three or four bed rooms, and servants' ditto, in the W. or S.W. district. The neighbourhood of Berkeley, Portman, or Grosvenor squares preferred. Address, stating full particulars, to C. S., post-office, Duke-street, Manchester-square.

AN unfurnished HOUSE WANTED, in February, in the neighbourhood of Maidenhead; containing the usual reception rooms and eight or nine bed rooms; coach-house and stable, with inexpensive gardens and grounds to keep up. Rent, with rates and taxes, not to exceed £100 per annum. Address W.W., 4, Belgrave-place, Brighton.

A COTTAGE WANTED, to RENT, unfurnished, containing at least two sitting rooms and five bed rooms, with large garden and stable, within 20 miles of London, on the Great Northern or Midland railways. Easy access to a station necessary, and an old-fashioned place preferred. Apply by letter, stating full particulars, addressed to Z., care of Mr. Roberts, advertising agent, No. 19, Change-alley, Cornhill.

COUNTRY RESIDENCE WANTED, to RENT, on LEASE, unfurnished, situate within about two or three hours' ride by rail of London, a few miles from a first-class railway station and market town, on a dry, healthy soil, in a good agricultural district and pleasant neighbourhood. The accommodation must consist of not less than three reception rooms and 12 or 13 principal and secondary bed chambers, with domestic offices, garden, and pleasure grounds of moderate extent, stabling for six horses, cottages for groom and gardener, and a home farm of 40 to 60 acres, with agricultural buildings and labourers' cottages. The counties of Berks, Hants, Wilts, and Beds are preferred. The eastern counties objected to. Particulars to be addressed to Messrs Norton, Trist, Watney, and Co., 62, Old Broad-street, Royal Exchange.

COUNTRY RESIDENCE WANTED, to RENT on LEASE, furnished or unfurnished, with shooting, and in a hunting country. Should be on a dry, healthy soil, in a pleasant neighbourhood, and within seven miles of a town and railway station. A small farm attached would be an advantage. The accommodation must consist of not less than three or four reception rooms, with 10 or 12 principal and secondary bed rooms, besides servants' bed rooms; stabling for 10 to 20 horses. Some of the counties between Durham and London preferred. Rent not to exceed £500 a year for house and shooting, exclusive of land. As such places are frequently let without being advertised or their vacancy being generally known, a commission of 5 per cent. on the first year's rent would be allowed to any solicitor, house agent, or other person giving the earliest information, if the after negotiation should result in a take. Address W. H., care of Messrs. Wiggins, Teape, and Co., 10, Aldgate, London, E.

LARGE HOUSE WANTED, unfurnished, on LEASE, within 12 miles of town. South side of London preferred, near a station. 14 bed and five reception rooms; gardens, and six to 12 acres; servants' hall, housekeeper's room, butler's pantry, offices; stabling. Full particulars Y. Z., J. B. Watson, Esq.'s, 9, Nottingham-place, W

PRIVATE HOUSE WANTED, in the neighbourhood of Tottenham-court-road, suitable for a home for working boys. Full particulars as to size and number of rooms and rent to be sent to A. O. Charles, Esq., 11, Buckingham-street, Strand.

TOWN MANSION WANTED, to PURCHASE, at the west-end, with or without furniture. Good stabling indispensable. Freehold preferred, but the short lease of one, otherwise suitable, would not be an objection. Direct particulars to Mr. Rearden, No. 92, Piccadilly.

TO HOUSE AGENTS and others.—WANTED, to PURCHASE a FREEHOLD, or long Leasehold, detached RESIDENCE, in the neighbourhood of the Crystal Palace. From £1,500 to £1,800. Leading thoroughfare preferred. Must contain seven or eight bed rooms, bath room, three sitting rooms above ground, billiard room (not absolutely necessary). Address L., Abbott's, 7, Little Tower-street, E.C.

UNFURNISHED HOUSE.—WANTED, within 10 or 12 miles of London, N., S., or W., a detached HOUSE, containing not less than three reception rooms and six bed rooms, and bath room, with complete domestic offices. The house must be well-built, and the rooms of handsome proportions. A good garden, with paddock and stabling, is requisite. The situation must be dry and healthy, and the drainage and water supply good and sufficient. Rent not to exceed £130. Address, with full particulars, including size of rooms and extent of grounds, Z., Warren's library, Edwardes-terrace, Kensington.

A Beautiful ESTATE, of about 260 acres, an old Mansion, and 14 Cottages, Freehold and land-tax redeemed; fine and salubrious elevation, greater part sloping to the River Tamer, overlooking a town. About 30 acres of the hanging lands are growing fine strawberries, the remainder fine feeding grounds and coppice, on which bullocks thrive remarkably well. Price, including timber, £16,500.—Roberts, Downes, and Co., 29, Bishopsgate-street, Bank, E.C.

FURNISHED HOUSE to be LET (immediate possession), containing bath, five bed, three reception rooms (newly decorated), kitchen, and scullery. Close to Notting-hill Station, healthy position. Good garden. Terms £10 per month. Apply to Mrs. Moyle, 21, St. Lawrence-road, Ladbroke-grove-road, W.

FURNISHED HOUSE to be LET, in Gloucestershire, for one or two years. Can be entered upon on short notice. Contains four sitting rooms and all offices on ground floor, 11 bed rooms; stabling, and a few acres of grass land and orchards. For full particulars direct to A. B. C., care of Mr. Hammond, Stationer, Knaresborough.

FURNISHED RESIDENCE (near Westbourne-park Station) to be LET, for six months or longer, at four guineas per week; five bed rooms, bath room, drawing room, double dining rooms, and complete offices, nicely furnished. Two good servants can be retained.—Messrs. Beard and Son, 110, Westbourne-grove.

FURNISHED.—Regent's-park.—A handsomely FURNISHED (13-roomed) VILLA; bath room, fernery, and perfect sanitary appliances, fitted under superintence of well-known sanitary engineer. Rent 10 guineas per week, for six months. Address A. R., No. 19, Princess-terrace, Regent's-park, N.W.

FURNISHED, semi-detached VILLA to be LET, about the 18th November, near Ladbroke-grove; contains five good bed rooms, three sitting rooms, bath room (hot and cold water); a large garden. If taken for a year or longer £12 per month. Apply to H., 96, Lancaster-road, Notting-hill, W.

FOR SALE, the LEASE of 88 years of an excellent HOUSE, and grounds, in perfect order within and without, containing three sitting, four good bed rooms, two dressing rooms, school room, and servants' rooms; good stabling, walled kitchen garden, glass houses, gardener's cottage, and eight acres of good pasture. It possesses unusual advantages, and is in the centre of Lord Leconfield's hunt. Apply to A. W. Phillips, Esq., Barton Rough, Petworth.

FREEHOLD INVESTMENT.—HOUSES, new, good position, two miles from Bank. To pay 7½. Purchase money £2,800, £3,700, or £6,500. Can be sold leasehold.—T. W., No. 108, Church-street, Paddington.

FREEHOLD HOUSES on SALE, close to Wimbledon-park and the railway station. One or more pairs, semi-detached. Price £750 each, or £1,450 the pair. Apply to Mr. Triggs, No. 26, Alexandra-road, Wimbledon.

FREEHOLD ESTATE, 750 acres, well timbered, lies in a ring fence, within two miles of station, 50 of London. There is a roomy old manor house, capable of great improvement, ample farm buildings. This is very suitable for a sporting man. Price only £17,500.—Roberts, Downes, and Co., 29, Bishopsgate-street, Bank, E.C.

FREEHOLD TOWN HOUSES, also long Leaseholds, most desirable for Trust Funds and Marriage Settlements.—Mr. Nosotti can offer several eligible HOUSES for the above:—Hyde-park, Freehold, £9,500; Beaufort-gardens, Freehold, £6,500; Queen's-gate, Freehold, with Furniture, £9,000; Belgravia, £8,000; Belgravia, £6,000; Belgravia, 6,000 guineas; Onslow-gardens, 8,000 guineas; Rutland-gate, £7,000; Queen's-gate, £4,500; Lancaster-gate, £11,500; Bayswater, £9,000; Kensington-gore, £9,000. Full particulars of Mr. Nosotti, Hyde-park-corner Estate offices, 31, St. George's-place, S.W.

HIGH-CLASS TRUST FUND INVESTMENT.—Bayswater.—Noble CORNER RESIDENCE, in the best position in a fashionable square. Let to a highly responsible lessee up to 1883, at £115 per annum, but worth £180 (large premium paid). Lease 63 years, at £3. Price £[illegible],800. Security equal to a ground-rent. Letters only, P. S., Gates' Library, Ladbroke-grove-road, W.

RENT £80.—To be LET (40, Grove-end-road, St. John's-wood), a BIJOU RESIDENCE, standing in centre of large garden. Main road. Well drained. South aspect. On view Tuesday, Thursday, and Saturday, from 2 p.m. to 4 p.m.

WINTER RESIDENCE, on the Hampshire Coast.—A most delightfully placed HOUSE, elegantly Furnished, commanding a splendid sea view, with the Needles, Christchurch Bay, and the west entrance to the Solent, has been intrusted to Messrs. Lumley for letting during the winter months at a nominal rent. To any gentleman's family without young children this offers a most agreeable residence for the time. Apply to Lumleys, Land Agents and Auctioneers, St. James's-street, Piccadilly. (18,813.)

FREEHOLD INVESTMENT.—Good FREEHOLD VILLA, with good garden; let for long term; £65 per annum. Price £970.—C. Willmott, 65, Goldhawk-road, Shepherd's-bush, W.

FURNISHED BIJOU RESIDENCE, large garden, near park and two stations, newly furnished; five bed and two reception rooms. Good kitchen. Rent three guineas.—Messrs. Osborne, No. 163, Queen's-road, Bayswater.

FURNISHED HOUSE.—A gentleman, having nine months since furnished a 10-roomed HOUSE, within one minute's walk of Chalk Farm Station, wishes to LET the same for a year, at £4 a week, or will Sell the Furniture for £350. Address, in first instance, Delta, post-office Chalk Farm-road, N.W.

FURNISHED RESIDENCE, in Warwick-square, in admirable order, and ready for immediate occupation. Well adapted for a Member of Parliament or a family requiring a first-class house. Contains four reception and 10 bed rooms, with very superior offices. Key to square. To be LET, for three years or for the season. Apply to Mr. Walther, 27a, Old Bond-street, Piccadilly, London, W

FOR SALE, LEASEHOLD, forming an entire place in the Borough, consisting of 12 substantial DWELLING-HOUSES, and a WAREHOUSE, held for 63 years unexpired, from Lady-day next, at a ground-rent of £89. Annual value £419. Always let. Net price £4,000. Apply to A. B., The Warehouse, 6, King's-place, Blackman-street, Borough, S.E.

FOR SALE, a FREEHOLD RESIDENCE, having ample accommodation for a gentleman's family, fitted in every way regardless of expense, and situate in a rural and very healthy district, easily accessible from the city, with the prospect of communication with the West-end by railway in the spring. There are in all about 12 acres of meadow land, including a garden of very pleasing but inexpensive character, with forcing houses, ample stabling, &c. Price of the freehold £8,750, three-fourths of which may remain upon mortgage. Apply to Messrs. Norton, Trist, Watney, and Co., 62, Old Broad-street, Royal Exchange.

THE nearly 15 years' LEASE and FURNITURE of a BIJOU RESIDENCE to be DISPOSED OF, in Great Cumberland-place, Hyde-park—five bed rooms, two pretty but small drawing rooms communicating by arched passage; on ground floor, a charming dining room, possessing all the quietness of the country, conservatory leading to bath room and lavatory, library fronting Great Cumberland-place, offices, consisting of butler's pantry, with bed, servants' kitchen, cook's kitchen, double wine cellar, small yard, &c. Lowest price 1,200 guineas. Rent £150. For permission to view apply by letter to M. W., care of Abbott, Barton, and Co., Advertisement Contractors, 269, Strand, W.C.

HOUSE WANTED, immediately, in the neighbourhood of Piccadilly. Rent about £200. No premium. Address R. W., 58, Redcliffe-road, South Kensington.

HOUSE WANTED, containing drawing, dining, five bed rooms and bath room. Must be close to a station; small garden. No basement preferred. Rent not over £60. N. or N.W. preferred.—79, Elsham-road, Kensington.

A FURNISHED, 10-roomed HOUSE WANTED, near Kensington-gardens or Hyde-park (on which side immaterial), for eight months or more. Rent under 150 guineas per annum.—Z., No. 53, Hollywood-road, S.W.

A FURNISHED HOUSE WANTED, in the immediate neighbourhood of Russell-square. Rent between £4 and £5 a week. Address F. V., MrParnell's, Stationer, 63, Southampton-row, W.C.

A FURNISHED HOUSE WANTED (worth about £100 per year unfurnished), within 50 minutes from Bank, with option to buy furniture at end of 12 months. Particulars to W., care of Housekeeper, 84, Lombard-street.

A SMALL, detached HOUSE or COTTAGE WANTED, to RENT, within 30 miles of London. Rent not to exceed £30 a year. Send particulars and order to view to B. L., care of Advertising offices, 150, Queen Victoria-street, E.C.

A SMALL HOUSE WANTED, to RENT (with option of purchase preferred), on two floors, with wash-house, two water-closets, &c., within five or six miles south of London, and near a railway station. Rent not to exceed £35. Address, prepaid, to R. G. F518, Address and Inquiry office, The Times Office, E.C.

A Detached HOUSE WANTED, with about 15 to 20 bed rooms, four reception rooms, and suitable domestic offices. Must be on high ground and near the Crystal Palace and railway stations. Not less than three acres of ground. Would either purchase or rent, on long lease. Address C., care of W. H. Steere, Auctioneer, &c., 5, Church-road, Upper Norwood, S.E.

A Detached DWELLING-HOUSE WANTED, to Purchase or Rent, containing seven bed rooms, bath room, and dressing room, and three reception rooms, with usual domestic offices on ground floor. About 30 minutes' rail from City; gravel or chalk soil. Price about £3,000, or corresponding rent. Early possession. Address S. N., 33, Duke-street, S.W.

BEXHILL, three-quarters of a mile from railway station. To be LET, with immediate possession, a PAIR of semi-detached VILLA RESIDENCES, very pleasantly situate. Pleasing views of sea and surrounding country. Each containing 10 rooms, and large garden. Rent £34 and £38 respectively. Further particulars of Messrs. Woodhams and Son, Estate Agents, Havelock-road, Hastings.

BUSH-HILL-PARK, Enfield.—To be LET, a gentleman's RESIDENCE, specially built on a most picturesque spot. Three reception rooms, seven bed rooms. Every modern convenience. Rent £120 per annum. Stables, &c., built to suit tenant if required. Other Smaller Houses in course of completion. To view address Mr. Flowers, the Bush-hill-park, Enfield.

BECKENHAM, Kent.—To be LET, at a nominal rent, in consequence of the owner going abroad, a comfortable detached RESIDENCE, standing in a nice garden, on a gravelly soil, and containing eight bed rooms, bath room, three reception rooms, and capital offices. Rent £120 on lease. Apply to Baxter, Payne, and Lepper, 69, King William-street, E.C., and Town-hall, Bromley, Kent. (4,364A.)

BRUGES.—An English lady wishes to LET her elegantly FURNISHED HOUSE, situate in the best and healthiest part of this city. It contains four sitting rooms, one of which can be used as a bed room, eight bed and dressing rooms, a large attic, and good offices. There is a small garden, with outhouse, and a grand piano by Broadwood will be left. The house is fitted with every regard to English comfort. Terms five guineas per week, or less if taken for a term. Address E. B., 67, Rue Nord du Sablon, Bruges.

BROMLEY, Kent.—To be LET, in this favourite locality, a convenient, detached RESIDENCE, containing 14 rooms. Large garden and conservatory. Rent £110 per annum. Particulars and orders to view of Messrs. Inman Sharp and Harrington, Auctioneers, 16, Abchurch-lane, City.

CHISLEHURST.—WANTED, a Furnished, or partially furnished HOUSE, on gravel, by year or on lease; three reception rooms and water-closet on ground floor, six or seven bed rooms. Rent not to exceed £150 per annum. Send replies to G. F. T., 33, Norfolk-street, Strand, W.C.

SMALL FURNISHED HOUSE WANTED, at Forest-hill, Sydenham, or vicinity, for few months or longer. Not less than four bed rooms. Careful tenant. Rent must be very moderate. Address M., care of Mr. Albery, Stationer, Horsham.

VILLA RESIDENCE WANTED, within an easy distance of London—one that has been inhabited. Reception rooms and one bed room must be large. Commission to agents. Rent not to exceed about £70 per annum. Particulars to X. X., 36, Prince's-street, Stamford-street, Blackfriars.

SPECIAL OFFER to LANDOWNERS.—A very superior FAMILY MANSION, not mortgaged, in South Kensington, of the value of £15,000, would be EXCHANGED for a landed estate, with or without a residence. If the landed estate is of more value a few thousand pounds in cash would be given too. Apply to Messrs. Dowsett and Woods, 70, Lincoln's-inn-fields.

FURNISHED RESIDENCES, Kensington, 2½ guineas a week upwards; unfurnished, £60, £80, £100, £150, £200 per annum upwards, to be LET or SOLD.—Morley and Bate, House Agents, Auctioneers, opposite Earl's-court Station, London.

HYDE-PARK and BAYSWATER ESTATES.—Messrs. CARTWRIGHT and Co. invite the attention of the nobility and gentry to their REGISTERS of furnished and unfurnished HOUSES to be LET and SOLD.—Estate Agency and Survey offices, No. 23, Leinster-terrace, Lancaster-gate, Hyde-park, W.

HYDE-PARK and PORTMAN ESTATES.—Messrs. FREDERICK A. MULLETT, BOOKER, and Co.'s REGISTER of the principal select, furnished and unfurnished RESIDENCES to be LET or SOLD may be inspected daily at their Auction and Estate Agency offices, Albion-house, Hyde-park-square (the corner of Albion-street), W.

KENSINGTON.—Morley and Bate, House Agents and Auctioneers, 185, Earl's-court-road, facing station, have unfurnished HOUSES for SALE or to LET, at £60, £80, £100, £150, £200, and upwards; Furnished Houses, at from 2½ guineas.

TO be LET, a most desirable HOUSE, for a small family, situate in the very best position in New Barnet, the most healthy suburb of London, newly decorated throughout. Good garden. Immediate possession for Christmas quarter. Rent £60. Apply B. J. Mills, Oakwood, Lyonsdown, New Barnet, N.

TO be LET or SOLD, Putney-hill (best part), handsome, detached FAMILY RESIDENCES. Three reception rooms, billiard room, conservatory, eight to 10 bed rooms, dressing and bath rooms, and every modern convenience. Matured gardens and trained fruit trees. Rents, one at £138 10s., one at £150, and one at £200 per annum. Apply to Messrs. Jennings and Burton, Solicitors, 17, Gracechurch-street, E.C.

Clothing

FREE of CHARGE.—MOURNING.—Goods are sent free of charge, for selection, to all parts of England (with dressmaker if desired), upon receipt of letter, order, or telegram; and patterns are sent, with book of illustrations, to all parts of the world. The Court and General Mourning Warehouse, 256 to 262, Regent-street, London. The largest mourning warehouse in Europe, PETER ROBINSON'S.

ARTICLES de LUXE.–RICH FRENCH VELVET MANTLES, trimmed with real lace or fur, at a reduction of from 10 to 15 guineas on each mantle. Sealskin Mantles proportionately cheap. JAYS'.

DRESSES for EVENING.—Messrs. JAY confidently invite attention to their present STOCK of EVENING DRESSES. Black and black and white tulle skirts, of the most fashionable kinds, are kept ready for immediate wear, any of which can be made up in a few hours, by French or English dressmakers employed at Jay's.

MOURNING.—Messrs. JAY have always at command experienced dressmakers and milliners who act as travellers, so that, in the event of immediate mourning being required, or any other sudden emergency for dress, one can be despatched to any part of the kingdom on receipt of letter or telegram, without any expense whatever to the purchaser. All articles are marked in plain figures, and charges are the same as if the goods were bought for ready money at the warehouse in Regent-street.—Jay's, the London General Mourning Warehouse, 247, 249, and 251, Regent-street.

NOTICE.–SPENCER, TURNER, and BOLDERO having bought by private contract the STOCK of Messrs. Trotman and Co., of 58, Archer-street, Westbourne-grove, who are retiring from the trade, will offer the same for SALE on Wednesday next, the 5th inst., at 10 o'clock. The stock consists of GENERAL DRAPERY, silks, shawls, mantles, fancy dresses, linens, longcloths, hosiery, haberdashery, ribands, lace, &c.—60, 61, 65, 67, 70, 71, 72, 73, and 74, Lisson-grove; 2, 4, 18, 19, 20, 21, and 22, Duke-street, N.W.

STOCK of a DRAPER.—Z. SIMPSON and Co., having purchased by public tender of Messrs. Honey, Humphrys, and Co., accountants to the estate, the entire STOCK of Mr. David Thomas, of Merton, draper, they will offer the same at large discounts from Mr. Thomas's cost, this day and during the week. Particulars already advertised. Z. Simpson and Company will offer with the above a large stock of fancy goods, suitable for Christmas presents, at an extraordinary discount off regular prices.—65 and 66 (late 48, 49, 50, and 53), Farringdon-street, E.C.

ON Monday, January 3d, 1870, the SALE of £15,900 worth of GOODS will be commenced at this establishment; a portion of the said goods comprising stock to the value of £8,800, lately the property of Wright and Morris, general export merchants, of St. Helen's (insolvents), and bought under a bill of sale by Baker and Crisp, at a reduction from the cost of three-sevenths, or about 8s. 9d. in the pound sterling.—BAKER and CRISP'S general drapery, silk-mercery, and fancy goods warehouse, 198, Regent-street. Detailed catalogue on application.

ANNUAL SALE of WINTER STOCK, at Reduced Prices.—GASK and GASK (late Grant and Gask) will offer for SALE, on Monday next, and during the month, their Autumn and Winter STOCK, at greatly reduced prices, the object being to sell the goods very cheap at once, rather than keep them over until another season. Plain and fancy silks, silk costumes and long skirts, dress fabrics of all kinds, costume skirts in all the new materials, ball and evening dresses, petticoats, shawls, mantles, opera cloaks, lace and fancy goods, French millinery, &c. Patterns forwarded to the country. Every article marked in plain figures the lowest price for ready money.—58, 59, 60, 61, 62, Oxford-street; 3, 4 and 5, Wells-street, London.

MESSRS. SWAN and EDGAR have the honour to announce that they have just purchased the whole of the extensive STOCK of rich-coloured GLACE SILKS of a Paris and Lyons manufacturer of the highest eminence. These goods, having been manufactured during the present year, comprise all the fashionable colours, and will be offered as follows on Monday, January 3d, 1870:—Quality No. 1—63s. 6d. the dress, or any length cut; original price 15f. per metre. Quality No. 2—78s. 6d. the dress, or any length cut. Quality No. 3—comprising 58 shades in ponit de sole glacé, of the widest width and richest quality manufactured, from four to 5½ guineas the full dress; original price 25f. per metre. This on examination will be found to be one of the most important and valuable collection of silks Messrs. Swan and Edgar have ever had to offer. Together with the above, and preparatory to a general stock-taking on January 31st, the greater part of their Stock of Fancy Goods in every department will be offered at a great reduction in price.—9 to 11, Piccadilly, and 39 to 53, Regent-street.

NEW YEAR'S GIFTS.—SEAL JACKETS, the most desirable and elegant present for the winter season, from 5½ guineas. Silks, a choice assortment of plain colour French silks, suitable for evening costumes, from 2½ guineas the dress. Bonnet's noted black silks, warranted to wear well, from 3 guineas. Dresses, rich corded silk poplins, from 29s. 6d. the dress; wool Tartan camlets, from 9s. 11d. the dress; ball dresses and opera cloaks, from 12s. 9d.—ALFRED BUTLER, Leinster-house, 113 and 115, Westbourne-grove.

FLANNEL DRESSING-GOWNS.—Special.—CHAS. AMOTT and Co. will SELL this day, 300 all-wool FLANNEL GOWNS, at 18s. 9d. and 1 guinea, containing 12 yards of flannel, and worth 2 guineas. 200 engravings of chemises, night gowns, drawers, camisoles, stays, &c., post free.—Chas. Amott and Co., 61 and 62, St. Paul's, London.

INDIAN OUTFITS.—An account of what is really necessary for the outfit of ladies, gentlemen, and children for the long sea and overland routes, with much valuable information on many topics useful for the voyage, and a few words on the new Brindisi Route. "Ladies going abroad will find the little work under notice of considerable value."—Queen.—ADDLEY BOURNE, 37, Piccadilly.

THRESHER and GLENNY, Outfitters, only establishment in London, next door to Somerset-house, Strand. N.B. Lists of necessary outfit for every purpose and appointment to India, China, and the colonies, will be forwarded on application.

STOCKINGS, Socks, and warm Under Clothing, for ladies, gentlemen, and children. The largest and best assorted stock in London, at strictly economical prices, at LODGE and SON'S, family hosiers and shirtmakers, 53, Oxford-street, W.

H. J. NICOLL'S OVERCOATS for Gentlemen. Pilot cloths, 25s., 42s., and 52s. 6d.; Melton cloths, 42s., 52s. 6d., and 63s.; beaver Witney cloth, 31s. 6d., 42s., 63s.; treble milled cloth for driving, 105s., 115s. 6d.; real fur seal, lined silk, 26 guineas; fur beaver, lined silk, 84s.; quilted, 126s.

Trousers for dress, 28s., 35s.; for walking, 14s. to 30s.

Dress coats, 52s. 6d., 63s.; frock coats, 63s. to 84s.; morning coats, from 42s. to 63s.

Real fur seal waistcoats, lined satin cloth, 52s. 6d.; ditto, lined with quilted silk, 63s.

H. J. NICOLL'S SPECIALITIES in WINTER DRESS for BOYS,

Knickerbocker suits, from	21s.
Morning suits, from	25s.
Evening dress suits, from	55s.
Highland suits, from	31s. 6d.

Frieze Cloth Overcoats:—Four years of age, 15s. 6d.; six years, 17s.; eight years, 18s. 6d.; 10 years, 20s.; 12 years, 21s. 6d.; 14 years, 23s.; and 16 years, 24s. 6d., &c.

Milled Melton, Pilot, and Witney Overcoats:—Four years of age, 22s. 6d.; six years, 14s. 6d.; eight years, 16s. 6d.; 10 years, 18s. 6d.; 12 years, 30s. 6d.; 14 years, 32s. 6d.; and 16 years, 34s. 6d.

Specialities in hats, shirts, hosiery, &c., suitable for each dress.

For every article one fixed and moderate price is charged for cash payments. Garments are kept ready for immediate use, or made to order in a few hours.

H. J. NICOLL'S RIDING HABITS, in various coloured tweed cloths, £3 3s.; melton cloths, £4 4s.; superfine cloths, £6 6s.; riding trousers, from 21s.; hats, with lace falls, 21s.; promenade jackets, in great variety, serge, waterproof tweed, and melton travelling costumes, £1 11s. 6d., £2; with skirts, 20s., 25s.

Scarlet, blue, and other coloured Waterproof Cloth Shawls, 21s.

Real Fur Seal Jackets, 24 inches long, lined with quilted silk, £9 9s.; ditto, 27 inches long, £10 10s.

SERVANTS' LIVERIES. The best, at moderate prices; treble-milled Cloth Overcoats, and milled cloth Frock Coats, thoroughly waterproof, for grooms and coachmen.

H. J. NICOLL, Merchant Clothier to the Queen the Royal Family, and the Courts of Europe.

LONDON .. .. .. { 114, 116, 118, 120, Regent-street, W.
41, 44, 45, Warwick-street, W.
22, Cornhill, E.C.

BRANCHES .. .. { 10, Mosley-street, Manchester.
50, Bold-street, Liverpool.
39, New-street, Birmingham.

EVENING and BALL DRESSES.—New Figured French Tarlatans, in stars, crescents, spots, and other new devices, the lightest, prettiest, and most brilliant dress of the season, 3s. 11½d. the dress. Patterns free.—JOHN HOOPER, 52, Oxford-st., W.

REAL SEALSKIN JACKETS.—SEWELL and Co.'s recent purchases will give ladies the advantage of buying a really good SEALSKIN JACKET at very low prices.—Compton-house, Frith-street, Soho-square, W.

NEW YEAR FESTIVITIES.—BALL and EVENING SKIRTS tastefully made and trimmed in all colours from 21s. Crystallized Tarlatans, at 10s. 6d. the dress. Tulle and Net Skirts fashionably trimmed, from two guineas.—SEWELL and Co., Frith-street, Soho-square, W.

BALL and EVENING DRESSES.—Special novelties, beautifully made and trimmed. More than 20 designs, in perfect taste, from one guinea and upwards, carefully packed in box, free, for all parts. Descriptive illustrations, post free, on application.—PETER ROBINSON, 103 to 108, Oxford-street, London.

OPERA MANTLES.—Every description of Opera Mantle and Opera Jacket now fashionable, suitable for the theatre, evening wear, or for weddings, from 10s. 6d. each to the most elaborately embroidered.—PETER ROBINSON, 103 to 108, Oxford-street, London. Illustrated Manual free on application.

FREE of CHARGE.—MOURNING.—Goods are sent free of charge, for selection, to all parts of England (with dressmaker if desired), upon receipt of letter, order, or telegram; and patterns are sent, with book of illustrations, to all parts of the world. The Court and General Mourning Warehouse, 256 to 262, Regent-street, London. The largest mourning warehouse in Europe, PETER ROBINSON'S.

ANNUAL SALE of WINTER STOCK, at reduced prices.—GASK and GASK (late Grant and Gask) are now SELLING their autumn and winter STOCK at greatly reduced prices. Plain and fancy silks, silk costumes and long skirts, dress fabrics of all kinds, costume skirts in all the new materials, ball and evening dresses, petticoats, shawls, mantles, opera cloaks, lace and fancy goods, French millinery, &c. Patterns forwarded to the country. Every article marked in plain figures the lowest price for ready money.—58, 59, 60, 61, 62, Oxford-street; 3, 4, and 5, Wells-street, London.

SELLING OFF.—G. W. JONES' choice FANCY STOCK of FLOWERS, Feathers, Ribands, laces, falls, millinery, hats (seal, felt, &c), French and English jewellery, jet, tortoise-shell, ivory goods, with an extensive assortment of Paris fans, at prices that must command a quick clearance. N.B. 101, Oxford-street.

HOLBORN VALLEY IMPROVEMENTS.—"The Corporation v. Holdich."—The National Linen Warehouses, 105, Fleet-street, corner of Farringdon-street, foot of Ludgate-hill, city.—These premises being bought by the Corporation for the new street to the Holborn-circus, Messrs. WM. HOLDICH and Co. are compelled to SELL the whole of their large and welll assorted STOCK at a great reduction, compensation being allowed by the Corporation for the loss thereon. The Warehouses will be Closed, for the purpose of re-marking the stock, on the Friday and Saturday previous to the sale, on Monday next, the 24th inst., and following days, when the entire stock must be cleared out without reserve. Doors open at 10 o'clock and close at 6.—The National Linen Warehouses, 105, Fleet-street, corner of Farringdon-street, foot of Ludgate-hill, city.

THRESHER and GLENNY, Outfitters, only establishment in London, next door to Somerset-house, Strand. N.B. Lists of necessary outfit for every purpose and appointment to India, China, and the colonies, will be forwarded on application.

GENTLEMEN'S DRESS.——HAMILTON and KIMPTON, tailors and overcoat makers, 105, Strand. New goods from the best manufacturers in the west of England, at a fair price.—No. 105, Strand, opposite Exeter-hall.

GEORGE HOBSON respectfully invites the attention of the public to his superfine West of England woaded Black Cloths for FROCK and DRESS COATS:—

Black frocks coats ..	£3 3s. 0d.	Dress coats	£2 15s. 0d.
Ditto	3 13s. 6d.	Ditto	3 3s. 0d.
Ditto	4 4s. 0d.	Ditto	3 13s. 6d.

All the new materials for winter overcoats and morning coats. Superior fit and workmanship are the characteristics of this establishment.

GEORGE HOBSON'S NEW TROUSERS for the present season, Price 16s.—No. 57, Lombard-street.

DRESS SUITS, four guineas, 4½ guineas, and five guineas, to order at a few hours' notice. Excellence with economy. GEORGE HOBSON, 57, Lombard-street. Established in the XVIIIth century.

LILLICRAPP, Court Furrier, 27, Davies-street, Berkeley-square, W.—Real FUR SEALSKIN CLOAKS, jackets, and coats, vests for hunting, and driving gloves; Astracan jackets, velvet mantles trimmed with various kinds of fur, cloth coats lined with fur. Carriage wrappers in great variety. Skins dressed and mounted. Furs taken in exchange.—Lillicrapp, furrier, by special appointment to H.R.H. the Prince of Wales

MOURNING for WIDOWS and DAUGHTERS,

THE BEST and CHEAPEST in the KINGDOM. Furnisher to the Queen.

PUGH'S, 163 and 165, Regent-street.

WOOL SERGES EXTRAORDINARY.—A MANUFACTURER'S STOCK, now selling at little more than half-price. Beautiful colours, wide width, price 7¾d per yard. Patterns free.—JOHN HOOPER, 52, Oxford-street, W.

EVENING and BALL DRESSES.—Thousands of beautiful WHITE, WASHING STRIPED GRENADINES are now offering at 3s. 11½d. the dress, or 6d. per yard. Starred tarlatans at 3s. 11½d. the dress. Patterns free.—JOHN HOOPER, 52, Oxford-street, W.

HILDITCH'S SILKS.—Stock-taking, 1874.—Previous to receiving the new goods for the Spring, Messrs. Hilditch are now selling a considerable portion of their STOCK of SILKS at reduced prices. Coloured gros grains from 3s. 6d.; remnants and cut lengths under 16 yards much under value.—G. and J. B. Hilditch (late of Ludgate-hill), Silk Warehouse, 11 and 12, Cheapside. Patterns sent to residents in the country.

HILDITCH'S BLACK SILKS, new price list, January, 1874. Patterns sent to the country and abroad.—Silk Warehouse, 11 and 12, Cheapside. Established 1760.

NON-CRUSHING TULLE.—Elegant and cheap EVENING DRESSES at Messrs. JAY'S, made of black tulle, which will neither tumble nor get out of condition in the carriage or the ball room. Designed by the best Paris modistes, and made up at the London General Mourning Warehouse, by une Couturière Française or an English dressmaker.—JAYS'.

TWO POUNDS TWELVE SHILLINGS and SIXPENCE EACH.—Fashionably made up WINTER BLACK STUFF COSTUMES, full quantities, and trimmed after models from the best houses in Paris, 2½ guineas.—JAYS'.

FASHIONABLE BLACK SILK COSTUMES, 6½ guineas each.—Black Silks.—Ladies in search of this useful material will find a choice selection at Messrs. JAY'S for £5 5s. the dress or 7s. 6d. the yard. Costumes from the best French models made to price and order with only the additional cost of trimmings.—JAYS', the London General Mourning Warehouse, 243, 245, 247, 249, and 251, Regent-street, W.

RICH FRENCH GROS de LONDRES SILKS, all colours, 3s. 11d. per yard; new Canéle striped silks, 3s. 3d.; extra rich coloured and black Lyons gros grain silks, 6s. 6d. and 7s. 6d.; silk costumes, woollen costumes, evening costumes, a large collection, from 16s. 6d. to 30 guineas; new ball and evening dresses, one guinea. —GASK and GASK, 58, 59, 60, 61, 62, 63, Oxford-street; 1, 2, 3, 4, 5, Wells-street.

BLACK ASTRACAN FUR JACKETS.—A few first-class qualities clearing out much below cost price. Seven guinea jackets for five, 10 guinea jackets for seven, 12 guinea jackets for 8½.—At PETER ROBINSON'S Mourning Warehouse, 256 to 262, Regent-street.

STOCK-TAKING SEASON, February, 1874.—During this month we intend offering for SALE, at greatly reduced prices, a considerable PORTION of our STOCK, to make room for our new spring goods.—WM. CHURTON and SON, 91 and 92, Oxford-street.

SAMPLES sent for six stamps, with Illustrated Price List.—PAPER COLLARS, wrists, and fronts for ladies and gentlemen, of the best quality.—EDWARD TANN, 308, High Holborn, London.

ÆGIDIUS, a new elastic over-shirt, which will entirely dispense with the old-fashioned coloured flannel. The Ægidius is perfectly shrinkless. Patterns of the material and self-measure free per post for two stamps. Sole makers, the inventors of the Eureka, RICHARD FORD and Co., 41 and 44, Poultry, E.C.

GENTLEMEN'S DRESS (105, Strand), of the best materials, for frock and walking coats, winter suits and overcoats, at HAMILTON and KIMPTON'S, Tailors and Overcoat Makers, 105, Strand, opposite Exeter-hall.

H. J. NICOLL'S celebrated SOVEREIGN TWEED OVERCOATS (waterproof yet evaporable), or, with silk lapels, one guinea each, are further improved by the insertion of pockets so constructed as to allow expansion on the inside without showing any appearance of bulging from the exterior. This useful invention was registered by H. J. Nicoll, Jan. 7, 1874, and these overcoats can only be obtained at his several addresses—in London, 114, 116, 118, and 120, Regent-street, and 22, Cornhill. Manchester, 10, Mosley-street; Liverpool, 50, Bold-street; Birmingham, 39, New-street.

HIGH-CLASS fashionable CLOTHING for gentlemen paying cash, at a fractional advance only on the cost of production. Exclusively to order, and of the best quality. Price lists on application.—LAWRANCE D. PHILLIPS and Co., Military and Court Tailors, 13, George-street, Hanover-square, W.

LAWRANCE D. PHILLIPS and Co., Military and Court Tailors, wish it to be distinctly understood that they only use materials of the best quality, and employ workmen of the highest experience.—13, George-street, Hanover-square, W.

LAWRANCE D. PHILLIPS and Co., Military and Court Tailors, wish it to be distinctly understood that the great reduction in their prices is solely attributable to the absence of bad debts and the risks and responsibilities inseparable from a credit trade.—13, George-street, Hanover-square, W.

WANTED, LEFT-OFF CLOTHING.—Mr. and Mrs. LEWIS DAVIS, 2, Crawford-street, Baker-street, W., offer special facilities to ladies and gentlemen having LEFT-OFF CLOTHING to dispose of. They attend any time or distance, they purchase goods of every description, in large or small quantities, they pay cash in every instance, and punctuality is strictly regarded. They will be happy to receive commands, either verbally or by letter at their only address, 2, Crawford-street, Baker-street, W. It is respectfully requested that the address may be noted and kept for reference. Cards forwarded on application. Bankers—National Provincial Bank of England. Established 1800. Terms cash.

BLACK GROS GRAIN SILKS, the richest quality, wide width, sacrificed at 4s. 6d. the yard.—HARVEY and Co., Lambeth-house, Westminster-bridge. Patterns free.

JAPANESE.—The largest and most varied stock, chiefly the German make, excellent for wear, at prices hitherto unknown, beginning at 10d. the yard. The same has been sold at 2s. 6d.—HARVEY and Co., Lambeth-house, Westminster-bridge. Patterns post free.

BLACK and COLOURED VELVETEENS.—Widest, at 2s., 2s. 6d., and 3s. 6d. The quality at 2s. 6d. is bright and silky. This firm (the first to place velveteens before the public) have sold many thousand dresses, and never heard a complaint. Patterns post free.—HARVEY and Co., Lambeth-house, Westminster-bridge.

MERINO.—After all, there is no dress which gives such entire satisfaction as French Merino. Softest wool, very fine and wide, in brilliant colours, all at 2s. the yard. The quality has been scrupulously kept up, and can be had only at Lambeth-house, Westminster-bridge. Patterns post free.—HARVEY and Co. Established 50 years.

REGENT-HOUSE, 238, 240, 242, Regent-street, 26 and 27, Argyll-street.

ALLISON and COMPANY'S ANNUAL SALE of SURPLUS STOCK commenced Monday, 29th ult., and will continue for a few weeks. An inspection is respectfully solicited. Patterns free.

WOOL SERGES EXTRAORDINARY.—A manufacturer's stock now selling at little more than half price. Beautiful winter colours, wide width, price 7¾d. per yard. Patterns free.—JOHN HOOPER, 52, Oxford-street, W.

EVENING and BALL DRESSES.—Thousands of beautiful white washing striped GRENADINES are now offering at 2s. 11½d. the dress, or 4½d. per yard; starred Tarlatans at 3s. 11½d. the dress. Patterns free.—JOHN HOOPER, 52, Oxford-street, W.

THE LAST WEEK of J. PARTON and SON'S ANNUAL SALE of DRAPERY. The whole of their stock greatly reduced. A discount of 2s. in the pound allowed on all parcels above 20s.—41 and 43, Buckingham Palace-road, Pimlico, S.W.

ONE THOUSAND made BALL DRESSES, from one guinea (always in stock). Descriptive illustrations post-free on application.—PETER ROBINSON'S, 103 to 108, Oxford-street, London, W.

INDIA SHAWLS.—EVERINGTON and GRAHAM receive consignments by every mail from Cashmere, in all new designs. Ladies purchasing in England save all duties to which they are subject in other countries.—India Shawl Warehouse, 19 and 21, Ludgate-hill, near St. Paul's. N.B. Rich Black Lyons Silks, manufactured by C. J. Bonnet, from 5s. per yard, upwards.

HALF-YEARLY SALE, at reduced rates.—HOWELL, JAMES, and Co. hold their Half-yearly Sale THIS DAY, and continue the same for 30 days from Jan. 12. Large quantities of valuable MERCHANDIZE are offered in all the departments at greatly reduced rates. Detailed catalogues forwarded post free.—5, 7, 9, Regent-street (near Pall-mall).

HALF-YEARLY SALE.—HOWELL, JAMES, and Co., 5, 7, 9, Regent-street (near Pall-mall).—The STOCK of elegant PLAIN, BLACK, and COLOURED SILKS being unusually large, Messrs. H., J., and Co. have decided to reduce the prices very considerably. Upwards of 10,000 yards of rich black silks are placed on their counters daily, until the beginning of February, at the following prices (much below their value) :—4s. 6d., 5s. 6d., 6s. 6d., 7s. 6d., 8s. 6d., 9s. 6d., 10s. 6d. the yard wide width. Patterns post-free. Five per cent. discount for cash.—5, 7, 9, Regent-street (near Pall-mall).

WINTER SALE.—ALFRED BUTLER begs to announce that his ANNUAL WINTER SALE is now in progress, as ladies begin to be aware that they purchase BLACK SILKS, rich Velvet Mantles, and Costumes, dress materials, household linens, and muslin curtains, at prices so far below their ordinary purchases at other times, every year is attended with greater success. Dress Serges, 6¾d. the yard; Diagonal Cloths, 11¾d. During the sale patterns of these goods cannot be sent, as the colour selected will most likely be sold out.—ALFRED BUTLER, Leinster-house, 113 and 115, Westbourne grove, W.

GASK and GASK'S SALE of SURPLUS STOCK, and the remainder of choice goods from the Vienna Exhibition, at greatly reduced prices. All the immense stock of rich French silks and velvets, Paris silk and woollen costumes, Austrian bronzes, Indian goods, Scotch, English, and foreign dress fabrics, Paris mantles and jackets, Russian sealskins, sables and furs, Brussels laces, Paris millinery, French gloves, soiled linens, curtains, &c. All the surplus stock from all the departments and all that remains from the Vienna Exhibition will be sold, without exception, very cheap. Patterns free.—58, 59, 60, 61, 62, 63, Oxford-street, and 1, 2, 3, 4, 5, Wells-street.

GENERAL NOTICE.—MARSHALL and SNELGROVE beg to announce to their patrons and the public generally that their usual SALE, at the close of the Winter Season, is now being proceeded with, and will be continued until the last week in January. During the whole of this time Messrs. M. and S. hope to be constantly visited by purchasers desirous of obtaining cheap goods in excellent condition. Among the many lots they are showing at the various counters, particular attention is directed to about 850 polonaises, beginning at 12s. 9d. each, and well adapted for the coming spring; also 400 cashmere and cloth tunics, with jacket and skirt, from 42s. each, worth much more and suitable for immediate wear. These, with the largest purchase they have ever made in black, coloured, and rich fancy silks, remarkably cheap, will no doubt be soon cleared. In the other departments goods of daily requirement will also be found at remarkably low prices. N.B. Some rich Brussels lace and a maker's stock of plain and embroidered cambric handkerchiefs.—Marshall and Snelgrove, Vere-street and Oxford-street.

THE CITY LINEN WAREHOUSES, 49 and 51, Ludgate-hill, London.—The ANNUAL STOCK-TAKING SALE of SURPLUS STOCK, Winter Goods, and Remnants, commenced on Monday, the 12th inst., and will be continued during the month. A lot of Irish Damask Table Linen and Cambric Handkerchiefs very cheap. A quantity of Lace Curtains much below value. A very cheap lot of white Quilts, Austrian and other Blankets, Tapestry Table Covers, Cretonnes, Chintzes, Bath Coatings, and Fancy Flannels; some ends of Sheetings, Towellings, Tea Cloths, &c., at half-price. All goods marked in plain figures.

WINTER OVERCOATS, of the very best materials and workmanship, at HAMILTON and KIMPTON'S, Tailors and Overcoat Makers, 105, Strand, opposite Exeter-hall.

H. J. NICOLL, Merchant Clothier and Outfitter. London—114, 116, 118, 120, Regent-street, and 22, Cornhill. Manchester—10, Mosley-street. Liverpool—50, Bold-street. Birmingham—39, New-street. Young Gentlemen's Outfits on their return to school. The stock comprises tasteful designs in suits for younger boys, and Regulation Suits, as worn at Eton, Harrow, and other great schools. Overcoats in warm materials from one guinea. Shirt, Hosiery, and Hat Department.—Great care has been taken in the selection of winter stock, and with special reference to the colours being suitable for each dress. Whether in hats, hose, ties, or other articles, they will be found to harmonise with the particular tint of dress selected. The shirts and underclothing are of a superior quality, while the prices are most moderate for cash payments.

TO GENTLEMEN.—EVENING DRESS SUITS of the highest finish and fashion, at H. J. NICOLL'S several addresses, viz.:—114, 116, 118, 120, Regent-street, and 22, Cornhill, London; 10, Mosley-street, Manchester; 50, Bold-street, Liverpool; and No. 39, New-street, Birmingham.

HER MAJESTY'S DRAWING ROOM, March 25th.—Miss LEONORA GEARY will RECEIVE, and also attend LADIES, to prepare them for presentation to Her Majesty, up to Wednesday, March 25th.—14, Grafton-street, New Bond-street.

HER MAJESTY'S LEVEES and DRAWING ROOMS.—Every REQUISITE for the above, including Court suit, Deputy-Lieutenant and every other uniform, in elegant and superior style, to be had on HIRE at NATHAN'S, the celebrated Court Costumiers, of 23, Tichborne-street, Regent street, only. Their splendid and portable Theatre, with every requisite, on Hire.

HER MAJESTY'S LEVEES, &c.—The new COURT DRESS, Deputy-Lieutenant's, naval and military uniforms made to order, or on hire, at SIMMONS', Court Costumier, No. 8, King-street, Covent-garden, only.

SABLE TAIL (real), wide **FLOUNCING**, &c., cost £70, price £36; Sable Skin ditto, cost £30, price £16 16s.; set finest electro-plated Entrée Dishes, cost £16 16s., price £8 8s.; diamond Earrings, Bracelets, Rings, Studs, &c. A lady wishes to SELL the above. All are new, and can be sent anywhere on approval.—Mrs. Cowper, Wheatley, near Oxford.

H. J. NICOLL'S NEW GUINEA PALETOT of finely twilled West of England Tweed, rendered by their special process showerproof yet evaporable; suitable for summer and autumn wear.

LADIES' ULSTERS.—Messrs. NICOLL would draw attention to their specialité PRINCESS ULSTER, at the price of 2½ guineas, made from soft Scotch cheviot, and designed in accordance with the new costume models for this season.

SHOOTING SEASON, 1879.—EDMISTON'S NEW SHOOTING CAPE allows perfect freedom to the arms when firing; carried on the back, by undoing a button falls over the shoulders ready for use. Price from 15s. 6d. See Field, Sept. 7th and Oct. 5th, 1878.—Sole Manufacturers, Edmiston and Son, 14, Cockspur-street, Pall-mall, London, S.W. (opposite the Haymarket).

HOWELL, JAMES, and Co., Silk Merchants to the Queen and Royal Family, have just purchased, under most exceptional circumstances, a very large quantity of

THE RICHEST PLAIN BLACK SILKS, the renowned manufacture of

MESSRS. BONNET and Co., of Lyons and Jujurieux.—Howell and James, with a view to encourage cash payments, will place the whole of these superb SILKS on their counters on Monday next, Nov. 3, and during the month, marked in plain figures, at 6s. 6d, 7s., 8s. 6d., 9s., and 10s. 6d. These prices are from 2s. to 4s. per yard under the usual retail rates. Howell, James, and Co. will be happy to send patterns to the country; but they strongly recommend ladies residing in town to inspect and choose from the pieces.—HOWELL, JAMES, and Co., 5, 7, and 9, Regent-street, and 10, Charles-street, St. James's-square.

MADAME ELLIOT'S stylish DRESSES, from 63s.; Children's Dresses, beautiful material, 25s. 6d. complete.

MADAME ELLIOT'S CORSETS, splendid shape, will suit and improve any figure. Special corsets for ladies inclined to embonpoint; also another speciality for slight figures. Young ladies' corsets from 5s. 6d.—8, Great Portland-street (four doors from Oxford-street).

NEW WINTER DRESSES—Scarboro' Tweed Serges. Price 7¾d. per yard. Patterns free.—JOHN HOOPER, No. 52, Oxford-street, W.

MANUFACTURER'S STOCK of LADIES' WINTER DRESSES SELLING OFF at one quarter off the cost, consisting of French Foule Wool Serges in the new rich fashionable, warm, dark colours. Price 7¾d. per yard. Patterns free.—JOHN HOOPER, 52, Oxford-street, W.

DRAPERY, Cloaks, Costumes, &c.—MARSHALL and SNELGROVE are now showing some beautiful COSTUMES in Satin de Laine, &c., trimmed broché jardinière, at 58s. 6d. each; a variety of Braided Serge Costumes, at 52s. 6d.; the New Sark Wool Costume; Silk Costumes trimmed Cachemire Oriental, at 7½ guineas; French Costume Cloth in assorted colours, at 11½d.; Serge, Cachemire de Rheims, Merinoes, &c.; Cashmere Cloaks lined imitation sable, at 4½ guineas; Ulster and Waterproof Cloaks, Fur-lined and Fur-trimmed Cloaks, from 52s. 6d. to 120 guineas. Inspection solicited.

MOURNING WAREHOUSE, Vere-street, W.— MARSHALL and SNELGROVE.

Black Vigognes, 47 inches wide, 2s. 9d.
Black Damascenes, 3s. 9d.
Black Broché Grenadines, 3s. 9d. and 4s. 6d.
Black Merinoes and Cachemires d'Ecosse, from 2s.; Hosiery, Gloves, Jet, and Silver Ornaments, Millinery, &c. Mourning Dressmaking on the shortest notice. Patterns free. Orders by post or telegram promptly attended to. Funerals furnished.

FANCY and GENERAL DEPARTMENT.—300 AUSTRIAN STRIPED BLANKETS, at 5s. 6d., 7s. 3d., and 8s. 6d. Linseys, unbleached calicoes, flannels, blankets, and all goods for charities, at manufacturers' prices. The New Beaded Velvet Necklet, in the varieties of steel, gold, jet, &c., free by post, at 3s. each.—MARSHALL and SNELGROVE, Vere-street, Oxford-street, and Henrietta-street.

SILKS, Velvets, Laces, Sables, Sealskins, Guns, Indian Shawls, Mantles, Dresses, Gentlemen's Attire, Cloths, Doeskins, Linens, Carpets, &c., SOLD by AUCTION four days in each week, at DEBENHAM, STORR, and SONS' Great Mart, King-street, Covent-garden, London, W.C. Valuables of all kinds included in suitable sales on short notice.

ANTIQUE EASTERN EMBROIDERIES.—HOWELL, JAMES, and Co. are now unpacking several bales of ANTIQUE TURKISH and other interesting kinds of EMBROIDERIES, recently collected by their agents in Janina, Rhodes, Mytelene, &c., and will offer them for sale on Monday next, Nov. 3, and during the month, at prices varying from 2s. to 10s. 6d.—Howell, James, and Co., 5, 7, 9, Regent street, and 10, Charles-street, St. James's-square.

CHRISTMAS PRESENTS.—A. BLACKBORNE and Co. respectfully request the favour of an inspection of their display of PARISIAN NOVELTIES; also in Five-o'clock-tea Aprons, real Black Lace Veils, real Spanish Lace Fichus and Scarves, Black Spanish Mantillas, new fashionable Lace Sleeves, Old Lace Setts, Modern Lace ditto, finest Cambric Lace Handkerchiefs, Caps, Fans, &c. all in best taste and well adapted as most acceptable Christmas presents.—35, South Audley-street, Grosvenor-square.

MADAME ELLIOT.—Stylish COSTUMES and DRESSES, from two guineas. Elegant bonnets and hats, from 15s. 6d. A choice collection of out-door jackets and polonaises.—8, Great Portland-street, Regent-circus, opposite the London Crystal Palace Bazaar.

MADAME ELLIOT, speciality in DRESSMAKING. Costumes, morning and evening dresses elegantly made up, from 10s. 6d. Style and fit guaranteed.—8, Great Portland-street, Regent-circus, opposite London Crystal Palace Bazaar.

SPECIAL NOTICE.—Change of Ministry.—Gentlemen requiring DIPLOMATIC or COURT UNIFORMS for the approaching session, will oblige by placing their orders as early as possible.—LAWRANCE D. PHILLIPS and Co., Court Tailors, No. 13, George-street, Hanover-square, London, W.

GENTLEMEN'S DRESS (105, Strand), of the best materials, for frock and walking coats, travelling suits and overcoats, for the present and coming season, at fair prices for cash payments, at HAMILTON and KIMPTON'S, 105, Strand, opposite Exeter-hall.

THE HYTHE BOOT (by Royal Letters Patent) is admirably adapted for the farm, sportsman, or tourist. Newmarket and all kinds of hunting boots (first-class only). Also spurs of the best finish. Lasts and boot-trees made on anatomical principles.—JOHN EVANS, 69, Great Queen-street, Lincoln's-inn-fields, W.C.

HOWELL and JAMES—5, 7, 9, Regent-street, and 10, Charles-street, St. James's-square, London.

HOWELL and JAMES beg to announce the completion of most important purchases of new and seasonable Merchandise, adapted for the present period and for Christmas gifts, and, with the view to meet the general desire for economy, they will offer them at a greatly reduced scale of profit, which will enable purchasers to obtain the very highest-class goods at relatively cheaper rates than is usually paid for inferior articles.

HOWELL and JAMES—Elegant Llama Costumes, for evening wear, £2 12s. 6d., all colours, fully trimmed with lace.

HOWELL and JAMES—Black Grenadine Costumes, trimmed black satin, £2 12s. 6d.

HOWELL and JAMES—Parisian Costumes, 3½ to 6½ guineas.

HOWELL and JAMES—Ball Costumes, from £1 1s. Illustrations free by post.

HOWELL and JAMES—Striped Grenadine Robes, in cream, white, pink, and blue, with gold and silver, from

HOWELL and JAMES—Two and a half guineas. Illustrations free.

HOWELL and JAMES—Black Net Dresses, from £1 8s. 6d.

HOWELL and JAMES—Costume Department, 10, Charles-street, St. James's-square.

HOWELL and JAMES—Splendid Silk Costumes, black and coloured, £10 10s.

HOWELL and JAMES—Parisian Mantles, 4½ to 7½ guineas.

HOWELL and JAMES—Sealskin Paletots, finest quality.

HOWELL and JAMES—Cloth Paletots, trimmed Fur.

HOWELL and JAMES—Fashionable Jackets, trimmed Fur, 4½ to 250 guineas.

HOWELL and JAMES—Cashmere Cloaks, lined Fur, from £2 12s. 6d.

Travel Overseas

AROUND the WORLD in NINETY DAYS, by steam and rail, by land and sea, via North America, Japan, China, Ceylon, India, Egypt, and continent of Europe, or vice-versa.—By authority of the various mail steamship and railway lines comprising the above routes, FIRST-CLASS PASSAGE COUPON TICKETS are now issued for the ROUND JOURNEY, at one reduced and inclusive fare, with privilege of stopping at any point.

The route will be over the Great Union and Central Pacific Railway to San Francisco, passing through some of the grandest and most interesting scenery in the world. From San Francisco the tourist will be taken to Japan and China by the Pacific Mail Steamship Company, and thence by the Peninsular and Oriental Company, via Galle, Madras, Calcutta, and Bombay (over the Great Indian Railway), to Southampton, or London via Brindisi. Fares £200 and upwards.

H. Starr and Co., 22, Moorgate-street, London. Agents, Union and Central Pacific Railway. PacificMail S.S. Company, &c.

PARIS and BACK, 24s.—The GENERAL STEAM NAVIGATION COMPANY'S fast STEAMSHIPS leave London-bridge-wharf for BOULOGNE daily (Mondays excepted):— 1st Jan., at 12 noon; 2d, at 1; 4th, at 2; 5th and 6th, at 3 a.m. Fares:— London to Boulogne—Saloon, 11s.; fore cabin, 8s. Return tickets (available for one month), a fare and a half. London to Paris—first-class, 25s.; saloon and second class, 21s.; fore cabin and second class, 18s.; fore cabin and third class, 15s. Return tickets (available for 14 days), £2 8s., £1 16s., £1 12s., and £1 4s.—Offices, No. 71, Lombard-street, and 37, Regent-circus, Piccadilly.

COOK'S TOURS to EGYPT, the Nile, Suez Canal, Palestine, Turkey, Greece, Italy, &c.—Arrangements for approaching Special Tours to the East, and for Tourists' Tickets, available at all times, for Italy, &c., will be found in the CHRISTMAS SUPPLEMENT to COOK'S EXCURSIONIST, now ready, price 2d., by post 3d., which also contains Notes of Explanation of Mr. Cook and his Tourists in reference to the statements of Dr. W. H. Russell in his Diary in the East; Dr. Guthrie on Cook's Tours, &c. Tourist office, 98, Fleet-street, E.C.

RIVER PLATE.—GENTLEMEN are invited to JOIN Mr. HENLY'S AGRICULTURAL COLONY, near Fraile Muerto. Apply to Mr. T. Henly, Calne, Wilts.

FORWARDING AGENCY.——Messageries Impériales of France.—SPECIE, Merchandise, and Parcels FORWARDED daily, at through rates, to PARIS, Lyons, Marseilles, and most parts of Europe, by mail steamers of the Messageries Impériales to the ports of the Mediterranean and Black Sea, India, China, Japan, Brazil, and River Plate. Reduced rates. Apply to B. W. and H. Horne, Moorgate-street, London, E.C.

BREMEN.—Direct Route to Hanover, Brunswick, and Central Germany.—The NORTH GERMAN LLOYD'S fine, first-class, screw steamer FALKE, Capt. N. BUNDISEN, will be despatched on Thursday, Jan. 6, calling at Blackwall (weather permitting), at 12 noon. Fares to Bremen—£2 and £1; return tickets, £3 and £1 10s. Apply at Chaplin's Universal Office, Regent-circus, W.; or to Phillipps, Graves, Phillipps, and Co., St. Dunstan's-house, Cross-lane, Great Tower-street, E.C.

BRUSSELS, Cologne, Hamburg, Berlin, Leipsic, Dresden.—Reduced Fares to Antwerp—chief cabin, £1; fore cabin, 15s.; return tickets, available one month, £1 10s.—The renowned steamship BARON OSY, entirely restored and redecorated, J. F. VAN DIEPENDAEL, Commander, leaves St. Katharine's-wharf, near the Tower, every Sunday at 12 o'clock noon, returning from Antwerp every Wednesday at 12 o'clock noon. Applications for the shipment of merchandise must be made to the London agents, Messrs. Simon and Lightly, 123, Fenchurch-street, where, and at 108, New Bond-street, berths may be secured and every information obtained.

STEAM direct from LIVERPOOL to MADRAS and CALCUTTA, through the Suez Canal, sailing on 8th January.—The fine new Clyde-built screw-steamer WAVERLEY, BOYSON, Commander, 644 tons register. This steamer offers a favourable opportunity to shippers, as she steams fast, and when loaded will not exceed 14 feet draft of water. A large portion of her cargo is already engaged. For freight apply to Stodart, Brothers, 30, Tower-buildings, Liverpool. Freight 70s, and 10 per cent., payable on delivery of bills of lading. To be followed by the steamer RIGA.

CALCUTTA direct.—The splendid clipper ship DUKE of ATHOLE, 1,000 tons, Capt. W. CUNNINGHAM, will leave the East India Docks 10th January. Has very superior accommodation for passengers. Apply to Messrs. Grindlay and Co., No. 55, Parliament-street, S.W.; to the owners, Messrs. Montgomerie and Greenhorne, 17, Gracechurch-street; or to F. Green and Co., No. 140, Leadenhall-street, E.C.

STEAM to CALCUTTA, via Suez Canal.—THOS. and WM. SMITH will despatch the following fast and powerful SCREW STEAMERS, built by them expressly for the India Trade:—

Hotspur.. ..	1,081 tons register	400 h.p.	Jan. 20th
Crosby	1,500 tons register	500 h.p.	March 5th
Blue Cross ..	1,038 tons register	400 h.p.	April 16th

For freight apply to Messrs. Grindlay and Co., 55, Parliament-street, S.W.; or to Thos. and Wm. Smith, 1, Crosby-square, E.C.

TRIESTE ROUTE to INDIA.-Weekly Service.-Reduced Fares: first-class £13; second class, £9.-The STEAMERS of the AUSTRIAN LLOYD's STEAM NAVIGATION COMPANY leave Trieste for ALEXANDRIA every Saturday, in correspondence with the Peninsular and Oriental Company's lines to India, China, and Australia. Baggage shipped from Southampton for Suez. Packages and parcels forwarded. For further information apply to Hickie, Borman, and Co., agents, 127, Leadenhall-street, London, or Oriental-place, Southampton.

OVERLAND ROUTE via MARSEILLES.—SERVICES MARITIMES des MESSAGERIES IMPERIALES of FRANCE.—French Mail Steam Packets leave Marseilles as follows:—

September 4 .. October 3 .. October 30 .. November 27 .. December 25 ..	For	Alexandria, Aden, Mauritius, Seychelles, Reunion, Point de Galle (Ceylon), Pondicherry, Madras, Calcutta, Singapore, Batavia, Saigon, Hongkong, Shanghae, and Japan.

9th, 19th, and 29th of every month for Alexandria.

For passage, freight, and information apply to B. W. and H. Horne, No. 4, Moorgate-street, London; G. H. Fletcher and Co., Liverpool; at the offices of the Services Maritimes des Messageries Impériales, in Paris, Lyons, Bordeaux, and Marseilles; or to Smith and Co., Rotterdam. Passengers eastward of Suez securing their berths in London are entitled to the conveyance of their luggage free to Marseilles.

COLOMBO.—The SHOOTING STAR, A1 10 years, 900 tons, West India Docks. Will not carry manure. Has splendid accommodation for passengers.—Henry Ellis and Sons, 17, Gracechurch-street, E.C.

BRISBANE, Queensland.—BLACK BALL LINE.—Under an arrangement of the Queensland Government Land Orders, value £30, are given to all Classes of Passengers by this line.—The favourite Australian trader PLANET, A1 at Lloyd's, 1,200 tons, has a spacious poop saloon, and most comfortable accommodation for all classes. Will carry an experienced surgeon. To be followed at monthly intervals by the celebrated clippers RAMSEY and YOUNG AUSTRALIA. For terms of passage, &c., apply to Jas. Baines, Taylor, and Co., 60, Castle-street, Liverpool; or to T. M. Mackay, Son, and Co., 1, Leadenhall-street, London.

NEW ORLEANS.—The magnificent steamers of the NORTH GERMAN LLOYD leave HAVRE for NEW ORLEANS every alternate Saturday, calling at Havana. Next departure the NEW YORK, 3,000 tons, 700-horse power, from Havre, on Saturday, January 15. Through fares from London via Southampton:—first-class, £23; steerage, £9. For freight or passage apply to Keller, Wallis, and Postlethwaite, 16 and 17, King William-street, city, London, E.C., or at Southampton; or to Phillipps, Graves, Phillipps, and Co., St. Dunstan's-house, Idol-lane, London, E.C.

STEAM to HAVANA and NEW ORLEANS.—The HAMBURG AMERICAN COMPANY'S splendid mail STEAMSHIPS are appointed to sail as under:—

Ships.	Tons.	H. p.	From	Date.
Bavaria	2,500	700	Havre	18th January, 1870.
Teutonia	2,500	600	Havre	15th February.
Saxonia	3,000	700	Havre	15th March.

The passenger accommodation and table of these well-known steamers are of a very superior order. Outward cargo and passengers forwarded (at through rates from London), by the boats, leaving Southampton three times a week, for Havre. Fares from Southampton—first cabin, upper salooon, £27; lower saloon, £18; steerage, £8 10s.

For freight or passage apply to Brostrom and Co., 2, Rue Scribe, Paris; or to Smith, Sundius, and Co., Plymouth, Southampton, and No. 17, Gracechurch-street, London.

HAMBURG LONDON STEAMSHIP COMPANY.—The splendid, fast steamers Capella, Captain P. Witt' 1,000 tons; and Wega, Captain C. F. Nomens, 1,000 tons.—The steamer WEGA will leave from off Horselydown, with goods and passengers, for Hamburg, on Friday morning. Passengers walk on shore and on board in Hamburg. Fares:—saloon, £2; fore cabin, £1 5s. Goods cleared and forwarded if addressed to Drolenvaux and Bremner, 40, Seething-lane, E.C.; or in Hamburg, to Pearson and Laugnese, of whom may be had full particulars.

PARIS, Rouen, Havre, Honfleur, Caen, Trouville, by the SOUTH-WESTERN COMPANY'S commodious, large, and fast MAIL STEAMSHIPS, every Monday, Wednesday, and Friday, from Southampton Docks, at 11.45 p.m. The last train leaves Waterloo Station, London, at 9 p.m., and goes into docks alongside ship. Return tickets—London to Paris and back, within one month, 55s. first class; 39s. second class. London to Havre, Honfleur, or Trouville and back, available for the return journey within one month, 40s. first class; 30s. second class, including steward's fees. The steamers leave Havre for Southampton every Monday, Wednesday, and Friday, at 8.30 p.m., instead of midnight, as hitherto.

ST. MALO, via Southampton.——The SOUTH-WESTERN COMPANY'S new, fast, and commodious steamers ALICE and CÆSAREA, or other steamers, leave Southampton for St. Malo every Monday, Wednesday, and Friday. For hours see South-Western Time Table-book. Return tickets, available for one month, 40s. second-class; 52s. first-class, including steward's fees.

WINTER SERVICE.—Change of Days of Sailing.—LONDON and the CHANNEL ISLANDS, via Southampton, by SOUTH-WESTERN RAILWAY.—Shortest and Quickest Route.—By the Royal Mail Steamships, every Monday, Wednesday, and Friday. Last train from Waterloo at 9 p.m. Returning from Jersey every Monday, Wednesday, and Friday at 6.45 a.m., calling at Guernsey, for Southampton and London. The fast screw steamship St. Malo or Griffin (or other steamer) will also leave Southampton on Thursdays at 11.45 p.m. for Guernsey and Jersey; last train from Waterloo at 9 p.m., returning from Jersey every Saturday morning at 6.45 and calling at Guernsey for Southampton and London.

Return tickets (available to return within a month), 38s. second-class, 45s. first-class, including steward's fees. Third-class tickets are also issued between London and Guernsey and Jersey by all boats. Single journey (available for four days), 20s.; double journey (available for a month), 30s.

EDINBURGH and NEWCASTLE.—The GENERAL STEAM NAVIGATION COMPANY'S splendid STEAMSHIPS leave London and Continental Wharf, 92 and 93, Lower East Smithfield, as under:—For Edinburgh every Wednesday and Saturday—Jan. 7th, at 2 p.m.; 10th, at noon. Fares—saloon, 20s.; fore cabin, 15s.; return tickets, 30s. and 22s. 6d. For Newcastle, every Wednesday and Sunday, at 9 morning. Fares—saloon, 12s.; fore cabin, 8s.; return tickets, 18s. and 12s.—Offices, 71, Lombard-street, and 37, Regent-circus.

FREE EMIGRATION to QUEENSLAND, Australia.—Owing to the great demand in the Colony for labour, the Agent-General will GRANT, under the new Immigration Act, passed on the 2nd August, 1872, FREE PASSAGES to AGRICULTURAL LABOURERS (married and single) and to FEMALE DOMESTIC SERVANTS, without undertaking to repay the cost of passage, and assisted passages to mechanics and other eligible persons at lower rates than the cost of passages to Canada or United States.

£20 Land Order Warrants per adult issued to persons paying their own full passage to the Colony.

Further information on application to the Agent-General, Queensland Government Offices, 32, Charing-cross, London.

JAPAN and CHINA.—San Francisco Mail Route.—The PACIFIC MAIL STEAMSHIP COMPANY will despatch their magnificent STEAMERS, of 3,000 tons burden and upwards, with Mails and Passengers from San Francisco, on the 1st and 16th of every month, for Yokohama, Hiogo, Nagasaki, Shanghai, and Hongkong, returning from Hongkong on the 12th and 27th of every month.

The Company's Steamers also leave New York twice a month (via Panama), for San Francisco and intermediate Pacific ports. For through fares and other information apply to H. Starr and Co., Agents, 22, Moorgate-street, London.

CHEFOO, Tientsin, and Newchwang, viâ Singapore and Hongkong, the new ocean steamship YENTAI, 100 A 1; last shipping day 5th January; South West India Docks.—Robertson and Co., 5, Newman's-court, Cornhill, E.C.

STEAM from SOUTHAMPTON to BATAVIA, via Suez Canal.—Steamship Company Nederland's Mail Service to Dutch East Indies, under contract with Netherlands Government.

The magnificent Clyde-built steamship PRINS VAN ORANGE, 2,500 tons, 1,600 effective horse-power, and 400 nominal horse-power, is appointed to sail from Southampton to Padang, Batavia, and Sourabaya on the 19th January. Fares:—First-class, £58 and upwards; second-class, £33. Apply to J. Rankine and Son, Glasgow; or to the General Agents of the Company, Keller, Wallis and Postlethwaite, 16 and 17, King William-street, London, E.C.; 73, Piccadilly, Manchester; and at Southampton.

STEAM to NEW YORK.—Notice.—This Company takes the risk of insurance (up to £100,000) on each of its vessels, thus giving passengers the best possible guarantee for safety and avoidance of danger at sea. The most southerly route has always been adopted by this Company to avoid ice and headlands.—The NATIONAL STEAMSHIP COMPANY (Limited) despatch their first-class screw STEAMSHIPS from Liverpool, calling at Queenstown, as follows:—GREECE, Wednesday, Jan. 7; Italy, Wednesday, Jan. 14, 1874. Saloon passage, 12, 15, and 17 guineas, according to accommodation. Return tickets, 25 guineas. Steerage passage at reduced rates. Apply to Mosses and Mitchell, 55, Gracechurch-street; to W. S. Rowland, 445, Strand, London, W.C.; Smith, Sundius, and C., No. 33, Gracechurch-street, London; and at the Company's offices, Nos. 21 and 23, Water-street, Liverpool.

WEST INDIES.—The ROYAL MAIL STEAM PACKET COMPANY despatch a STEAMER on the 25th o each month, from SOUTHAMPTON, calling at the following ports on the outward voyage—Barbadoes, Trinidad, La Guayra, Porto Cabello, Curacoa, Santa Marthe, Savanilla, and Solon.

Rates of passage—first-class, £30; second-class, £20 and upwards.

Larne, 26th January, 1874.	Essequibo, 25th March
Severn, 25th February, 1874.	

N.B. Tourist tickets for the round voyage are issued by these steamers.

For further information as to rates of passage, freight, &c., apply to J. K. Linstead, Royal Mail Steam Packet Company, Southampton; or to J. M. Lloyd, Secretary, 35, Moorgate-street, E.C.

LONDON to GOTHENBURG.—Regular Line.—The first-class steamer Prins Oscar, Carl XV., or Albert Edward leaves Millwall Docks every week. CARL XV. on Thursday, Nov. 6. Excellent passenger accommodation. Fares—Saloon, £3 3s.; second cabin, £2 2s.—W. E. Bott and Co., 10, Mark-lane, E.C.

THE GENERAL STEAM NAVIGATION COMPANY'S STEAMSHIPS leave Irongate and St. Katharine's-wharf, near the Tower, for

HAMBURG.—Tuesday, Thursday, and Saturday:—Nov. 1, at noon; 4th, at 1 p.m.; 6th, at 2 p.m. Saloon, £2 5s.; fore cabin, £1 9s. Return:—Saloon, £3 8s.; fore cabin, £2 4s.

ANTWERP.—Tuesday and Saturday, at noon. Saloon, £1; fore cabin, 12s. 6d. Return:—Saloon, £1 11s.; fore cabin, 19s. 3d.

OSTEND.—Wednesday and Sunday—Nov. 2, at 2 p.m.; 4th, at 3 p.m.; 5th, at 4 p.m. Saloon, 16s.; fore cabin, 12s. 6d. Return:—Saloon, £1 7s. 6d.; fore cabin, 19s.

BOULOGNE.—Nov. 1, at midnight; 4th, at 3 p.m.; 5th and 6th, at 4 p.m.; 7th, at 5 p.m.; 9th, at 7 a.m. Saloon, 12s.; fore cabin, 8s. 6d. Return:—Saloon, 18s. 6d.; fore cabin, 13s.

HAVRE.—Thursday, Nov. 6th, at 9 a.m. Saloon, 13s.; fore cabin, 9s. Return:—Saloon, 20s. 6d.; fore cabin, 14s.

BORDEAUX.—Thursday, Nov. 6th, at 2 p.m. Saloon, £3; fore cabin, £2. Return:—Saloon, £5; fore cabin, £3 6s. 8d. The magnificent new steamships Kestrel, Bitterne, and Lapwing, with splendid passenger accommodation, are now on this station.

OPORTO.—Every fortnight. Chief cabin passengers only. Single fare £4 4s.; ladies 10s. extra.

A steam tender conveys passengers free of charge to and from the ships when necessary. Steward's fees are included in the above fares.

The Company undertake all shipping and delivery business in London, and make through rates, including all charges between all ports. For particulars apply to the Secretary, 71, Lombard-street, London, E.C.

DOVER and OSTEND MAIL PACKETS, the fastest in the Channel. From Dover twice daily (including Sundays), viz., at 8.40 a.m. and 10.25 p.m., after arrival of mail and boat express trains from London. These packets also leave Ostend twice daily (including Saturday), at 10 a.m. and 6 p.m., after arrival of Cologne and Brussels mail trains.—Office, 53, Gracechurch-street, E.C

STEAM to AUSTRALIA and NEW ZEALAND.—COLONIAL LINE.—The magnificent, new, full-powered screw steamship TE ANAU, 2,500 tons burden, 2,000 h.p. effective, 100 A1 at Lloyd's, commanded by Capt. CAREY (late of the s.s. Rotorua), will be despatched from the Clyde (Greenock) for Melbourne and Dunedin on the 13th December. This superb steamship has just been built by Messrs. Wm. Denny and Brothers, Dumbarton, expressly for the passenger trade. She has a superb saloon and state rooms, furnished in the most sumptuous manner, while the social hall and smoking room on deck offer attractions seldom met with on board ship. The Rotomahana, a sister ship, has just made the passage to Melbourne (under steam) in 41 days. Fares:—First class, 50 to 70 guineas; second class, 25 to 30 guineas. No other classes taken. Carries a surgeon. Apply to John Henry Flint, 112, Fenchurch-street, London.

Furnishings

FURNISH on the NEW HIRE SYSTEM.—"A novel and ingenious method, and within the reach of all."—Vide Public Press.—GENERAL FURNISHING COMPANY: offices, 9, Southampton-street, Strand. Prospectus, with press opinions, post free.

FURNISH YOUR HOUSE or APARTMENTS throughout on MOEDER'S HIRE SYSTEM. Cash prices; no extra charges; large, useful stock to select from. All goods warranted. Illustrated price catalogue, with terms, post free.—249 and 250, Tottenham-court-road. Established 1862.

FURNITURE.—Hire System.—The largest stock in the kingdom to select from of all descriptions of general FURNITURE, Carpets, and bedding. Parties desiring to furnish on this convenient system should apply for illustrated catalogue and prospectus of terms to Manager, Hire Department, 71 Brompton-road, S.W

FURNISHING EXHIBITION.—Visitors to London should inspect the extensive display of DECORATIVE ARTICLES of every description for the complete furnishing of a house of any class, with a view to artistic taste combined with utility. The goods are conveniently arranged in separate departments, all communicating, and visitors are conducted through the spacious show rooms and galleries without the slightest importunity to purchase. Lowest prices consistent with guaranteed quality.—OETZMANN and Co., 67, 69, 71, and 73, Hampstead-road, near Tottenham-court-road and Gower-street Station. Established 1848. A detailed Catalogue, the best furnishing guide extant, post free. The establishment is visible from Tottenham-court-road. Close at 7, and on Saturdays at 4 o'clock.

VIENNA EXHIBITION.—The Diploma of Honour.—The sole highest honour for ENGLISH FURNITURE has been awarded to JACKSON and GRAHAM, Interior Decorators, Cabinetmakers, Upholsterers, and Carpet Manufacturers, 30 to 38, Oxford-street, W.

PRIEST'S, noted for superior SECOND-HAND and NEW FURNITURE, largest stock in the world for the drawing, dining, library, and bed rooms; also office furniture, cylinder, pedestal, leg tables, clerks' desks, and every requisite for the counting-house.—Tudor-street, Blackfriars.

NOTICE. Excellent Opportunity to those about to Furnish.—Genuine SALE of first-class FURNITURE, by order of the executors of the late Mr. George Diack, of 212 and 213, Oxford-street. The whole of this extensive and elegant stock now on sale at a very great reduction in price. All goods marked in plain figures, for ready money only.

SIDEBOARDS, Bookcases, Library and Dining Tables, also Wardrobes of all kinds and sizes, other furniture for bed chambers, dining and drawing rooms, and library, principally second-hand, by the best makers, and Turkey carpets, all at very moderate prices. The largest stock in London, at SPILLMAN'S extensive warehouse, 14, Newcastle-street, Strand, near Somerset-house.

MESSRS. T. H. FILMER and SON, Upholsterers, Decorators, &c., 31 and 32, Berners-street, beg respectfully to solicit a visit to their FURNITURE SHOW ROOMS and GALLERIES, the largest in the United Kingdom, containing every variety of furniture, marked in plain figures, of the best manufacture and designs. Plans taken and estimates prepared free of any charge. Illustrated priced catalogues of bed-room furniture, easy chairs, couches, sofas sent post free on application.

HEWETSON and THEXTON'S ILLUSTRATED CATALOGUE of CABINET FURNITURE, with prices, sent free by post on application. Bed-room furniture in various woods.—Hewetson and Thexton, Manufacturers, 200, 203, and 204, Tottenham-court-road. (N.B. Nearly opposite the chapel.)

HEWETSON and THEXTON send free by post on application designs of their special set of MEDIÆVAL DINING-ROOM FURNITURE in American ash, at £30; also of their special set of polished deal bed-room furniture (Mediæval), with bedstead and bedding, at £12 10s. Hewetson and Thexton recommend the attention of all to this furniture who are wishful to furnish in good taste at little cost. For country parsonages, moderate-sized dining rooms, &c., this furniture is admirably adapted.—HEWETSON and THEXTON, Manufacturers, 200, 203, and 204, Tottenham-court-road. (N.B. Nearly opposite the chapel.)

ANTIQUE CARVED OAK FURNITURE for immediate DISPOSAL, at less than a moiety of its cost—a complete suite of this rare and costly furniture, adapted for a large dining room, in the best preservation and of a very splendid description. It comprises a sideboard 8 feet long, with lofty plate-glass back, richly carved, representing animals and other subjects in a very elaborate and artistic style, and is a masterpiece of art; 12 Elizabethan chairs, and a pair of carving chairs covered in real morocco, and a long set of telescope dining tables (to dine 16 persons). Price of the above 90 gs., originally cost more than double. To be seen at Lewin Crawcour and Co.'s, Upholsterers, 71, 73, 75, and 81, Brompton-road, London.

EBONIZED and GOLD DRAWING ROOM SUITE, covered in rich regina blue figured silk, to be SOLD, at a greatly reduced price, in consequence of the owner leaving England; has never been in use, and is of the highest possible manufacture and of the most elegant design. It consists of a very handsome centre ottoman, double-end settee, two easy chairs, and six drawing room chairs upholstered in the best manner, and four very handsome and unique occasional chairs covered in rich tapestry. The above for 75 guineas, original price 120 guineas. There are also belonging to the same suite a splendid cabinet in ebonized and gold and fitted with Sèvres china medallions mounted in or-moulu, occasional and centre tables same style, and a large chimney-glass to correspond; price of the above 40 guineas, cost 75 guineas. Also a superb piano, by an eminent maker, of most brilliant tone, 7-octaves, with all the latest improvements, in magnificent ebonized and gold case, price £44. This really fine lot of furniture is well worthy of inspection, and to be seen at LEWIN CRAWCOUR and Co.'s, Upholsterers, 71, 73, 75, and 81, Brompton-road.

LEWIN CRAWCOUR and Co., 71, 73, 75, and 81, Brompton-road, complete HOUSE FURNISHERS. Established 1810.

LEWIN CRAWCOUR and Co.'s magnificent display of DECORATIVE ARTICLES and REQUISITES for the entire FURNISHING of all descriptions of RESIDENCES is unequalled. A house of any extent furnished in three days.

NEW GREAT SHOW ROOMS NOW OPEN.

LARGEST in the KINGDOM.

LEWIN CRAWCOUR and Co.'s incomparable complete BED ROOM SUITES, warranted enamelled to represent the choicest wood at 6½ guineas, including a convenient wardrobe, are marvels of cheapness and elegance.—Vide Public Press One hundred suites always in stock.

CARPETS.—The most splendid assortment.

CURTAINS.—All the latest Novelties.

LEWIN CRAWCOUR and Co. invite noblemen and gentlemen furnishing to view their new great show rooms, containing such an assemblage of high-class FURNITURE and UPHOLSTERY as cannot elsewhere be seen, at prices unrivalled for cheapness.

BEDSTEADS.—500 in Iron and Brass in a separate department.

BEDDING.—Every description manufactured on the premises.

BED-ROOM FURNITURE, in suites in every variety of style and wood.

DINING-ROOM FURNITURE. Numerous suites, oak and mahogany.

DRAWING-ROOM FURNITURE, in suites. All descriptions in walnut and ebonized and gold.

LIBRARY and BOUDOIR FURNITURE of every kind.

ILLUSTRATED CATALOGUE GRATIS.

ILLUSTRATED CATALOGUE (Latest Edition).

LEWIN CRAWCOUR and Co. deliver free to any part of the Kingdom at London prices. A saving of 25 per cent. to country purchasers. Travellers sent free to submit patterns and give estimates.—71, 73, 75, and 81, Brompton-road, London. Established 1810.

FILMER and SON'S BEDSTEADS, Bedding, and Bed Room Furniture. An Illustrated Catalogue sent, post free, containing prices of 1,000 articles of Bed Room Furniture. 31 and 32, Berners-street, Oxford-street, W.

FILMER and SON'S various new and beautiful FABRICS for DRAWING, Dining Room, and Library CURTAINS and FURNITURE, Carpets of every description, and interior decorations of all kinds. Plans taken and estimates given free of any charge.—31 and 32, Berners-street, Oxford-street, W.

WHOLESALE and EXPORT CABINET, Upholstery, and Bedding WAREHOUSES. G. M. and H. J. STORY, 33, London-wall, and 2, Coleman-street, city (late R. Loader and Co., of Finsbury). Patent Billiard Dining Tables.

SECOND-HAND OAK DINING-ROOM SUITE, in morocco, a great bargain. The suite comprises eight massive chairs, two comfortable easy chairs, spring stuffed lounge, extending dining table (extra leaves), and enclosed sideboard, all in good order. Price 42 guineas. To be seen at LEWIN CRAWCOUR and Co.'s, upholsterers, 73 and 75, Brompton-road, Knightsbridge.

HEWETSON and THEXTON send free by post an Illustrated Priced Catalogue of their CABINET FURNITURE, as adapted for the entire furnishing of genteel residences. Bed-room furniture in porcelain colours, &c.—Hewetson and Thexton, manufacturers, 200, 203, and 204, Tottenham-court-road, W. (N.B. Nearly opposite the chapel).

DRAWING-ROOM FURNITURE, of very superior manufacture and design, highly finished, and covered in rich silk brocade.—A SUITE of the above, nearly new, is OFFERED, a great bargain; is well adapted for a first-class residence, and comprises magnificent 6ft. cabinet, very large chimney-glass, handsome centre and sofa tables, six elegant drawing-room chairs, an easy and lady's chair, and a very pretty double-end settee en suite. The whole to be sold at the very low sum of 60 guineas. To be seen at the BELGRAVE FURNITURE COMPANY, 12, Sloane-street, S.W.

TO PARTIES FURNISHING.—An excellent SUITE of OAK DINING-ROOM FURNITURE, of modern and elegant design, is offered, an unusual bargain, and consists of 12 chairs, with stuffed backs, on castors, in green morocco; a pair of comfortable easy chairs, and a handsome couch to match; a noble set of telescope dining tables, with richly carved moulding legs, and a very handsome sideboard, with lofty plate-glass back. The above is in the best condition, and well adapted for a first-class residence. Price 75 guineas; about half its cost. To be seen at the Belgrave Furnishing Company's, 12, Sloane-street, S.W.

DRAWING-ROOM, Dining-room, and Library FURNITURE.—JACKSON and GRAHAM respectfully invite families about to furnish to visit their spacious show rooms and manufactory. The stock will be found unrivalled, the prices are marked in plain figures, and the manufactory is fitted with machinery worked by steam power, together with all other means and appliances to ensure superiority and economize cost.—29, 33, 34, 35, 37, and 38, Oxford-street.

BEDSTEADS, Bedding, and Chamber Furniture.—JACKSON and GRAHAM have devoted spacious showrooms to this department, in which superior BEDSTEADS of brass, iron, and various woods, in every style, together with complete suites of Bed-room Furniture, of painted and polished deal, mahogany, walnut, and other fine, fancy woods, plain and inlaid, may be seen. They respectfully invite a visit by families about to furnish.—29, 33, 34, 35, 37, and 38, Oxford-street.

BED-ROOM FURNITURE, in Polished Deal.—GEORGE MADDOX'S SUITES, comprising wardrobe, chest of drawers, washstand, dressing table, toilet glass, pedestal towel horse, and three chairs complete. 12 guineas (£12 12s.) Illustrated catalogues sent post free.—21, Baker-street, W.

LOOKING GLASSES for the DRAWING ROOM .. .. £4 4s. 0d.
Looking Glasses for the dining room .. .. .. £4 4s. 0d.
Looking Glasses for the library .. .. .. £2 10s. 0d.
Looking Glasses for the bed room .. .. .. £1 1s. 0d.
Double gilt frames and best plates.

Auctioneers, builders, restaurant proprietors, and others, during refurnishing (to clear out), will be supplied considerably under wholesale prices. Upwards of 100 glasses, of the choicest designs, new and second-hand.—The COMMERCIAL PLATE-GLASS COMPANY, 78 and 79, Fleet-street. Famed for having exhibited in the Great Exhibition, 1851, the largest and purest plate ever seen.

CURTAINS.—Damasks, Reps, Brocatelles, Cretonnes, Satins, and every description of material used for upholstery. 10,000 yards of cretonne, chintz (fast colours), at 10½d. per yard. The new Shanghae satin, double width, 6s. 6d. per yard.—MAPLE and Co., 145, 146, 147, Tottenham-court-road.

DON'T BEAT your CARPETS; have them thoroughly cleansed and colours revived. 3d., 4d., &c., per yard. Bed and mattrass purifiers, silk dyers, and general cleaners.—METROPOLITAN STEAM BLEACHING and DYEING COMPANY, Wharf-road, City-road, and 472, New Oxford-street.

FURNITURE, a great Bargain.—A very superior SUITE of DRAWING-ROOM FURNITURE, in fine Italian walnut, equal to new, covered in rich silk, 38 guineas, warranted; comprises a beautiful large size console cabinet, a fine oval centre table, the top richly inlaid with marqueterie, on richly carved pillar and claws, a pretty sofa table to match, six drawing-room chairs, easy chair, indulgent ditto and comfortable settee, spring stuffed and covered in rich silk, Louis XIV. style, a pretty and unique whatnot, large chimney glass in gilt frame, and two handsome papier-mache occasional chairs. To be seen at LEWIN CRAWCOUR and Co.'s, upholsterers, Nos. 73 and 75, Brompton-road; established 1810. N.B. Also a fine and complete oak dining-room suite, nearly new, in morocco, 38 guineas

HOWARD and SONS' EASY CHAIRS and SOFAS. Patent No. 3,135. The best manufactured.—26 and 27, Berners-street, Oxford-street, W., and Cleveland Works.

HOWARD and SONS' MACHINE-MADE TABLES, for all purposes. Cheaper and better than hand-made.—26 and 27, Berners-street, Oxford-street, W., and Cleveland Works.

BOOKCASES and LIBRARY TABLES, of all kinds and sizes; also Furniture, principally second-hand, by the best makers, suitable for every description of house, offices, or chambers. The largest stock in London at the extensive warehouses, 14, Newcastle-street, Strand, nearly opposite Somerset-house.

TURKEY and other EASTERN CARPETS, at moderate prices, at 14, Newcastle-street, Strand, nearly opposite Somerset-house.

OFFICE, Library, and House FURNITURE of every description, mostly second-hand, by first-rate makers.—At PRIEST'S extensive furnishing warehouses, 1 and 2, Tudor-street, New Bridge-street, Blackfriars, E.C., leading to the Temple.

TOPLIS and SONS, cabinetmakers and upholsterers, are offering their STOCK of FURNITURE at greatly reduced prices, in order to make room for alterations; well known to be one of the best manufacturers in the trade. Show rooms and factory, Nos. 8 and 9, Berners-street, Oxford-street.

HOUSE FURNISHING.—DRUCE and Co.'s CARPET and DAMASK DEPARTMENT comprises every make of curtain fabrics, carpets of Turkey, Persian, Axminster, velvet pile, Brussels, tapestry, and all other manufactures, together with cretonnes, chintzes, poplins, silks, &c., at exceedingly low prices. Brussels carpets 1s. per yard under the usual charge. Down quilts, from 5s. 6d. each to £5 15s.

HOUSE FURNISHING.—DRUCE and Co. have SUITES of DINING-ROOM FURNITURE, in pollard oak, plain oak, mahogany, walnut, and other woods; in addition to which there are 150 Sideboards from £4 4s. to 100 guineas to select from, and 100 sets of extending dining tables from 60s. to £50; mahogany dining-room chairs, covered in real morocco and stuffed with horse-hair, from 20s. each

HOUSE FURNISHING.—DRUCE and Co.'s DRAWING-ROOM FURNITURE is arranged in suites of amboyna wood, walnut and rosewood; irrespective of which there are 500 easy chairs, settees, and convertible centre ottomans to choose from; console tables and mirrors in great variety, cabinets and cabinet tables of the best Parisian and Florentine manufacture, too, card, occasional, and centre tables of every description.

HOUSE FURNISHING.—DRUCE and Co.'s CHAMBER FURNITURE DEPARTMENT contains no less than 24 entire suites of bed room furniture, fitted up in 24 separate rooms, and varying in price from 84s. per suite to £120. These suites are in mahogany, walnut, birch, polished pine, Siberian ash, Hungarian ash, enamelled pine, and other fancy woods, and are in addition to their general stock of bed room furniture, which is complete in every respect. Down Quilts, from 5s. 6d. each to £5 15s.

HOUSE FURNISHING.—DRUCE and Co.'s premises extend over a ground area of more than an acre. Every article is guaranteed, and intending purchasers are respectfully invited to inspect their stock before deciding elsewhere.—68, 69, and 58, Baker-street, and 3 and 4, King-street, Portman-square.

CONVERTIBLE OTTOMANS, for centre of rooms, to form two settees and two easy chairs, a great improvement on the ordinary ottoman. Only of FILMER and SON, upholsterers, Nos. 31 and 32, Berners-street, Oxford-street, W.; factory, 34 and 35, Charles-street. An illustrated catalogue post free.

BEDSTEADS, Bedding, and Chamber Furniture.—JACKSON and GRAHAM have devoted spacious showrooms to this department, in which superior BEDSTEADS of brass, iron, and various woods, in every style, together with complete suites of Bedroom Furniture, of painted and polished deal, mahogany, walnut, and other fine, fancy woods, plain and inlaid, may be seen. They respectfully invite a visit by families about to furnish.—29, 33, 34, 36, 37, and 38, Oxford-street.

THE COMMERCIAL PLATE-GLASS COMPANY, 78 and 79, Fleet-street, exhibitors of the immense plate in the Exhibition, 1851 invite an inspection of their superior assortment of CHIMNEY GLASSES and CONSOLE TABLES (beautiful designs); the Excelsior, new design, elegant glass, five guineas. Picture frames, and all descriptions of carving and gilding. The largest and greatest variety in the kingdom. Re-gilding and re-silvering. Silvered plates cut for the trade. Estimates given. A large quantity of second-hand glasses in good preservation. Catalogues free on application at 78 and 79, Fleet-street.

TURKEY, Indian, Persian, and other CARPETS.—Best qualities only. Cash prices.—GREGORY and Co., 212, 214, and 216, Regent-street, London, W.

WATSON, BONTOR, and Co., Importers.

TURKEY CARPETS.

INDIAN CARPETS.

WATSON, BONTOR, and Co., 35 and 36, Old Bond-street, W.

CORK CARPET.—TRELOAR and SONS, 69, Ludgate-hill, E.C., invite attention to this highly decorative, sanitary, and economical floor covering. Description, price, and sample per post.

LINOLEUM.

LINOLEUM, a remarkable Floorcloth.

LINOLEUM, carpet-like appearance.

LINOLEUM, unequalled for wear, warm and soft to the feet.

LINOLEUM. Extraordinary sales, ever increasing. By all Furnishing Houses, town or country.

LINOLEUM. Beware of imitations. Look for the Trade Mark on the back of the cloth, and the words F. Walton's Patents.

LINOLEUM.—ARTHUR E. TAYLOR and Co., 36, Strand, W.C.

GOOD FLOORCLOTH.—TRELOAR and SONS, 69, Ludgate-hill.

BED and MATTRESS PURIFIERS and CARPET CLEANERS.—Bleachers of quilts and blankets, every size, 1s. each; silk dresses dyed, only two prices, 5s. 6d. and 6s. 6d. Price lists. —METROPOLITAN STEAM BLEACHING and DYEING COMPANY, Wharf-road, City-road, and 472, New Oxford-street.

FURNITURE, Pianos, Plate, Linen, Libraries, and other household effects PURCHASED, for cash, at a fair price; executors and others thereby saved the delay and expense of an auction. Estimates given free of charge. Goods warehoused. Executions paid out. Apply to Mr. HOLLINGSWORTH, 13, High Holborn. Established A.D. 1856.

SECOND-HAND FURNITURE (also new) WANTED, to PURCHASE, for cash, to ship. Whole houses preferred. No charge for estimate or removal.—WM. WAINE, Wholesale and Export Upholsterer, 131 to 139, Newington-butts, S.E.

HINKS' DUPLEX LAMP and the NEW SILBER LAMP. The largest and best assortment of these celebrated lamps is to be seen at the special West-end Agency.—HASKELL and Co., No. 280, Oxford-street, London, W. Both to be seen burning in a dark room. Prospectus post free.

TWO special SUITES of FURNITURE.—C. NOSOTTI has received instructions from a gentleman in Lisbon to DISPOSE OF TWO SUITES of FURNITURE, recently made to his order and finished in the most costly manner regardless of expense, and which are now to be sold considerably under cost price:—No. 1. A suite of walnut bed room Furniture, inlaid with coloured woods, tastefully ornamented with solid brass mountings, chased and electro-gilded, and including sofas, easy and other chairs, stuffed and covered in rich silk. No. 2. A suite of Boudoir Furniture, in choice sycamore, incised with blue and ornamented with elegant brass mountings, electro-gilded, and includes a causeuse, easy and other chairs covered in embroidered satin buton d'or. It would be impossible to find in England the equals of these suites for beauty of design or finish. May be viewed on application at Nosotti's Decorative and Upholstery Works, 397, 398, 399, and 399a, Oxford-street.

NOSOTTI'S ARTISTIC FURNITURE. Exclusive designs. Moderate prices.

NOSOTTI'S choice SILKS and CRETONNES, at Manufacturers' Prices.

NOSOTTI'S SPECIAL BED-ROOM FURNITURE. Moderate prices.

NOSOTTI'S PARISIAN PAPERHANGINGS, Plain and Decorative Painting. Moderate prices.

NOSOTTI'S LOOKING-GLASSES and GILT OBJETS d'ART. Moderate prices.

NOSOTTI'S BRONZES and CLOCKS.—A choice collection direct from the most eminent manufacturers, in Paris. Prices most moderate. Entrance, 397, 398, 399, and 399a, Oxford-street. 13 show rooms.

FOREIGN CLIMATES.—NOSOTTI'S LOOKING-GLASSES and ARTISTIC FURNITURE, &c., specially manufactured for all climates. Great care in paking to insure safe arrivals. The highest foreign references permitted. Prices most moderate. Entrance 397, 398, 399, and 399a, Oxford-street. 13 show rooms.

NOSOTTI'S Moderate Charges, superior manufacture, novelties, and exclusive designs, consequent on his having the most eminent artists and skilful workmen employed at his manufactories.—1, 2, 3, and 4, Great Chapel-street, 20, Dean-street, and Portland-mews.

CABINET FURNITURE.—DRUCE and Co. have re-arranged their stock, and have SUITES of DINING-ROOM FURNITURE in mahogany, oak, pollard oak, and walnut, from £15 to £220 per suite, and suites of drawing-room furniture in walnut and amboyna, also ebonized and gilt; in addition to which there are 100 sideboards to select from, varying in prices from 84s. to £100; 50 sets of dining tables, from 63s. to £50; 500 easy chairs and 100 settees and ottomans, all manufactured and stuffed upon the premises, so that the quality and materials can be guaranted.

CHAMBER FURNITURE.—DRUCE and Co. have 70 entire SUITES of BED-ROOM FURNITURE on show, in mahogany, oak, walnut, birch, ash, pitch pine, polished pine, and inlaid woods, varying in price from 84s. per suite to £150; irrespective of which they have every description of bed-room requisites, comprising brass and iron bedsteads and bedding, all manufactured by them, and composed of the best and purest materials only.

CRETONNES, Chintzes, &c.—DRUCE and Co. are showing CURTAIN FABRICS of all kinds, at prices much below the average. Purchasers are respectfully invited to inspect their stock, the whole of which is conveniently arranged for inspection and marked in plain figures at the lowest cash prices. Shippers and the trade supplied.—68, 69, and 58, Baker-street; 3 and 4, King-street, Portman-square.

CARPETS.—GRAHAM GROSSMITH and Co.'s MANUFACTURERS' SURPLUS STOCKS of best BRUSSELS at less than wholesale prices. G. G. and Co. call the special attention of hotelkeepers and others requiring carpets for purposes where price and quality is more an object than new designs.—32, Newgate-street, City.

HIGH-CLASS CARPETS.

GRAHAM GROSSMITH and Co.'s British Indian and Turkey CARPETS, combining durability with the rich subdued effects of the Oriental carpets, at about half the cost. G. G. and Co. make to any size exact copies of customers' own foreign carpets without extra charge. London warehouse, 32, Newgate-street.

SUPERIOR CARPETS.—Cash Prices.—WAUGH and SON, Designers and Manufacturers, Importers of Foreign Carpets, Curtain Fabrics, &c., Upholsterers and Interior Decorators London Carpet Warehouse, 3 and 4, Goodge-street and 65 and 66, Tottenham-court-road. Established 1760.

THE TRELOAR COCOA-NUT FIBRE MATS "may claim for themselves a place of honour of their own amid the art manufactures of our day."—Art Journal. Manufactory, No. 69, Ludgate-hill.

CAUTION.——TRELOAR'S CORK CARPET. Special manufacture and designs for sitting and bed rooms to be obtained only at the Ludgate Carpet Warehouse, 69, Ludgate-hill.

NOTICE.—The ORIENTAL FIBRE MAT and MATTING COMPANY beg respectfully to inform drapers, upholsterers, and house furnishers generally that, after the 14th inst., their patent manufactures may be obtained through any of the wholesale warehouses, or direct from the Company's works. Prices, terms, &c., on application, with trade card, to the Manager, Highworth, Wilts.—Feb. 6, 1874.

SECOND-HAND FURNITURE, also New, WANTED, to PURCHASE, for cash, to ship. Whole houses preferred. No charge for estimate or removal.—WM. WAINE, Wholesale and Export Upholsterer and General Furnishing Warehouseman, Nos. 131 to 139, Newington-butts.

NOTWITHSTANDING the great Advance in the Price of Materials, BARTHOLOMEW and FLETCHER continue selling their solid, substantial, unsurpassed MAHOGANY DINING-ROOM CHAIR, in real leather, upholstered all hair, at one guinea. Every article marked in plain figures.—217, 219, Tottenham-court-road.

DINING TABLES, Sideboards, Bookcases, Dinner Waggons, Sets of Chairs, Easy Chairs and Couches, Pedestal, Cylinder, and Leg Writing Tables in mahogany and oak, some of Messrs. Gillow's make, drawing-room cabinets, gilt and other furniture, wardrobes, and every article for bed-room use, in the extensive Show Rooms at WILLSON'S, 68, Great Queen-street, Lincoln's-inn-fields.

SIDEBOARDS, Bookcases, Library and Dining Tables, also Wardrobes of all kinds and sizes, other furniture for bed chambers, dining and drawing rooms, and library, principally second-hand, by the best makers, and Turkey carpets, all at very moderate prices. The largest stock in London, at SPILLMAN'S extensive warehouse, 14, Newcastle-street, Strand, near Somerset-house.

ONE HUNDRED and FIVE POUNDS.—The finest CARVED OAK SIDEBOARD in the City of London to be SOLD for 100 guineas; suitable for a nobleman's mansion or a club-house. To be seen at 72, Gracechurch-street, London.

DINING, Drawing, Library, Bed Room, and Office FURNITURE, second-hand and new, of every description, by Gillow and other eminent makers. Largest stock in the world for really well-made furniture, at PRIEST'S, Tudor-street, Blackfriars, E.C.

DINING TABLES, Sideboards, Bookcases, Dinner Waggons, Sets of Chairs, Easy Chairs and Couches, Pedestal and Leg Writing Tables in mahogany and oak, some of Messrs. Gillow's make, drawing-room cabinets, gilt and other furniture, wardrobes, and every article for bed-room use, in the extensive Show Rooms at WILLSON'S, 68, Great Queen-street, Lincoln's-inn-fields.

TWO special SUITES of FURNITURE.—C. NOSOTTI has received instructions from a gentleman in Lisbon to DISPOSE OF TWO SUITES of FURNITURE, recently made to his order and finished in the most costly manner regardless of expense, and which are now to be sold considerably under cost price:—No. 1. A suite of walnut bed room Furniture, inlaid with coloured woods, tastefully ornamented with solid brass mountings, chased and electro-gilded, and including sofas, easy and other chairs, stuffed and covered in rich silk. No. 2. A suite of Boudoir Furniture, in choice sycamore, incised with blue and ornamented with elegant brass mountings, electro-gilded, and includes a causeuse, easy and other chairs covered in embroidered satin buton d'or. It would be impossible to find in England the equals of these suites for beauty of design or finish. May be viewed on application at Nosotti's Decorative and Upholstery Works, 397, 398, 399, and 399a, Oxford-street.

SECOND-HAND FURNITURE.—Houses Completely Furnished.—A. Jenkins and Co. have for SALE several MAHOGANY and OAK DINING ROOM SUITES in leather; Drawing room Suites in rep, Cretonne velvet, silk, &c.; Bed room Suites in polished pine, walnut, and mahogany, iron and brass bedsteads, sideboards, dining tables, walnut and mahogany wardrobes, some handsome cabinets, and a quantity of soiled looking-glasses, to be sold great bargains.—A. JENKINS and Co., 167, Fleet-street, E.C. (next to Anderton's Hotel). Established 1812.

THE BEST HOUSE to BUY FURNITURE.—At LAW, BROTHERS', corner of Great Eastern-street and Curtain-road, Shoreditch, London. Wholesale and Export Furnishing Warehouse. Shippers liberally dealt with.

BED-ROOM SUITES (NINETEEN), removed from an hotel; never been used; in real birch or mahogany; each suite comprising wardrobe with two doors, fitted with drawers and hangings, duchesse dressing table, chest of drawers, large marble-top washstand, towel rail, and three chairs; 10 guineas the lot, worth treble.—DAVIS and Co., Second-hand Furniture Warehouses, Nos. 255, 256, 253, 258, Tottenham-court-road, W., near Oxford-street

CHAIRS, 50 dozens, removed from a club-house in condition equal to new, stuffed seats and backs, in real leather Spanish mahogany frames, to be SOLD, together or separately, at 21s. per chair, originally cost 55s.—DAVIS and Co., Secondhand Furniture Warehouses, 255, 256, 257, and 258, Tottenham-court-road, W. Catalogues post free.

WM. WAINE'S New and Second-hand FURNITURE, Warehouses and National Supply Stores, 131 to 139, Newington-butts, London, S.E., comprises dining, drawing, and bed room suites, carpets, pianos, pictures, billiard tables, carriages, &c., and every household requisite, 300 pieces Brussels carpets, from 2s. per yard. Lot Tapestry Brussels, from 1s. 3d. per yard; 500 new and choice patterns, 1s. 4½d.; 750 Axminster rugs, 4s. 9d.; 300 skin rugs, 8s. 11d.; 250 pieces cretonnes, 3½d. per yard. Large lot of very superior damasks at 3s. 6d., worth 4s. 9d.; 2,500 pairs real Witney blankets, from 4s. 11d. 1,200 oil paintings much under value; 6,000 pieces wall papers, from 6d. each. The whole vast assortment should be seen. N.B. Second-hand furniture purchased for cash to ship. Whole houses preferred. Estimates free. All goods warranted, and delivered free.

HOWELL and JAMES - 9, Regent-street, and 10, Charles-street.

HOWELL and JAMES have devoted a spacious salon for the exhibition of rare and costly specimens of Eastern industry, which they are selling at merely nominal prices. Two thousand pieces of embroidery, suited for cushions, antimacassars, chair covers, imported from Constantinople, all ancient and artistique pieces. 2s., 2s. 6d., 3s. 6d., 4s. 6d., 5s. 6d., 6s. 6d., 7s. 6d., 8s. 6d. and 10s. 6d. each piece.

HOWELL and JAMES are showing some rare specimens of Oriental rugs.

HOWELL and JAMES——Ancient Daghestan Rugs, 38s. 6d. to 45s.

HOWELL and JAMES—Smyrna Rugs, 16s. 6d.

HOWELL and JAMES—Antique Bed Covers, and a quantity of lengths, from

HOWELL and JAMES—three to six yards, are marked 10s. 6d., 15s. 6d., and 21s.

HOWELL and JAMES send PATTERNS of all PIECE GOODS free by post, and sample parcels into the country by rail on approval, at their own risk.

HOWELL and JAMES, 5, 7, 9, Regent-street. and

HOWELL and JAMES—10, Charles-street. St, James's-square.

FURNISH on the NEW HIRE SYSTEM (Reg.).—The New Hire System is quite distinct from anything yet attempted. Houses, apartments, and offices can be furnished throughout without increased yearly expenditure, the furniture becoming the absolute property of the hirer. The public Press directs the attention of merchants, traders, and others to these advantages. Prospectus, with numerous Press opinions, post free.—The GENERAL FURNISHING COMPANY. Offices, 9, Southampton-street, Strand.

LINOLEUM.—STAINES.—See TRADE MARK

LINOLEUM.—STAINES.—on back of the Cloth.

LINOLEUM.—STAINES.—Avoid Counterfeit

LINOLEUM.—STAINES.—and Inferior Makes.

LINOLEUM.——STAINES.——The ORIGINAL CLOTH.

LINOLEUM.—STAINES MAKE.—Of all Furnishing Houses.

LINOLEUM.—STAINES MAKE.—Orders for Shipping

LINOLEUM.—STAINES MAKE.—and Wholesale to be addressed to

LINOLEUM MANUFACTURING COMPANY (Limited), 144, Queen Victoria-street, London, E. C.

LIBERTY and Co.—GIFTS from the EAST.

LIBERTY and Co.—ILLUSTRATED CATALOGUE POST FREE.

LIBERTY and Co.—GIFTS from the EAST—India, China, Japan.

LIBERTY and Co.—ILLUSTRATED CATALOGUE POST FREE, upon application.

LIBERTY and Co.—INDIAN, Chinese, and Japanese.—Bric-a-brac—Ornaments, Toys, Silks, Carpets, Embroideries, Furniture—quaint, rich, useful, or decorative. The largest and most comprehensive stock in Europe. Prices from 1s. to £5. Illustrated priced catalogue post free on application.—Liberty and Co., East India-house, 218, Regent-street, 42 and 43, King-street, and 2, Argyll-place, London, W.

LIBERTY and Co.—ILLUSTRATED CATALOGUE will be sent post free.

LIBERTY and Co.—GIFTS from the EAST—Japan, China, India.

LIBERTY and Co—ILLUSTRATED CATALOGUE may be had post free.

LIBERTY and Co., East India-house, 218, Regent-street, London, W.

Horses & Carriages

THE NEW PATENT PERITHRON.—The patentee begs to call attention to these useful little carriages, exhibited at the Cattle Show, and much approved for their elegance and utility. This invention overcomes the difficulty experienced by a lady in stepping over the wheel to the much-prized front seat. To be seen at Tattersall's, Baker-street Bazaar, and Crystal Palace. Stanhope Phaetons or T Carts can be constructed with the Perithron seat. Apply for drawings to S. SMITH, East Suffolk Carriage Works, Halesworth.

MINIATURE BROUGHAMS.—R. STRONG, Coachbuilder, 29, 30, and 31, Long-acre, the original builder of these elegant little CARRIAGES, made of the best English woods, respectfully informs the nobility and gentry that the hickory and steel carriages sent to him to be broken up will be on view five weeks longer, when they will be destroyed. R. Strong freely admits using hickory in the construction of his carriages in the year 1865, but as soon as he perceived the utter worthlessness of the wood for carriage building purposes he replaced all hickory wheels on his clients' carriages with wheels made of the best English woods free of charge, meeting his customers fairly without trying to throw the blame on the users, or driving them to incur legal expenses, depending on the uncertainty of the law to shirk the responsibility.

COLTS and UNTRACTABLE HORSES BROKEN, easy mouthed and temperate, by Dumb Jockeys. Blackwell's Patent Whalebone and Guttapercha Jockeys, 64 shillings. Blackwell's Safety Spring Driving and Riding Reins, 12 shillings. Blackwell's Anti Crib-biting Straps, invaluable and simple, 18 shillings. BLACKWELL, saddler, 259, Oxford-street, W., near the Marble Arch.

WEIGHT-CARRYING HUNTER, the property of the breeder—a Bay Horse, five years old, 15 hands 3 inches high, well up to 18 stone, a very clever fencer. To view apply to Mr. Thomas Laurie, Brewery, Winchester. Price £210.

BOY'S HUNTER.—To be SOLD, a BAY BLOOD COB, 14.1 high, up to 11 stone over any country, carries a lady, very clever, temperate, and fast. Price 90 guineas. Veterinary examination allowed. To be seen at E. Fowler's Royal Belgrave Riding School, Gillingham-street, Eccleston-square, S.W.

AT Messrs. TATTERSALL'S, Jan. 5th, VICTOR, box No. 87, a handsome Bay Gelding, six years old, 15.3, a fine mover, and has been hunted. Also Tudor, box No. 88, a Bay Gelding, 15.3, regularly hunted with the Lecistershire hounds, and very fast.

GENUINE HORSES for SALE, the property of a gentleman:—Weight-carrying Hunters, nine years old, 16 hands whole, brown, sound and quiet, fast and clever, snaffle bridle, 100 guineas; also a beautiful Chestnut Mare, 15h. 3in., rising six years, splendid action, light mouth, steady, and would make good leader in a team, warranted sound, quiet to ride and drive, single and double, and free from all vice and tricks, 200 guineas. Both can be tried; hunter over fences in neighbourhood. Apply Coachman, 41, Victoria-mews, New Finchley-road.

RIDING TAUGHT in 12 lessons, price £2 2s., at ANGLE'S North London Riding Academy, 1, Tyndale-place, Islington. Subscriptions, monthly, £2 10s.; or quarterly, £5 6s. Lessons from 9 a.m. to 9 p.m.

RIDING.—Ladies and gentlemen may learn this delightful exercise in a few LESSONS at the ROYAL BELGRAVE RIDING SCHOOL, Gillingham-street, Eccleston-square, the largest and best in London. Hours for ladies, from 11 to 4; for gentlemen, from 7 till 11 in the morning, and from 4 till 8 at night. Hunting Lessons as usual.—EDWARD FOWLER, Proprietor.

HORSES—a Pair of remarkably handsome Landau, Brougham, or superior Riding Bay Geldings, six years old, 15 hands 3 inches high, step well together, with splendid action, in double and single harness. They are an excellent match, with black points, and sold for no fault. Price, with warranty of soundness, 120 guineas. Owner's servant has full particulars, at stable No. 3, Northumberland-mews, Southampton-buildings, Holborn.

HORSE (TUBAL CAIN)—a handsome, first-class Brougham, Phaeton, or Riding Bay Gelding, six years old, height 15.3, with superior action, breeding, and substance; well known with the Queen's hounds, a good hunter, and master of 15 stone. Warranted sound and free from vice. A few days' trial allowed. Property of a gentleman. Price £50. Owner treated with.—Stable, 14, Tavistock-mews, Bedford-street, Bedford-square, W.C.

HUNTERS.—To be SOLD, a STUD of first-class HUNTERS. No. 1. Bay Gelding, 15.3, up to 13 stone, carries a lady, 90 guineas; No. 2. Bay ditto, 15.2, up to 13 stone, carries a lady, 60 guineas; No. 3. Bay ditto, 15.3, up to 11 stone, 90 guineas; No. 4. Bay ditto, 15.2, up to 11 stone, 50 guineas. The above are in regular work, and hunted up to the present time. To be seen at E. FOWLER'S Riding School, Gillingham-street, Eccleston-square, London, S.W.

A DARK CHESTNUT or GRAY PONY WANTED, about 12.2, quiet in harness, with good action. Address A. W. M., 30, Great George-street, Westminster.

CHILD'S PONY, the property of a little boy going to school, a fast walker, will go from walk into canter, and is used to trotting along with a leading rein. Price 30 guineas. At Mr. Mostyn's, 19, Green-street, Park-lane.

FOR SALE, the property of a gentleman, a PAIR of BAY HARNESS HORSES, 15.2, perfectly quiet to drive, and with good action. Price 150 guineas. Apply at Wm. Banks's Commission Stables, King's-mews, Gray's-inn-road.

FOR SALE, by Private Contract, the property of a deceased Baronet, a PAIR of CARRIAGE HORSES, dark brown, 16 hands, and fashionable Landau, by Peters. Particulars at No. 28, Brook-street, Bond-street.

FOR SALE, a PAIR of DARK BROWN MATCH HORSES. Have been driven together for six years, and sold through death. Horses and harness 100 guineas. To be seen at Tansley's Livery Stables, Holland-road, Hove.

FOR SALE, a first-class HARNESS or MATCH HORSE, without fault (the property of a gentleman), 16 hands high, black, five years old, fine action, very gentle, docile temper, and exceedingly handy. Apply to the Coachman, before 2 p.m., 4, Eglon-mews, St. George's-square, Primrose-hill, N.W.

PHAETON or LIGHT BROUGHAM HORSE.—For SALE, a DARK BROWN GELDING, very well bred, with capital action; nearly 16 hands. He is a good hack and hunter. Price 70 guineas. Apply at the owner's Stables, 41, Hyde-park-gardens-mews, W., or by letter to the coachman there.

LADY'S PARK HACK, a long, low, and remarkably handsome black mare. Is the property of and has been regularly ridden by a lady; is perfectly quiet, with fine knee action. She is also very clever as a hunter. At Mr. F. Mostyn's, 19, Green-street, Park-lane.

NOTICE.—To be SOLD, ONE of the lightest and grandest Cee and under-spring BAROUCHES in London, Cost 300 guineas, price 130 guineas. Owner left England. Nearly new.—154, Piccadilly, W.

NOTICE, —— A nearly new MINIATURE BROUGHAM. 75 guineas, cost 140. By order of the lady who had it built.—154, Piccadilly, W.

NOTICE.—A LANDAU, of finest workmanship, cost 220 guineas, price little over half. Harness if required. Only run three months.—154, Piccadilly, W.

NOTICE. — An officer wishes to SELL his PHAETON; no further use for the same. Nearly new; 45 guineas.—154, Piccadilly, W.

IMPORTANT NOTICE.—For SALE, an elegant MINIATURE LANDAU, finished in best style, built to order, 180 guineas. Will be sold, by order of the Executors, for 135 guineas. It has never been used. Fittings for one or a pair. Also a handsome T cart. 40 guineas (cost £75 two months since). Three years' warranty will be given.—S. Harris, 13, Orchard-street, Oxford-street.

BROUGHAM.—A lady, leaving England, wishes to DISPOSE OF this elegant LIGHT CARRIAGE for 70 guineas. Built last season. Cost 145 guineas. Scarcely soiled. Mats and water-proof apron. Fully warranted.—13, Orchard-street, Oxford-street.

A WAGGONETTE, changes to a Stanhope phaeton. Only in use two months. Cost 80 guineas. To an immediate purchaser 45 guineas.—S. Harris, 13, Orchard-street, Oxford-street.

FOR SALE, a well-matched PAIR of handsome BROWN CARRIAGE HORSES, both five years old, with good action, warranted sound. Perfectly quiet under all circumstances to ride and drive in single or double harness. Apply to the Coachman Wood Lea, Bedford-hill, Balham, S.W.

FOR SALE, an exceedingly handsome, high-stepping GELDING, rising six years, perfectly sound, very strong, and very free goer both in harness and saddle. Reason for selling going to keep a lighter pair and shorter than 16 hands. Price 100 guineas, and warranty given. Apply to Coachman, West-house, Congleton, Cheshire.

CHESTNUT GELDING—grandson of Blair Athol. Recommended to any lady wanting a perfect horse. He stands 15.1, is quiet and exceedingly handsome, with good action; rising five years. Can be seen at stables of owner and breeder, a private gentleman, 14, Winchester-mews, near Swiss-cottage Station, London, N.W.

VERY good HACK, eight years old, rich brown gelding, about 15.2, no white, well bred, fast, and good in all paces; has been carrying young ladies three years, and not been harnessed; believed to be sound and unblemished. Price 40 guineas. Apply to Mr. Tewson's Coachman, Grove-house, Walthamstow, five minutes' cab ride from Hoe-street Station, Great Eastern Railway.

PONY for SALE, a good stepper and very fleet, quiet to ride or drive, age eight, height 11.2. Also Pony-cart, Harness, and Pad, and girl's saddle if desired. Any warranty given or trial allowed. Only reason of owner parting with it, which he does with regret, being that he now resides in town, and has no more use for it. Apply at Owner's stables, Gloucester-mews, Gloucester-place, Hyde-park.

COBS, together or separate—a Pair of very handsome miniature brougham, phaeton, or riding Cobs, colour Bays, five years old, 14 hands 3 high; fast, with admirable action in harness or saddle; quiet for any timid lady or gentleman to ride or drive. Price moderate. Sold for no fault. The owner will warrant them sound, free from vice, and allow a few days' trial. They were examined by an eminent veterinary surgeon lately, and passed sound; certificate given to purchaser. To be seen at City Livery Stables, Tenter-street, Little Moorfields, City.

JOHN DARBY, Rugby, begs to give notice that, having completed his alterations, he will resume business at his stables in Church-street, Rugby, on Thursday, the 4th September, 1879, when he will have on show a number of HUNTERS of high character, principally bought in Ireland and at the Dublin Show, many up to weight; also some very good Servants' Horses, and an extraordinary Boy's Hunter.

THE DEFIANCE COACH HORSES.—Messrs. TATTERSALL will SELL by AUCTION, near Albert-gate. Hyde park, on Monday, Sept. 15, 1879, without reserve, 120 HORSES (horse a mile), comprising the entire stud of Carleton V. Blyth, Esq., the proprietor of the Defiance Coach, now running between Oxford, London, and Cambridge. nearly all of which have been in regular work in the coach throughout the season (six months). For further particulars see catalogue.—Wm. Banks, Secretary.—White Horse Cellars, Piccadilly.

ALDRIDGE'S, St. Martin's-lane.—Black Troop Horses.—Next Saturday, September 6, will be SOLD by Public AUCTION, witeout reserve, ELEVEN BLACK HORSES from Her Majesty's Regiment of 1st Life Guards. On view Friday.—W. and S. FREEMAN, Proprietors.

ALDRIDGE'S, St. Martin's-lane.—The Greenwich COACH HORSES will be SOLD by Public AUCTION, Wednesday, Sept. 10. Are now working the Greenwich Coach, and can be seen daily running in the coach up to Wednesday, Sept. 3. On view at Aldridge's the day before and morning of sale.—W. and S. FREEMAN, Proprietors.

BARBICAN REPOSITORY. — Sales by Auction every Tuesday and Friday.—To-morrow (Tuesday), commencing at 11, will be SOLD upwards of 160 HORSES of various descriptions, suitable for professional gentlemen, tradesmen, cab proprietors, and others; active young cart and van horses for town and agricultural purposes; also a large assortment of new and second-hand carriages, cabs, carts, harness, &c.—HERBERT RYMILL, Proprietor.

BARBICAN REPOSITORY.—Irish Horses from Waterford and Limerick.—Mr. RYMILL will SELL by AUCTION, To-morrow (Tuesday), TWENTY-FIVE quick-stepping, useful YOUNG HARNESS HORSES and HACKS, suitable for professional gentlemen, jobmasters, cab proprietors, tradesmen, and others, the property of Widger and Ryan.

BLACK TROOPERS from Her Majesty's Regiment of Royal Horse Guards.—Mr. RYMILL will SELL by AUCTION. at his Repository, Barbican, on Tuesday, Sept. 9, TWENTY long-tailed BLACK TROOP HORSES, supernumeraries of the above Regiment, by order of the Commanding Officer. On view.

LIGHT LANDAU, for one horse. Has been only used a few times. 90 guineas cash will be taken by owner for it. To be seen at Dunstan's Coach factory, 193, Marylebone-road.

LIGHT, stylish **MAIL PHAETON**, fully furnished with pole and shafts, patent break, &c., for SALE, by order of the owner, at a great sacrifice. On view at the Grosvenor Carriage Factory, 176, New Bond-street, W., opposite Burlington-gardens.

LANDAU, highly finished, light, and suitable for a hilly country, almost new. As an immediate SALE is desired a very low cash offer will be accepted. On view at the Grosvenor Carriage Factory, 176, New Bond-street, W., opposite Burlington-gardens.

THE GROSVENOR COUPE.—ONE of these elegant, compact LITTLE BROUGHAMS, which has scarcely been used, for SALE, at a considerable reduction in price, at the Grosvenor Carriage Factory, 176, New Bond-street, W. Also a Circular-fronted Brougham, may be had a bargain for cash.

VICTORIA—one of these elegant carriages, as built for H.R.H. the Princess of Wales. It has been only a few times in use, and is for SALE at a very low price. On view at the Grosvenor Carriage Factory, 176, New Bond-street, W.

BROCKELBANK'S REGISTERED REVERSIBLE WAGGONETTE and STANHOPE PHAETON, can be changed in a minute; fitted also with the Patent Dividing Front Seat. The most perfect carriage of the kind yet introduced.—Islington-green.

W. CLARK, 232, Oxford-street, London.—His PATENT HORSE CLIPPERS are all stamped with his name, both on the plates and on the handles, wooden and iron. All purchasers are requested to insist on such name and address being so stamped, as none others are genuine.

SPECIAL NOTICE.—W. CLARK begs to inform the public that he has invented a SMALL HORSE-CLIPPING MACHINE, worked by one hand only, to be used in conjunction with the above well-known clipper. By this admirable invention the operator, having one hand at liberty, can hold the animal in any desired position, and thereby prevent injury to himself and to the machine.

HARROW.—Omnibus Horses.—In consequence of the Harrow and London Omnibus discontinuing running for the winter season, Messrs. W. and S. FREEMAN, Proprietors of Aldridge's, St. Martin's-lane, will SELL by Public AUCTION, Wednesday next, 26 HORSES which have been working in the Harrow omnibus. They are hard working, well-conditioned machiners, and are suitable for tramways, omnibus, and cab work, &c. On view at Aldridge's on Tuesday, November 4th.—W. and S. FREEMAN.

FOR SALE, a **STANHOPE PHAETON**, light and well built, with let-down step over front wheel, nearly new. Price £35. Apply to Coachman, 31, Queen's-gate-mews, South Kensington.

WAGGONETTE OMNIBUS, by Peters, and Victoria, both painted and lined blue, in condition as new. Standing at 3, Davies-street, Berkeley-square.

SUPERIOR BROUGHAM, by W. and F. Thorn, built last season, and scarcely distinguishable from new. Is light and of the best style, with all the latest improvements. Ranelagh-house, Lower Grosvenor-place, S.W., and 19, Great Portland-street, W.

ROYAL PATENT LANDAU and **WAGGONETTE**, with portable top to form omnibus. Both very light. Not used three weeks. Great sacrifice in price. At the Royal Carriage Gallery, No. 137, New Bond-street.

ELEGANT LIGHT BROUGHAM, 70 guineas, and Victoria, with back and front shifting seats, 60 guineas; both in splendid condition. Apply to the Manager, Royal Carriage Gallery, No. 137, New Bond-street.

BROUGHAM—a remarkably light carriage, built to order, and having been used but a few times is in every way like new, for SALE, at a very moderate price, at the Burlington Carriage Factory, 176, New Bond-street, W., opposite Burlington-gardens.

HENRY HEFFER and Co. have several of their celebrated MINIATURE BROUGHAMS, Second-hand, in condition almost equal to new, which may be hired for the winter months, with option to purchase.—100 to 104, Long-acre.

ELEGANT VICTORIA, nearly new, the property of a lady of title, for SALE, at exactly half its original price. On view at the VICTORIA CARRIAGE WORKS, 24 and 25, Long-acre, W.C.

BROUGHAM, price 60 guineas, by one of the best London builders, light, fashionable, and in splendid condition, on SALE at the VICTORIA CARRIAGE WORKS, 24 and 25, Long-acre, W.C.

THE THREE-YEARS' SYSTEM.—CARRIAGES of all sorts SOLD on the three-years' system of payment, at the VICTORIA CARRIAGE WORKS, 24 and 25, Long-acre, W.C.

Books, Magazines & Music

ANNALS of an EVENTFUL LIFE, a Novel, in 3 vols., is just ready. Hurst and Blackett, publishers, No. 13, Great Marlborough-street.

THE DUKE'S HONOUR. By EDWARD WILBERFORCE, Author of "Social Life in Munich," &c. In 3 vols. Is now ready at all the libraries. Hurst and Blackett, publishers, 13, Great Marlborough-street.

FORGOTTEN by the WORLD, a Novel, in 3 vols., post 8vo., is now ready, and may be had of all booksellers and at all the libraries. Hurst and Blackett, publishers, 13, Great Marlborough-street.

NOBLESSE OBLIGE, by SARAH TYTLER, Author of "Citoyenne Jacqueline," &c., in 3 vols. "Whatever Miss Tytler publishes is worth reading. Her book is origina and rich in observation."—Pall Mall Gaz. Hurst and Blackett, publishers.

THE UNKIND WORD, and other Stories, by the Author of "John Halifax," 2 vols. "We can call to mind nothing from the author's pen that has a more enduring charm than the fresh and graceful sketches in these volumes."—United Service Mag. Hurst and Blackett, 13, Great Marlborough-street.

DEBENHAM'S VOW. By AMELIA B. EDWARDS, Author of "Barbara's History," &c. 3 vols., at all the libraries. "A clever book. The story is fresh and interesting, and most of the characters are natural, while some of them are charming."—Saturday Review. Hurst and Blackett, publishers.

FAIRY FANCIES. By LIZZIE SELINA EDEN. Illustrated by the Marchioness of HASTINGS. 1 vol., 10s. 6d., elegantly bound. "This volume is exactly one of those which most profoundly touch and stir the truest Christmas feelings—of goodwill, not to man alone, but to all the mysterious worldly associations amid which man lives."—Telegraph. Hurst and Blackett, publishers.

GUY VERNON. By the Hon. Mrs. WOULFE. Now ready, in 3 vols. "A good novel in every sense of the word. It is a very interesting, graceful, stirring, and touching story, told in a clear, flowing style, and whose principal personage is a very lovable creature. Violet Harcourt is a creation of which any novelist might be proud."—Examiner. Hurst and Blackett, publishers.

GWENDOLINE'S HARVEST,

AN original and interesting NOVEL in CHAMBERS'S JOURNAL, on New Year's-Day.

GWENDOLINE'S HARVEST.

WHAT is the "HOLY GRAIL?"—See CHAMBERS'S ENCYCLOPÆDIA, under article "Grail."

EVENINGS with HOMER: The Heroes of the Iliad. Price 6d. By J. SHIRLEY. Simpkin, Marshall, and Co., London. Order through any bookseller.

NEW EDITION of HOLMES'S SURGERY.—The Second Volume, comprising all the Treatises in the Previous Edition relating to General and Special Injuries, will be ready on January 6, price one guinea. London, Longmans, Green, and Co.

MR. MILL on the IRISH LAND QUESTION.—CHAPTERS and SPEECHES on the IRISH LAND QUESTION. By JOHN STUART MILL. Ready on January 5, in 1 vol. post 8vo. London, Longmans and Co.

JOURNAL des DEMOISELLES, 16s. par an; Revue des Deux Mondes, 50s.; etc. Almanachs pour Rire, Comique des Cocottes, etc., 6d. chacun. Abonnement à la librairie, 2s. 6d. par mois. Catalogues gratis. —P. A. ROQUES, 51, High Holborn, W.C.

THE ACADEMY.—The Fourth Number of The ACADEMY, a New Literary Review and Monthly Record of Literature, Learning, Science, and Art, will be published on Saturday next, January 8th. Advertisements should be received for insertion not later than the 3d instant. John Murray, Albemarle-street.

THE FREE CHURCH PENNY MONTHLY MAGAZINE gives every information on the anti-pew and offertory movement, originated, and for 12 years conducted in London and throughout England, by the National Association, 16, Northumberland-street, W.C., and St. John's-street, Manchester. Parker, 377, Strand.

THE NEW CHRISTMAS STORY, "Christmas Eve with the Spirits;" or, "The Canon's Wanderings through Ways Unknown, with further Tidings of Scrooge and Tiny Tim." Original Illustrations, cloth extra, gilt edges, &c., 2s. 6d. At all libraries and booksellers in town or country; or free by post direct from the publishers, at 2s. 6d. Bull, Simmons, and Co., publishers, &c., 9, Wigmore-street, Cavendish-square, W.

NOTICE.—The GARDENER'S CHRONICLE and AGRICULTURAL GAZETTE will, on and after the 1st January, 1870, be printed in larger type. Several new features will be introduced, and woodcuts will be given more frequently than hitherto. Among other changes the agricultural portion will be considerably enlarged. Published by William Richards, 41, Wellington-street, Strand, London, every Saturday, 5d. (and 6d. stamped).

THE MONTHLY PACKET for January, 1870, contains:—The Pillars of the House; or, Under Wode Under Rode. A tale, by the Author of "The Heir of Redclifte." Chap. I.—Hymn-Poems on Notable Texts. By the Rev. S. J. Stone. No. 1—The River of God—The Child's Crusade. Chaps. I. and II. By Evelyn Tod—The Spots on the Sun. By R. A. Proctor, B.A.—London's Twelve Days Prayer. By Ivanoona—Traditions of Tirol. No. XI., and other aricles. Price 1s. London, J. and C. Mozley, 6, Paternoster-row.

THE POPULAR SCIENCE REVIEW, Jan., 1870, price 2s. 6d., contains—The Heat of the Moon, by J. E. Carpenter, F.R.A.S.—Under Chloroform, by W. B. Richardson, M.D., F.R.S.—Relation of the Deep Atlantic Deposits to the White Chalk of the Crustaceous Period, by Prof. Ansted, F.R.S.—What is Wine? by A. Dupré—On Some interesting Points in the History of Polyzoa, by Rev. T. Hincks—The Fertilization of Dedynamia, by Dr. Ogle—Reviews of Books, Summary of the Quarter, &c. London, Robert Hardwicke, 192, Piccadilly, W.

THE MONTHLY MICROSCOPICAL JOURNAL and TRANSACTIONS of the ROYAL MICROSCOPICAL SOCIETY for January, price 1s. 6d., contains:—Structure of Scales of certain Insects of the Order Thysanura, by J. S. M'Intyre, F.R.M.S.—Organisms in Mineral Infusions, by C. S. Wake, F.A.S.L. Markings on Podura Scale, by G. Royston Pigott. M.D.—Cultivation, &c., of Microscopic Fungi, by R. L. Maddox, M.D.—Jottings by a Student of Heterogeny, by Metcalfe Johnson, M.R.C.S.—Mode of Examining the Microscopic Structure of Plants, by R. W. M'Nabb, M.D.—Microscopic Examination of Milk under certain conditions, by J. B. Dancer, F.R.A.S.—New Books, Progress of Microscopic Science, Notes and Memoranda, Correspondence, Proceedings of Societies, Bibliography, &c. London, Robert Hardwicke, 192, Piccadilly, W.

THE CONTEMPORARY REVIEW: Theological, Literary, and Social. Half-a-crown, monthly. Contents for January:—

1. The Roman Curia. By the Rev. Professor Cheetham.
2. Lovers of the Lost. By Josephine E. Butler.
3. Cathedral Reform in Ireland. By J. C. MacDonnell, Dean of Cashel
4. Hegel and his Connexion with British Thought. By T. Collyns Simon, LL.D.
5. A Few Thoughts on the Laity. By a Layman.
6. Mr. Tennyson's New Poems. By the Dean of Canterbury.
7. A Nonconformist's Vindication. By Herbert S. Skeats.
8. Notices of Books.

Strahan and Co., 56, Ludgate-hill.

THE ARGOSY MAGAZINE. Edited by Mrs. HENRY WOOD. 6d. monthly.

THE ARGOSY MAGAZINE. Opinions of the Press:—"The Argosy keeps its hold on all who appreciate a high-class magazine."—Paisley Gazette. "The Argosy is the best magazine of light literature we have seen."—Portsmouth Times. "An excellent periodical."—Examiner. "The Argosy is equal to any shilling magazine."—Clare Journal. "We do not wonder that the Argosy holds its own."—Queen. "The Argosy is one of the marvels of the day."—London Scotsman. "The Argosy has a very remarkable contributor in Johnny Ludlow. His papers possess some of the finest humour and pathos, some of the deepest insight into human nature we have met with for many years."—Spectator. "The Argosy is a complete fount of amusement."—Brighton Gazette. 6d. monthly.

NOTICE.-BESSY RANE, Mrs. HENRY WOOD'S new Serial Story, is now commenced in the ARGOSY MAGAZINE. 6d. monthly.

THE ANGEL at the WINDOW. By BERTHOLD TOURS. This much-admired, new song may be had in B flat, for soprano or tenor, also in G., for contralto or baritone. Sent for 2s. Duff and Stewart, 147, Oxford-street.

THE NEW PART SONG for FOUR VOICES.—GOD BLESS OUR SAILOR PRINCE. Written by the Author and Composer of "What are the Wild Waves Saying?" Post free for two stamps. "It has the true marine ring."—Stamford Mercury. The song, 3s.; piano solo, 3s.; post free 18 stamps each. London, Sole Publishers, Robert Cocks and Co.

CIRO PINSUTI'S NEW SONGS. Post free at half-price, in stamps. Don't forget me. Words by Miss Helen Marion Burnside. 3s. In Shadow Land. Words by Rea. 3s. What Shall I Sing to Thee. Words by Rea. 3s. London, Sole Publishers, Robert Cocks and Co.

MOLLOY'S LATEST SONGS.—The Ride (in three keys), 4s. each. The Brook and the Wave, 4s. London, Robert Cocks and Co., New Burlington-street. Order of all music-sellers. Post free, 24 stamps each.

A BIRD SANG in a HAWTHORN TREE. New Song by J. L. HATTON. "For soprano, is exceedingly original, quaint, and truly charming, a song that will add to its composer's fame."—Queen, Dec. 20. Sent for 2s. Duff and Stewart, 147, Oxford-street.

UNDER the MISTLETOE. Juvenile Quadrille on Popular Melodies. By CHARLES GODFREY. "Very pretty and very easy; just the thing for juvenile players. The illustrated title-page is exceedingly good."—Orchestra. Sent for 2s. Duff and Stewart, 147, Oxford-street.

THE MAGIC SPELL (the Fairy's Fancy Fair). New Song by W. C. LEVEY. Sung by Miss Russell. Encored every evening at the Theatre Royal, Drury-lane. Sent for 2s. Duff and Stewart, 147, Oxford-street.

ABSENCE and RETURN. FRANZ ABT'S New Song. "One of Franz Abt's latest and most taking compositions.—Graphic, Oct. 25. Sent for 2s. Duff and Stewart, 147, Oxford-street.

THE VILLAGE CHURCH. New Song. By J. L. HATTON. "One of those simple, unaffected little ditties which will please all alike—for who does not love fresh melody, true expression, and chaste harmony."—Queen, Dec. 6. Sent for 2s. Duff and Stewart, 147, Oxford-street.

POPULAR SONGS in the PANTOMIMES:—

Belle of the Ball	Eaton-square
Have you seen the Shah?	First she would
The Scamp. Sung by M'Dermott	Wait till you get it. Sung by Clark
It's very aggravating	I wish I was
Love Song. Leybourne	Under the mistletoe.

18 stamps each. Hopwood and Crew, 42, New Bond-street.

HOW to DANCE.—COOTE'S BALL-ROOM GUIDE for HOME PRACTICE fully explains how to learn dancing without a master. Illustrated with the figures. Post free 13 stamps.—Hopwood and Crew, 42, New Bond-street.

W. H. CALLCOTT'S RUSSIAN MELODIES for the pianoforte, inscribed, by express permission, to H.R.H. the Duke of Edinburgh. Price 4s. London, Brewer and Co., No. 23, Bishopsgate-street within.

COME to OUR FAIRY BOWER, by Sir JULIUS BENEDICT, as sung with immense applause at Rivière's Concerts. Solo or Duet. Price 4s. Stanley Lucas, Weber, and Co., No. 84, New Bond-street.

NOTICE.—OLD TIMES REVIVED, by F. TROLLOPE, Author of "An Old Man's Secret," "Broken Fetters," in 2 vols., is this day published by Mr. Newby.
2. Lady Flora, by Selina Bunbury, in 2 vols., this day.

NOTICE.—FORSAKING ALL OTHERS, a Novel, by EMMA PICKERING, 2 vols., just ready.
2. Peccavi! a Novel, by Arthur Griffiths, Captain 63d Regiment, in March.

THE CHEAPEST BOOKS in the world are The COTTAGE LIBRARY, 1s. each, and The Wide, Wide World Library, 1s. 3d. each. Catalogues free on application to Milner and Sowerby, 44, Paternoster-row, London.

PUNCH and JUDY, price 1d.—On and after Feb. 2 PUNCH and JUDY will be published on Wednesday, in time for the early trains, instead of Saturday, as heretofore. To be had at all newsagents' and railway stations. Office, No. 7, Garrick-street, W.C.

THE JOURNAL of HORTICULTURE: a Weekly Illustrated Paper, published every Thursday morning, at 5 o'clock. 3d.; stamped, 4d. A new volume commenced on Thursday, Jan. 6. Office, 171, Fleet-street, E.C. To be had of all booksellers.

The COOKERY-BOOK of the AGE.—The Edition de Luxe, super-royal 8vo., illustrated with large plates, beautifully printed in colours, and 161 woodcuts, cloth extra, £2 2s.; Household Edition, without the coloured plates, 10s. 6d.,

THE ROYAL COOKERY-BOOK. By JULES GOUFFE, Chef de Cuisine of the Paris Jockey Club. Translated and adapted for English use, by ALPHONSE GOUFFE, Head Pastry-cook to Her Majesty the Queen. "By far the ablest and most complete work on cookery that has ever been submitted to the gastronomil world."—Pall Mall Gazette. "The work is sumptuously produced. Each delicacy has been studied by the artist, from nature Apart from their scientific value, the coloured plates are charming works of art."—Athenæum. "Equal taste pervades all his work; and the casual reader will err if he fancies that there is any real amount of waste and extravagance in the preparation of his sumptuous dishes. Probably no English manual ever respected economy so much."—Saturday Review. London, Sampson Low, Son, and Marston, Crown-buildings, 188, Fleet-street.

THE EDINBURGH REVIEW, No. CCLXVII., January, is just published. Contents:—

1. Mr. Froude's History of Queen Elizabeth.
2. Geological Theory in Britain.
3. Memoirs of General Von Brandt.
4. Sir Charles Adderley on Colonial Policy.
5. John Calvin in Church and State.
6. London Topography and Street Nomenclature.
7. Veitch's Memoir of Sir William Hamilton.
8. The Prechristian Cross.
9. The Land Question in Ireland.

London, Longmans and Co.; Edinburgh, A. and C. Black.

THE QUARTERLY REVIEW, No. 255, will be published next Saturday. Contents:—

1. Mr. Tennyson's Holy Grail.
2. Life Assurance Companies.
3. Mr. Lecky's History of European Morals.
4. The Land Question in France.
5. Era of George the Second.
6. New Zealand and Our Colonial Empire.
7. Papal Infallibility.
8. Miss Austen and Miss Mitford.
9. The Byron Mystery—Mrs. Stowe's Vindication.
10. The Irish Cauldron.

John Murray, Albemarle-street.

TO AUTHORS.—Mr. HARDWICKE, 192, Piccadilly, begs to inform Authors that he has at his command the requisite means for bringing all WORKS PUBLISHED by him prominently before the public, both at home and abroad. Being practically acquainted with printing, and having been many years engaged in business requiring an intimate knowledge of the best modes of illustration, he is enabled to offer great facilities to gentlemen who intrust their works to him. London, 192, Piccadilly.

TEN THOUSAND ILLUSTRATED BOOKS, in rich ornamental bindings, at less than half-price, admirably adapted for Presents, Rewards, or School Prizes. The public will save money by making an early selection at JOHN FIELD'S great warehouse, 65 and 66, Regent-street. Catalogues post free.

FIELD'S magnificent GUINEA FAMILY BIBLE, 4to. size, beautiful, antique binding, metal rims and clasps, fine steel plates, 50,000 references, and family register. A splendid present. Only to be had at Field's Great Bible Warehouse, 65, Regent-street.

MUDIE'S SELECT LIBRARY.—NEW BOOKS.—Boxes and parcels of the best new books are forwarded daily from Mudie's Select Library to private families, book societies, and public institutions in every part of the kingdom. Prospectuses postage free on application.—Mudie's Select Library, New Oxford-street; city office, 4, King-street, Cheapside.

BOOKS BOUGHT, Libraries or small collections of old and new books Purchased; full value given, thereby avoiding the loss on sale by auction.—THOMAS BEET, bookseller, 15, Conduit-street, Bond-street, London, W.

WHITAKER'S ALMANACK for 1870. The best, most complete, and most useful Almanack ever published. May be had of all booksellers, stationers, and newsvendors. Price 1s., or neatly half-bound 1s. 6d.

OLD MOORE'S PENNY ALMANACK, for 1870, with Predictions of Great Political Events, and important Scientific Discoveries. Ask for Roberts's edition, and thus avoid the inferior imitations.

STRIKE of 10,000 WORKMEN in FRANCE—Prosecution of M. Rochefort—The Auteuil Tragedy: Latest Particulars—The Working Men of London to the Queen—The Pope on Ireland—Mr. Goschen and Emigration—Desperate Attempt to Murder a Sweetheart—Inquiry into the Fatal Fire in the City—Trials at the Middlesex Sessions—Law and Police Intelligence—Special Reports of the Markets—and Latest Telegrams from all Parts of the World.

SOLD EVERYWHERE.—LLOYD'S WEEKLY LONDON NEWSPAPER. Sale over half a million. 1d.

LIFE of the Rt. Hon. SPENCER PERCEVAL, including his Correspondence with numerous Distinguished Persons. By his Grandson, SPENCER WALPOLE. 2 vols. 8vo., with Portrait, 30s. "As a contribution to political and Parliamentary history Mr. Spencer Walpole's work possesses considerable value."—Saturday Review. "This important biography will at once take rank in our political literature, both as a faithful reflection of the statesman and his period, as also for its philosophic, logical, and dramatic completeness."—Post. Hurst and Blackett, 13, Great Marlborough-street.

VICTOR and VANQUISHED, by MARY CECIL HAY, is now ready at all the libraries, in 3 vols. "A story of thrilling interest."—Messenger. Hurst and Blackett, Publishers, 13, Great Marlborough-street.

BROKEN BONDS, by HAWLEY SMART, Author of "Breezie Langton," "False Cards," in 3 vols., will be ready on Friday, Jan. 23. Hurst and Blackett, Publishers, 13, Great Marlborough-street. Orders received at all the Libraries.

COLONEL DACRE, by the Author of "Caste," &c., at all the libraries, in 3 vols. "There is much that is attractive both in Colonel Dacre and the simple-hearted girl whom he honours with his love."—Athenæum. Hurst and Blackett, Publishers.

VOLS. III. and IV. of The HISTORY of TWO QUEENS, Catharine of Arragon and Anne Boleyn, by W. HEPWORTH DIXON, completing the work, are just ready. Hurst and Blackett, Publishers, 13, Great Marlborough-street.

THE EXILES at ST. GERMAINS. By the Author of "The Ladye Shakerley." Now ready, 1 vol., 7s. 6d. "The whole narrative is picturesque, graphic, and entertaining, as well as moral and pathetic."—Post. Hurst and Blackett, Publishers.

TRANSMIGRATION, by MORTIMER COLLINS, Author of "Marquis and Merchant," &c., is now ready at all the libraries, in 3 vols. Hurst and Blackett, Publishers, 13, Great Marlborough-street.

THE BLUE RIBBON. By the Author of "St. Olave's," &c. 3 vols. "The reader will be both pleased and interested in this story. It abounds in picturesque sketches of incident and character, clever dialogue, and touches of pathos and quiet good sense, which will surely make it popular."—Standard. Hurst and Blackett, Publishers, 13, Great Marlborough-street.

STRANGERS and PILGRIMS. Cheap edition, price 2s. boards, 2s. 6d. cloth gilt. Uniform with cheap edition of Miss Braddon's other novels.

STRANGERS and PILGRIMS. A Novel. By the Author of "Lady Audley's Secret," &c. Cheap edition, 2s. boards, 2s. 6d. cloth gilt. "The best piece of work Miss Braddon has done."—Athenæum. London, Ward, Lock, and Tyler.

ALL the YEAR ROUND. Conducted by CHARLES DICKENS. This week's number contains:—The continuation of the serial story, Young Mr. Nightingale—Tea with an Actress—Rosetta's Confessions. Also, the continuation of the serial story, At Her Mercy—Judith's Advice. And the following papers:—Old Fighting Ships: the Old Temeraire and the Venerable—Modern Roman Mosaics—the Eve of St. John—Les Gants Glacés—An Anecdote of the Fronde, 1650—Elbow Room. All the Year Round may be obtained of all Booksellers and Railway Bookstalls.

DOGS and DOG SHOWS.—See the COUNTRY, a Journal of Rural Pursuits (published every Thursday, price 2d., by post 2½d.), which also contains Articles, News, and Reports upon all matters of general interest connected with Fishing, Shooting, the Kennel, the Stable, Natural Science, Travel, Emigration, Farming, Gardening, Cage Birds, Bees, Poultry, Pigeons, Rabbits, Cricket, Racing, Athletics, Aquatics, Foot-ball, Golf, and other sports. The whole of the subjects are treated by gentlemen for gentlemen. A specimen copy for two penny stamps. Office, 32, Wellington-street, Strand, London, W.C.

METZLER and Co.'s CHRISTMAS NUMBER of DANCE MUSIC.—MUSICAL LIBRARY, No. 10. Quadrille, Long ago (on English tunes), C. Godfrey—Galop, Fleur de Lys, C. Godfrey—Polka, Fleur de Lys, Lindheim—Galop, the Bohemians—Waltz, Zoe, Ettling—Waltz, The Bohemians (from the new opera of), Offenbach—Galop, Dark Blue, H. W. Goodban—Quadrille, The Bohemians, Offenbach—New Waltz, Life in Vienna, Johann Strauss. Price 1s.; post free, 13 stamps. Metzler and Co., 37, Great Marlborough-street, London, W.

THE WEDDING ALBUM of DANCE MUSIC, containing the Princess Marie Galop, Ch. D'Albert; Clarence Waltz, W. H. Montgomery; Royal Alfred Quadrille, Dan Godfrey; Duchess Waltz, Arch. Ramsden; St. Petersburg Quadrille, Ch. D'Albert; Star of the North Polka Mazurka, Ch. D'Albert. [illegible]andsomely bound in boards, with illuminated gold cover, and pr[illegible] portraits of H. R. H. the Duke of Edinburgh and the Princess Marie Alexandrowna, thus forming a charming souvenir and elegant musical present. Price 10s. 6d., net. Chappell and Co., 50, New Bond-street.

FALSE HEARTS and TRUE. By Mrs. ALEXANDER FRASER, Author of "A Fatal Passion," &c. Now ready at all the Libraries, in 3 vols. Hurst and Blackett, Publishers, No. 13, Great Marlborough-street.

GODWYN'S ORDEAL. By Mrs. J. K. SPENDER, Author of "Pa.ced Lives," &c. On Friday, September 5, in 3 vols. Hurst and Blackett, Publishers, 13, Great Marlborough-street. Orders received at all the Libraries.

ETHEL GREY: a Novel. By W. S. HAYWARD, Author of "Hunted to Death." A story of woman's love, trials, and triumphs. "Ethel Grey" surpasses most novels; it is full of exciting interest, plot, and character. London, J. and R. Maxwell.

SOPHIE CREWE. A Novel. By FREDERICK TALBOT, Author of "Lottie's Fortune," &c. New cheap edition. Price 2s.; cloth, 2s. 6d.; postage, 4d. London, J. and R. Maxwell, Publishers, Milton-house, Shoe-lane, E.C.

VIXEN. Miss BRADDON'S recent Novel. Now ready. Uniform with the New Cheap Edition of Miss Braddon's other Novels. Price 2s., cloth 2s. 6d. (postage 4d.). London, J. and R. Maxwell, Milton-house, Shoe-lane, E.C.; and all Booksellers, &c.

THE MACHINERY MARKET, 1st of each month, price 6d.

EVERY BUYER of MACHINERY, every User of Machinery, and every one interested in machinery, at home or abroad, ought to see the MACHINERY MARKET. Machinery exporters should send it to their foreign houses.

THE SETTLEMENT of the EASTERN QUESTION. By a Russian General. Price 3d. London, Simpkin and Marshall.

HYDROSTHETICS of the CISTERN, Drain, and Sewer. The Philosophy of Pure Water and Sweet Houses. By THOMAS MORRIS, Architect. 6d. London, Simpkin, Marshall, and Co.

GRIEG, the Norwegian Composer—Commentary on Chopin's Piano Works, by F. Niecks—Great German Composers—Reviews, Concerts, &c.—See MONTHLY MUSICAL RECORD for eptember. Post free 2½d. Augener and Co., 86, Newgate-street.

THE NATIONAL CHURCH. Price one penny, post free 1½d.

1. The Rightful Liberty of a National Church.
2. The Altered Position of the Burials Question.
3. The Church Congress: Revised Programme.
4. Mr. Gladstone and the Irish Church.
5. The Convocation of Canterbury and the Prayer-book.
6. Diocesan Conference Register.
7. The Session of 1879.
8. A Raid upon Endowments.
9. Circular from the Local Government Board on the New Burials Act.
10. Street Accidents in London.
11. A Tale of Empty Chapels.
12. Notes of the Month—Reviews—Correspondence.

Annual subscription, post free, 1s. 6d. Offices, St. Stephen's Palace chambers, 9 Bridge-street, Westminster, S.W.

MACMILLAN'S MAGAZINE, No. 239, for September. Price 1s. Contents of the number:—

1. History and Politics. By Professor Seeley. No. II.
2. A Doubting Heart. By Miss Keary. Chapters XXXV.—XXXVI.
3. An Editor's Troubles. By William Minto.
4. Needlework in the German Schools. By Miss Heath.
5. Indo-Mediterranean Railway. By Commander V. Lovett Cameron, R.N.
6. Hellenic Studies. By C. T. Newton, C.B., D.C.L., LL.D., &c.
7. Haworth's. By Frances Hodgson Burnett, Author of "That Lass o' Lowrie's." Chapters XLIX.—LI.
8. Alms and Legs in France. By Winifrede M. Wyse.
9. Cyprus—Is it Worth Keeping? By R. Hamilton Lang, late H.M. Consul for the Island of Cyprus.

Macmillan and Co., London.

A NEW JOURNAL by Mrs. BRASSEY. For Mrs. Brassey's Journal in the Holy Land, see FRASER'S MAGAZINE for September.

FRASER'S MAGAZINE, September, 1879, No. 597. New Series, CXVII. Price 2s. 6d. Edited by Dr. JOHN TULLOCH, Principal in the University of St. Andrews. Contents:—

Mary Anerley: a Yorkshire Tale. By R. D. Blackmore. Chapter XI. Dr. Upandown. XII. In a Lane, not Alone. XIII. Grumbling and Growling.
Mr. Froude's Cæsar. By Professor W. Y. Sellar
My Journal in the Holy Land. By Mrs. Brassey
Tenant Right in Ireland
Cheneys and the House of Russell. By J. A. Froude
In the Corsican Highlands. By the Hon. Roden Noel
A Hungarian Episode: Zigeuner Music. By the Author of "Flemish Interiors"
Holiday Travel-Books
The Close of the Session.

London, Longmans and Co.

YOUNG Mrs. JARDINE. By the Author of "John Halifax, Gentleman." Now ready, at all the Libraries, in 3 vols. Hurst and Blackett, Publishers, 13, Great Marlborough-street.

LITTLE Miss PRIMROSE. By the Author of "St. Olave's," &c. On Friday, Nov. 7, in 3 vols. crown 8vo. Hurst and Blackett, Publishers, 13, Great Marlborough-street. Orders received at all the Libraries.

THE AMATEUR POACHER. By the Author of "The Gamekeeper at Home," "Wild Life in a Southern County.' Crown 8vo., 5s. London, Smith, Elder, and Co., 15, Waterloo-place.

NEW NOVEL.--SISTER. 2 vols. London, Smith, Elder, and Co., 15, Waterloo-place.

JOHN HAZEL'S VENGEANCE. By W. S. HAYWARD, Author of "Hunted to Death," &c. A story that is full of exciting interest, plot, and character. Price 2s.; cloth gilt, 2s.6d. London, J. and R. Maxwell, Publishers, Milton-house, Shoe-lane.

THE CHEVELEY NOVELS:—1. A Modern Minister, complete, 2 vols.; 2. Saul Weir, complete, 2 vols.; 3. In preparation. W. Blackwood and Sons, Edinburgh and London.

PROF. FOWLER'S SELF-INSTRUCTOR in PHRENOLOGY. 60th thousand, just published, 2s. each. Other phrenological books for sale. Consultations daily at Cook's-buildings, No. 107, Fleet-street.

A LETTER from ROYALTY. By GEORGE AUGUSTUS SALA. BOW BELLS ANNUAL. Now ready. One shilling, postage 2½d. All available talent, literary and artistic. London, John Dicks, 313, Strand. Booksellers and bookstalls.

COMMON SENSE PAPERS on FREE TRADE, Reciprocity, and Protection. No. 1, The Old Free Trade Agitation a Delusion and a Snare.—See the BRITISH EMPIRE national newspaper of Saturday, 1st November. Price 2d.—47, Fleet-street, London, E.C.

TREE PLANTING as an INVESTMENT, and the GENERAL MANAGEMENT of ESTATES.—Landed Proprietors, Farmers, and Agriculturists generally will find much valuable information in the November Number of the JOURNAL of FORESTRY and ESTATES MANAGEMENT. One shilling. J and W. Rider, 14, Bartholomew-close, London, E.C., and of all booksellers.

GOBLIN ROCK: the Tale of a Light at Sea. Ready first week in November, price 1s.—The above is the title of the CHRISTMAS ANNUAL of ONCE A WEEK, and is written by G. MANVILLE FENN, Author of "The Parson of Dumford," "Ship Ahoy," &c., with illustrations by J. Proctor, F. Waddy, and A. S. Fenn. The story rivals in interest the celebrated "Ship Ahoy!" of which 100,000 copies were sold. As applications already received show the certainty of a large demand, the trade is respectfully requested to send in orders without delay, so as to avoid disappointment.—Once a Week office, 19, Tavistock-street, Covent-garden. W.C.

MESSRS. CASSELL, PETTER, GALPIN, and CO.'S ANNOUNCEMENTS:—

Now ready, two volumes demy 8vo., cloth, 24s.,

THE LIFE of the Rt. Hon. W. E. GLADSTONE, M.P., D.C.L. By GEORGE BARNETT SMITH, Author of "Shelley, a Critical Biography;" "Poets and Novelists," &c.

Now ready, two volumes demy 8vo., cloth, 24s.,

ENGLAND; its People, Polity, and Pursuits. By T. H. S. ESCOTT. In this important work a comprehensive view is given of the present state of England with reference to Society, Politics, Commerce, Education, Administration, Religion, Science, Law, &c.

Second edition, now ready, demy 8vo., cloth, 21s.

WITH the ARMIES of the BALKANS and at GALLIPOLI in 1877-8. By Lieut.-Col. FIFE-COOKSON. With Maps, Plans, and Original Illustrations. "The illustrated anecdotes of personal adventure are very well told and amusing. . ."—Vanity Fair. "C'est un épitomé écrit par un homme de guerre qui a la conscience de sa responsabilité."—Le Constitutionnel.

COMPLETION of PICTURESQUE EUROPE.—Now ready, complete in five volumes royal 4to., cloth, £2 2s. each,

PICTURESQUE EUROPE. With 65 exquisite Steel Plates from Original Drawings by Birket Foster, E. M. Wimperis, P. Skelton, D. McKewan, R. P. Leitch, H. Fenn, &c.; and nearly 1,000 Original Illustrations by the best artists, with descriptive Letterpress.

Now ready, extra crown 4to., cloth, 7s. 6d.,

THE MAGAZINE of ART. New Volume. With an Etching for Frontispiece by H. Herkomer, A.R.A., entitled "Touched," and about 200 Illustrations by the first artists of the day.

Now ready, demy 4to., cloth gilt, 12s. 6d.,

THE INTERNATIONAL PORTRAIT GALLERY. Containing Portraits in Colours, executed in the best style of Chromo-lithography, of the Distinguished Celebrities of Foreign Nations, with Biographies from authentic sources.

Cassell, Petter, Galpin, and Co., Ludgate-hill, London.

LONGMAN and CO.'s LIST :—

SUNSHINE and STORM in the EAST ; or, Cruises to Cyprus and Constantinople. By Mrs. BRASSEY, Author of "A Voyage in the Sunbeam." With Two Maps and 114 Illustrations (including nine full size of page), engraved on wood by G. Pearson, chiefly from drawings by the Hon. A. Y. Bingham ; the cover from an original design by Gustave Doré. 8vo., price 21s.

THE PASTOR'S NARRATIVE ; or, Before and After the Battle of Worth, 1870. By Pastor KLEIN. Translated by Mrs. F. E. MARSHALL. Crown 8vo., with Map, price 6s. "Pastor Klein has done the world a service in sending forth his narrative, remarkable as it is in its detail, touching in its simplicity—a book which makes an indelible impression on the mind."—Nonconformist.

HURST and BLACKETT'S NEW NOVELS.
To be had at all the Libraries :—

Mrs. OLIPHANT'S NEW NOVEL.—Now ready, at all the Libraries, in 3 vols. crown 8vo.,

THE GREATEST HEIRESS in ENGLAND. By Mrs. OLIPHANT, Author of "Chronicles of Carlingford," "The Primrose Path," &c.

Mr. CHARLES QUENTIN'S NEW NOVEL.—Now ready, at all the Libraries, in 3 vols.,

THROUGH the STORM. By CHARLES QUENTIN. "There is more than the average of exciting incident in this decidedly interesting tale."—Athenæum.

C. KEGAN PAUL and CO.'S NEW PUBLICATIONS :—

Dedicated, by express permission, to Her Majesty the Queen,

TENNYSON'S SONGS, Set to Music by various Composers. Edited by W. G. CUSINS. The volume comprises 45 songs, and is issued in a handsome cloth binding, gilt leaves, price 21s., or in half morocco, price 25s. "A more suitable Christmas present could not be desired."—Academy.

Bound in limp parchment. antique, price 6s.,

TENNYSON'S IN MEMORIAM. A new edition, choicely printed on hand made paper, with a miniature portrait in eau forte by Le Rat, after a photograph by the late Mrs. Cameron.

With 82 Illustrations, crown 8vo., cloth, price 5s.,

THE CRAYFISH : an Introduction to the Study of Zoology. By Professor T. H. HUXLEY, F.R.S. Vol. 28.—International Scientific Series.

Crown 8vo., cloth, price 6s.,

NOTES of TRAVEL : Being Extracts from the Journals of Count Moltke.

Demy 8vo., with Portrait, cloth, price 15s.,

JOHN DE WITT—HISTORY of the ADMINISTRATION of JOHN DE WITT, Grand Pensionary of Holland. By JAMES GEDDES. Vol. I., 1623—1654.

Fourth and cheaper edition, crown 8vo., cloth, price 6s.,

THE GREAT FROZEN SEA. A Personal Narrative of the Voyage of the Alert during the Arctic Expedition of 1875-76. By Capt. ALBERT HASTINGS MARKHAM, R.N., late Commander of the Alert. With six full-page Illustrations, two Maps, and 27 Woodcuts.

No. 1, Paternoster-square.

MESSRS. MACMILLAN and CO.'S LIST :—

With Eight Illustrations by Walter Crane,

THE TAPESTRY ROOM : a Child's Romance. By Mrs. MOLESWORTH, Author of "Grandmother Dear," "The Cuckoo Clock," "Carrots," &c. Extra fcp. 8vo., 4s. 6d.

This day, in crown 8vo., price 6s.,

FRANCE SINCE the FIRST EMPIRE. By JAMES MACDONELL. Edited by his Wife.

Now ready, at all the Libraries,

NEW NOVEL, by CHARLOTTE M. YONGE :— MAGNUM BONUM ; or, Mother Carey's Brood. 3 vols. crown 8vo., 18s.

Now ready, at all the Libraries,

NEW NOVEL, by LADY AUGUSTA NOEL: FROM GENERATION to GENERATION. 2 vols. crown 8vo., 21s.

Edited by JOHN MORLEY.

ENGLISH MEN of LETTERS—HAWTHORNE. By HENRY JAMES. Crown 8vo., 2s. 6d.

Household

PLATE.—GOLDSMITHS' ALLIANCE, Limited, manufacturing silversmiths, 11 and 12, Cornhill, London, opposite the Bank. The best wrought SILVER SPOONS and FORKS, fiddle pattern, 7s. 4d. per ounce; Queen's Pattern, 7s. 6d. per ounce. Many other patterns, plain or highly ornamented:—

Fiddle Pattern.	oz.	s.	d.	£	s.	d.	Queen's Pattern.	oz.	s.	d.	£	s.	d.
12 Table Spoons	30 at	7	4	11	0	0	12 Table Spoons	40 at	7	6	15	0	0
12 Dessert ditto	20	7	4	7	6	8	12 Dessert ditto	25	7	6	9	7	6
12 Table Forks	30	7	4	11	0	0	12 Table Forks	40	7	6	15	0	0
12 Dessert ditto	20	7	4	7	6	8	12 Dessert ditto	25	7	6	9	7	6
2 Gravy Spoons	10	7	4	3	13	4	2 Gravy Spoons	12	7	6	4	10	0
1 Soup Ladle	10	7	4	3	13	4	1 Soup Ladle	11	7	6	4	2	6
4 Sauce ditto	10	7	10	3	18	4	4 Sauce ditto	12	8	0	4	16	0
4 Salt Spoons, strong gilt				1	0	0	4 Salt Spoons, strong gilt				2	2	0
12 Tea Spoons	10	7	10	3	18	4	12 Tea Spoons	14	8	0	5	12	0
1 Pair Sugar Tongs	..			0	15	0	1 Pair Sugar Tongs	..			1	5	0

A pamphlet, illustrated with 300 engravings, containing the prices of articles required in furnishing, gratis and post free on application.

For the use of committees, a work has been published with large lithographic drawings of plate kept ready for presentation.

SILVER-PLATED SPOONS and FORKS.—Especial attention is directed to the superior quality of those manufactured by the GOLDSMITHS' ALLIANCE, Limited, which, being plated on a hard, white metal, are only surpassed in durability by solid silver. Illustrated pamphlet of prices will be forwarded gratis and post free on application to the Goldsmiths' Alliance, Limited, manufacturing silversmiths, 11 and 12, Cornhill, London.

NEW YEAR'S PRESENTS.-RUMSEY'S ROYAL (IXL) JEWELLERY TABLETS, in fancy boxes, with brush and chamois complete, for ladies' toilets, gentlemen's jewellery, &c., at 2s., 2s. 6d., and 3s. 6d. each. Sold by jewellers, chymists, and perfumers; at all bazaars, in the French and Sheffield courts, and the central transept, Crystal Palace, Sydenham. Manufactory, 281, Clapham-road, S.W. "Honourable mention" awarded to W. S. Rumsey's General Preparations in the Dublin (1865) and the Paris (1867) Exhibitions.

ALBATUM, or White Rouge (free from mercury), is the best article known for cleaning all kinds of plate. In boxes, 1s. and 2s. each; by post, 1s. 4d. and 2s. 6d. Also Boot Polish for dress boots, patronized by the Royal Family.—BRADLEY and BOURDAS, 7, Pont-street, and 48, Belgrave-road, London, S.W.

WASHING WANTED. Shirts well stiffened and glazed, 3d. each; collars and small things, 6d. a dozen. References. Punctuality. Cart in town four times a week. 14 years' experience.—A. Syrett, 2, Victoria-terrace, Queen-square, Holloway.

WASHING WANTED, by a respectable laundress Large, open drying ground, plenty of water, and good reference given. Cart in town daily.—J. B., 33, Birchwood-cottages, Albion-road east, Hammersmith.

WASHING WANTED, by an experienced laundress—one or two families'. Has every convenience for the work. Good supply of water, and drying grounds open to the fields. Address Mrs. Hawkes, Mill-hill laundry, Park-road, Acton. Own covered van in town daily. Ladies are invited to inspect the premises.

WASHING WANTED, by an experienced laundress. Plenty of water and extensive drying ground. Conveyance in town daily. 16 years' reference. Terms moderate. Extensive premises, and inspection solicited.—Mrs. Head, Kenilworth Laundry, Acton.

THE latest DISCOVERY in LAMPS, to burn every kind of mineral oil.—The NEW PATENT BELMONTINE LAMP, with two flat wicks, which produces two separate flames in one burner, is the greatest discovery of the age; gives a light of 24 candles at a cost of one halfpenny per hour; wicks last three months, and require no cutting. Price 20s. complete.—WILLIAM H. HONEY, 263, Regent-street, three doors above Oxford-street-circus. Catalogues free

FURNISHING IRONMONGERY, of the best manufacture. Baths of every description, refrigerators, and ice-making apparatus, garden seats and wire arches, garden hose and engines, mowing machines and garden tools; a large and well-selected stock of tea and coffee urns, tea trays, cutlery, electro-plated wares, &c.—EVANS, SON, and Co.'s Show Rooms, facing the Monument, London-bridge.

ECONOMY in the KITCHEN.——WARREN'S PATENT COOKERS, Warren's Patent Corrugated Broilers. The first ensures a well-cooked joint or dish, making good meat delicious, and ordinary meat juicy and tender. The latter cooks a steak or chop, roasts chestnuts, makes an omelette in a most perfect manner. Descriptive sheet and prices may be had of all furnishing ironmongers in town and country.

STOVES (terra-cotta) for greenhouses, bed rooms, &c., give healthy heat 24 hours for 1d., without attention.—At Mappin and Webb's, 77, Oxford-street, and 71, Cornhill; Cunningham and Co., 480, Oxford-street, W.C.; and Davis, 238, Camberwell-road, London.—JOHN ROBERTS, patentee, Upnor, Kent.

STOVES of every description.—EVANS, SON, and Co.'s STOCK for the present season contains an immense variety, adapted for halls, warehouses, churches, and all other purposes. Arnott stoves, Gill stoves, gas stoves, &c., with the latest improvements. —Stove grate and cooking apparatus manufactory, facing the Monument, London-bridge.

AMERICAN COOKING and HEATING STOVES. —Before purchasing send for BROWN, BROTHERS, and COMPANY'S CATALOGUE (Copyright), post free. The largest and best stock in London, in operation daily at Brown, Brothers, and Company's warehouses, 470, Oxford-street, and 11 and 12, Thorney-street, W.C., two minutes' from the British Museum.

THE patent, self-closing COAL VASE, manufactured by FREDERICK WALTON and Co., Old Hall Works, Wolverhampton, is the most compact, useful, and simple yet introduced. May be obtained from all ironmongers in town and country.

OAKEY and SON'S EMERY and BLACK LEAD MILLS, Blackfriars-road, London, S.

OAKEY'S SILVERSMITH'S SOAP (non-mercurial), for Cleaning and Polishing Silver, Electro-plate, Plate-glass, Marble, &c. Tablets, 6d.

OAKEY'S WELLINGTON KNIFE POLISH. Packets, 3d. each; tins, 6d., 1s., 2s. 6d., and 4s. each.

OAKEY'S INDIARUBBER KNIFEBOARDS from 1s. 6d. each.

OAKEY'S GOODS SOLD EVERYWHERE by ironmongers, oilmen, grocers, brushmakers, druggists, &c.

DUNN'S REFINED PURE COLZA OIL, 4s. per gallon, is emphatically unequalled for purity and brilliancy of burning, in moderator and other lamps.—DUNN and Co., 151, Cannon-street, city. Delivered free eight miles.

YOUNG'S PARAFFIN LIGHT and MINERAL OIL COMPANY (Limited).—YOUNG'S CANDLES, used in all the Royal Palaces in Britain, awarded medals (Paris, London, and Dublin), unequalled for household use. May be had of all dealers.

WHY BURN BAD OIL when you can get STRANGE'S A.1. CRYSTAL OIL, 2s. 9d. per gallon? Send for a sample, which can be had gratis, and compare it with that you are using. All oil tested by Dr. Letheby.—Strange's A.1. Crystal Oil and Lamp Depot, 41, Cannon-street, city, E.C.

OIL, Soap, Grocery, and Candles.—Good HOUSEHOLD YELLOW SOAP, 3d., best 4d., 4½d., 5d.; fuller's earth scrubbing soap, much recommended, 2d.; oatmeal skin soap, 10d. per pound. Special low rates for groceries. Composite candles, 6d., 6¾d., and 7½d. per pound; transparent candles, 10½d. Finest colza oil, 3s. 9d. per gallon. General orders over £2 rail free. Cash lists free of J. R. GREAVES, 524, New Oxford-street.

CITY ITALIAN, Soap, Oil, and Candle DEPOT.— Great reduction in price for ready-money HOUSEHOLD SOAPS, dry and fit for use, railway carriage free, and no charge for the case if 1 cwt. or upwards be taken at one time. Railway carriage paid on mixed orders £5 value. Price list sent upon application. WHITMORE and CRADDOCK, Purveyors to the Royal Palaces No. 16, Bishopsgate-street, London.

CHIMNEY PIECES, in Marble or Carved Wood, in the Cinque Cento, Louis XVI., Queen Anne, Adam, and other styles.—BENHAM and SONS, 50, 52, 54, Wigmore-street.

STOVES, of every description, to correspond with the above, including many Specially Designed and Modelled by the late Alfred Stevens.—BENHAM and SONS, 50, Wigmore-street.

CHINA TILE PANELS, for Fireplaces, also to correspond with the above, from special private designs.—BENHAM and SONS, 50, Wigmore-street.

COOKING APPARATUS and HEATING APPARATUS, for large or small establishments.—BENHAM and SONS, 50, Wigmore-street.

ENGINEERING, of every description, for public and private institutions.—BENHAM and SONS, 50, Wigmore-street.

CLARKE'S PATENT PYRAMID NURSERY LAMP FOOD WARMERS. Sold everywhere.

No. 1 holds half-pint food, besides water .. .. 3s. 6d.
No. 2 three-quarters pint food, besides water.. .. 5s. 0d.
No. 3 one pint food, besides water .. .. 6s. 0d.
See that the Patentee's name is on the lamp.

CLARKE'S PATENT PYRAMID NIGHT LIGHTS are made expressly for burning in the Pyramid Nursery Lamp Food Warmers, which will not answer with any others. They are much larger than other night lights, give double the light, and are, therefore, very suitable for illuminating passages, lobbies, &c.

CLARKE'S PATENT PYRAMID NIGHT LAMPS render the burning a night light perfectly safe, entirely prevent flickering (so objectionable in all night lights not burned in a lamp). They are clean, portable, and useful for many purposes. Price 1s. each.

CLARKE'S PATENT PYRAMID NIGHT LIGHTS are best when newly made.—Consumers who find any difficulty in obtaining the PYRAMID NIGHT LIGHTS in good condition are requested to write to the Patentee, SAMUEL CLARKE, at the Manufactory, Albany-street, Regent's park, London, N.W.

COAL.—THORNICROFT and Co. deliver the best descriptions only. Best Wall's-end, 33s.; best Silkstone, 30s.; Lund-hill (much liked), 29s.; best Derby, 27s.; best kitchen, 26s.; best Hartley, 25s.; best steam, 26s.; coke, 20s. Railway depots, Great Northern, King's-cross; Midland, St. Pancras; Great Eastern, Whitechapel; London, Chatham, and Dover, Elephant and Castle.

COALS.—ALLIANCE CO-OPERATIVE COAL COMPANY (Limited).—Best Wall's-end, 33s.; Household, 28s.; Kitchen, 26s.—All coals are the best of each kind, and sold under their correct names, and full weight guaranteed. Members' 5s. tickets avail for one year from the first day of the current month.—35, Lincoln's-inn-fields, W.C.

COALS.—D. RADFORD.—Best Wall's-end, 35s.; Hartlepool, 34s.; Newcastle, 33s.; Talk-o'-th'-Hill, 31s.; Cooper's best Silkstone, 31s.; Silkstone, 30s.; Ruabon, 29s.; Chesterfield, 29s.; Barnsley, 28s.; Derby Brights, 28s.; seconds, 26s.; kitchen, 25s.; hard steam, 25s.; nuts, 25s.; coke 20s. per chaldron. Welsh smokeless, steam, and anthracite. Address orders to Paddington Station, W.; King's-cross Station, N.; or to New-wharf, Pimlico, S.W.

COALS.—JOHN BRYAN and Co., Nine-elms-wharf, Vauxhall, S.W.—Best Hetton's Wall's-end, 35s. per ton; best Newcastle, 33s.; Silkstone, 30s. Arrangements have been made for large supplies of this famous inland coal. Derby, 28s.; steam nuts, 27s. Delivered at Clapham, Brixton, Dulwich, Tulse-hill, Wandsworth, Belgravia, Kensington, or any part of London, at a short notice. Coke, 20s. Cash prices. Telegrams and orders by post promptly attended to.

COAL.—HERBERT CLARKE, Great Northern Railway, King's-cross, Holloway, Elephant and Castle, and Clapham Stations. Lambton Wall's-end, 35s.; H. C. selected, 32s.; best Silkstone, 31s.; Cooper and Co.'s Silkstone, 31s.; Double Diamond, 30s.; black Shale, 30s.; Silkstone, 29s.; Haigh Moor, 29s.; Derby, 28s.; Barnsley, 28s.; kitchen, 26s.; cobbles, 23s.; steam, 27s.; bakers', 24s.; nuts, 24s.; best coke, 16s. per 10 sacks. Herbert Clarke has no agents. Trucks of coal sent to country stations.

COAL.—Great Northern Railway.—The Silkstone and Elsecar Coal Owner's Company.—R. C. Clarke's best Old Silkstone, 31s.; Wharncliffe best Silkstone, 31s.; Athersley, 30s.; Newton Chambers, and Co.'s Silkstone, 31s.; Brazils, 30s.; Wombwell Main, 30s.; Earl Fitzwilliam's Elsecar, 28s.; Rosa Main, 28s.; Park-gate House, 26s.; nuts, 24s.; small coal screenings, 18s. Depots:—King's-cross, Holloway, and Elephant and Castle.—Manager, JAMES J. MILLER, King's-cross Station, N.

COALS.—LEA and Co.'s Best Wall's-end, Hetton or Lambton, by screw steamers and railway, 35s. per ton; Wall's-end seconds, 34s.; best Wigan, 31s.; best Silkstone, 31s.; new Silkstone, 29s.; Derby Bright, 28s.; Barnsley, 28s.; kitchen, 26s.; Hartley, 25s.; cobbles, 24s.; nuts, 24s. Coke, 20s. per 12 sacks. Cash. Delivered screened. Depôts—Highbury and Highgate, N., Kingsland, E., Beauvoir-wharf, Kingsland-road, Great Northern Railway, King's-cross, and Holloway; Midland Railway, Cambridge-street, N.W.; South Tottenham, N.; and 4 and 5, Wharves, Regent's-park-basin.

COAL.—RICKETT, SMITH, and Co. supply every description of coal brought to London. Best Wall's-end, 35s. ; selected, 32s. ; R. S. and Co.'s Silkstone, 31s. ; new Silkstone, 29s. ; Derby bright, 28s. ; Barnsley, 28s. kitchen coal, 26s. ; Hartley, 24s. ; cobbles, 24s. ; steam, 27s. ; nuts, 24s. ; coke, 20s. ; small, &c. Cash.—Coal Departments : Great Northern Railway, King's-cross ; Great Eastern Railway, Bishopsgate ; Midland Railway, St. Pancras-road ; London, Chatham, and Dover Railway, Clapham-road and Elephant and Castle Stations ; Bridge-wharf, Hampstead-road ; Regent's Canal-basin, Limehouse ; Warwick-road, Kensington ; and elsewhere at local prices.

COAL.—FINNEY, SEAL, and Co. supply to housekeepers but three descriptions of coal, viz.—The best Wall's-end, at 35s. ; the best Silkstone, at 31s. ; the best Pinxton, at 28s. ; second quality ditto, 27s. ; via London and North-Western, Great Northern, Midland, and Great Western Railways. Coke, 20s. per chaldron. The above are loaded under inspection, and double screened. Cash on delivery.—Paddington-basin, W., Warwick-road, Kensington, W., Regent's-park-basin, N.W., Chalk-farm-bridge, N.W., Kilburn-bridge, N.W., Victoria-wharf, Millbank, S.W. ; also at the Great Northern Railway, King's-cross, N., and Midland ditto, N.W., and elsewhere. All orders should be sent to the nearest depot.

COAL.—GEORGE J. COCKERELL and Co., Coal Merchants to the Queen and to the Royal Family. Best Wall's-end, 35s. ; best Inland, 31s. Best coke, 20s. Cash on delivery. The best Wall's-end supplied by G. J. C. and Co. are the best of the coals drawn from the Great Hutton Seam of Sunderland and Durham and Original Hartlepool and Tees Wall's-end only. All orders executed as early as possible at the advertised price of the day on which the order is given. Special rates quoted to country buyers for coals in truck.—Central office, 13, Cornhill ; West-end office, next Grosvenor Hotel (and Eaton-wharf), Pimlico ; Purfleet-wharf, Earl-street, Blackfriars ; Durham-wharf (and 108, High-street), Wandsworth ; Sunderland-wharf, Peckham—also at South Transept, Crystal Palace, and Bromley and Beckenham Stations, 1s. extra.

FIRES INSTANTLY LIGHTED. — PATENT FIREWOOD, Wheel or Square, entirely superseding bundle-wood. Adapted for any size grate. Extensively patronized in the houses of peers, hotels, clubs, public offices. Invaluable in large or small establishments. Sold by all Oilmen and Grocers. 500 squares packed for the country on receipt of post-office order, 12s. 6d. -STEVENSON and Co., Manufacturers, 18, Wharf-road, City-road.

LONDON SOAP and CANDLE COMPANY,
107, New Bond-street.

BEST and CHEAPEST HOUSE for all kinds of CANDLES, Soaps, Lamps, Oils, &c. Manufacturers' prices.

BOND-STREET SPERM CANDLES, 1s. per pound.
Beautifully transparent ; give a brilliant light.

VICTORIA SPERM and WAX CANDLES, 1s. 2d. per lb. The most perfect candle ever introduced ; will not bend.

PARLOUR or DRAWING-ROOM WAX CANDLES, 10d. per lb. Fit for state rooms of palaces, castles, clubs, hotels, &c.

CANARY and DOMESTIC WAX CANDLES, 9d. and 7d. per lb. Fit for nurseries, dressing rooms, housekeepers' rooms, &c.

DUPLEX, Moderateur, Reading, and other Lamps. —A choice, extensive, and varying Stock, from 5s. to £5. Lamp, Candle, and fancy shades, in all colours, &c.

FINEST FRENCH COLZA OIL, 3s. 6d. per gallon cash. Free from all acids or deposit, and suitable for all lamps.

PARAGON MINERAL OIL. 2s. 6d. per gallon cash. Water white. Brilliant in burning. Safest and best.

KEROSINE OIL, 1s. 6d. per gallon. Pale straw colour. Fit for stoves, out-door lamps, stables, &c.

HOUSEHOLD, Laundry, and Fancy SOAPS.
Manufacturers' prices.

BUY of the MANUFACTURER direct, pay ready money, and take 5 per cent. discount on all cash purchases.

LONDON SOAP and CANDLE COMPANY,
107, New Bond-street, London, W.

EDWARDS and SON'S SLOW COMBUSTION BRICK-BOTTOM BASKET GRATES, constructed on the principles recommended by Mr. Edwards in his publication, "Our Domestic Fireplaces," published by Messrs. Longmans.

EDWARDS and SON'S VENTILATING TILED KITCHENERS, constructed after the principles recommended by Mr. Edwards in his publication on "The Use of Fuel in Cooking," published by Messrs. Longmans.

EDWARDS and SON, Stove and Kitchen Range Manufacturers and Hot-water Engineers, may be CONSULTED on all matters relating to heating, ventilation, and smoky chimneys.

EDWARDS and SON 49, Great Marlborough-street, London, W Illustrated sheets forwarded

Hotels & Board Residence

HOTEL MIRABEAU, 8, rue de la Paix, Paris. First-class Family Hotel. Patronized by the Royal Family.

WINTER TERMS.—QUEEN'S HOTEL, near the Crystal Palace. Upper Norwood. Arrangements may be made for boarding, &c. Special rooms for wedding breakfasts.

IMPERIAL HOTEL, Dover. First-class family hotel, facing the sea, sheltered from east winds. Winter tariff—board, apartments, and attendance, three guineas per week. Full particulars forwarded on application to the Manager.

NOAKES' ROYAL OPERA HOTEL, opposite the grand entrance of Covent-garden Theatre. Dinners, from joint, 1s. 9d.; entrées, 2s. Suppers; private rooms; ladies' coffee room. Beds, 2s. Billiard rooms. A porter up all night.

NICE.—PALAIS MARIE CHRISTINE FAMILY HOTEL COMPANY (Limited). For tariff of this splendid hotel (formerly a Royal residence) address Packer, 23, King-street, Portman-square; or to the hotel, Nice.

WEST KENSINGTON STATION HOTEL, Russell-road, for families and gentlemen. Spacious coffee, reading, and billiard rooms; elegant drawing room. Private dinners on the shortest notice. Terms moderate.—Mr. T. NORRIS, Manager.

AMSTERDAM.—HOTEL RONDEEL, Proprietor, M. WOLTERS. This establishment, situate at Doelenstraat, in the centre of the town, is recommended to families and tourists. Every comfort. Moderate prices. Newly fitted up.

HAXELL'S ROYAL EXETER HOTEL, West Strand.—Special Notice.—Christmas Pantomimes, &c.—It is respectfully submitted to the patrons of the hotel that upon receipt of letter or telegram, places will be taken for them at any of the theatres.

HYDE-PARK HOTEL, Marble Arch, W., under new management, having been re-decorated and newly furnished. Suites of rooms from two guineas per week; bed, breakfast, and attendance, with use of coffee room, from £1 11s. 6d. do. The house stands unrivalled, having an uninterrupted view of the park.

WINTER TERMS.—QUEEN'S HOTEL, near the Crystal Palace. Upper Norwood. Arrangements may be made for boarding, &c. Special rooms for wedding breakfasts.

ABERYSTWITH.—The QUEEN'S HOTEL, facing the sea, will be found to be an eligible winter residence. Tariff and guide free on application to Mr. JOSEPH MANN, Manager.

HAXELL'S ROYAL EXETER HOTEL, West Strand. This old-established house, long known to travellers as a comfortable and inexpensive residence. Apartments, 2s. 6d.; drawing room suites, 8s. 6d. Attendance 1s. Ladies' coffee room.

IMPERIAL HOTEL, Great Malvern.—Very moderate terms for suites of APARTMENTS, Board, &c., during winter. Tariff on application. Covered way connects the hotel with the railway station.

NICE.—For tariff of the HOTEL des ANGLAIS, the new first-class hotel, facing the sea, and under English management, address the Secretary, Mediterranean Hotel Company (Limited), 6, Dove-court, Old Jewry, London; or to the Hotel, Nice.

NELSON'S PORTLAND HOTEL, Great Portland-street, London. Bed rooms, 2s., 2s. 6d.; private suites, 8s. 6d., 10s. 6d.; service 1s. per day. Ladies' coffee room. Visitors may reside en pension, at 8s. or 9s. per day. Tariffs forwarded.

NOAKES' ROYAL OPERA HOTEL, opposite the grand entrance of Covent-garden Theatre. Dinners, from joint, 1s. 9d.; entrées, 2s. Suppers; private rooms; ladies' coffee room. Beds, 2s. Billiard rooms. A porter up all night.

HYDE-PARK HOTEL, Marble Arch, W., under new management, having been re-decorated and newly furnished. Suites of rooms from two guineas per week, bed, breakfast, and attendance, with use of coffee room, from £1 11s. 6d. do. The house stands unrivalled, having an uninterrupted view of the park.

OXFORD.—CLARENDON HOTEL (late Clarendon Hotel Company), situate in the most central part of the city, and near to the principal Colleges and places of interest to visitors. Families and gentlemen will find this hotel replete with every comfort. Spacious coffee rooms. Private sitting and bed rooms en suite. Guides always in attendance.—JOHN F. ATTWOOD, Proprietor.

BOARD and RESIDENCE, in Gordon-square, W.C. Address A. B., 4, Torrington-place, Gordon-square, W.C. Gentlemen fond of music and a social evening will find a most desirable and comfortable home. Terms moderate.

BOARD and RESIDENCE REQUIRED, for two young gentlemen, within an easy distance of the Veterinary College, Camden-town. References required. Terms moderate. Address M. L., post-office, Lymington.

BOARD and RESIDENCE, for ladies and gentlemen. Terms from 30s. a week, and partial board £1 1s. Address M. R., Lohmann and Cockhead's library, 73, Norfolk-terrace, Bayswater.

BOARD, of the best description, in a family of position. Good cooking, extreme cleanliness, and every comfort requisite. A large bed room vacant. Dinner hour half-past 6. Address E. P., 13, Brunswick-square, W.C.

BOARD and RESIDENCE, for ladies and gentlemen, with all the comforts of a home, two minutes' walk from Kensington-gardens and Metropolitan Railway.—M. W., 38, Queen's-road, Bayswater, W.

BOARD and RESIDENCE (superior), in a beautifully situate house, overlooking Ladbroke-square. The arrangements are those of a private family.—A. Z., Boddington's library, Notting-hill-gate.

BOARD and RESIDENCE, 29, Norfolk-crescent, Marble Arch, Hyde-park. The situation is unexceptionable; every home comfort is provided. An excellent cook kept. References always required.

BOARD and RESIDENCE, Seaside. Ladies and gentlemen are received by the day or week. Winter terms from 25s. to 35s. per week. Reduced terms for two occupying the same room. Piano, smoking room.—The Misses Sankey, Folkestone.

BOARD and RESIDENCE, 8, Prince's-square, Bayswater. Superior accommodation, where a limited number are received. Five minutes' walk of Kensington-gardens. One Vacancy. Address O. Dinner hour 7 o'clock.

BOARD and RESIDENCE REQUIRED, in London, by a lady, for two days in the week, in a cheerful, superior family. Address, stating full particulars and yearly terms, to Z., Messrs. Ford's, stationers, Upper-street, Islington.

BOARD and RESIDENCE REQUIRED, by a lady and gentleman (mother and son), in the neighbourhood of Hyde-park. Send full particulars, with terms and number in house, to A. B., post-office, Winchester.

BOARD and RESIDENCE (superior appointments) – three reception, bath rooms; large house, hall warmed. Best suburb. Late dinner. Terms from four, married, seven guineas per month. References. France—13, Pembridge-crescent, Notting-hill-gate, W.

BOARD and RESIDENCE, near Crystal Palace.—A young married couple have a VACANCY for a gentleman or lady. Unusual facilities and the comforts of a refined and cheerful home. Near the railway station. Terms moderate. 6 o'clock dinner.—Veritas, Oakfield-hall, Gipsy-hill, Norwood.

BOARD and RESIDENCE (very superior), five minutes' walk from Lancaster-gate, Hyde-park west—spacious bed room, suitable to a married couple, very handsomely furnished and lighted with gas; there is an adjoining bed room, equally well fitted up. The house faces two well-cultivated gardens. Besides double drawing and dining rooms, each above 30 feet long, there are baths, a conservary, and smoking parlour. Further particulars obtained from G. D., post-office, Westbourne-grove. Private stabling close by.

AUX ETRANGERS.——BOARD and RESIDENCE OFFERED, with excellent opportunity of learning English. Address Dr. Bartels, 24, Rectory-grove, Clapham.

A GENTLEMAN, his mother, and sister, about taking a good house in the Alexandra-road, St. John's-wood, are desirous of MEETING a thoroughly respectable FAMILY, who would share accommodation and expenses. Address E. H., 2, Devereux-court, Temple.

BRIGHTON.—BOARD and RESIDENCE, Ashburnham-house, Waterloo-street, two doors from Brunswick-terrace. A good winter situation. References required. Reduced terms. Address S. P.

COMFORTABLE and refined HOME OFFERED, with young and musical society. Vacancy for married couple and one lady or gentleman. Address Leah, Ives', post-office, Stanhope-terrace, Glocester-road, South Kensington.

FOLKESTONE.—BOARD and RESIDENCE, combining the comforts of a home, with the social advantages of a select boarding-house. References exchanged. Address Miss Howard, 40, Sandgate-road, Folkestone.

HOME in PARIS.—A French Protestant clergyman's family admits a few BOARDERS. Address M. L., 64, Rue Perronet, Parc de Neuilly, Paris.

PARIS.—An English lady, moving in good French society, would be happy to RECEIVE TWO INMATES. Terms 200 guineas per annum. References exchanged. Address Me. F., No. 4, rue Pasquier.

PARIS, 24, rue Brunel, Avenue de la Grande Armée.—To YOUNG LADIES desirous of perfecting themselves in French and other accomplishments, a comfortable HOME, on moderate terms, is OFFERED by Mme. Raimbault (sister-in-law to Mr. Havet, Director of the Scottish Institution, Edinburgh).

PARTIAL BOARD is OFFERED to one or two gentlemen in a semi-detached villa on St. John's-hill, close to Clapham Junction. Terms from 18s. to 25s. per week. Address X. Y. Z., Benison's, St. John's-hill, New Wandsworth.

PARTIAL BOARD WANTED, in a respectable family, by a gentleman engaged during the day. Terms must be moderate. No lodging-housekeeper need apply. Address X. Y., post-office, 9, High Holborn.

PARTIAL BOARD (permanent) WANTED, by a bachelor, at home three days a week, in the house of a private family without children. W., N.W., or S.W. district. No boarding-house. State terms and full particulars. References exchanged. Address X. Y. Z., Messrs. Rogers and Co.'s, 120, Cheapside, E.C.

WALMER, Kent.—BOARD and RESIDENCE for ladies and gentlemen, in a large house facing the sea. Liberal table. Reduced terms, by the day or week, for the winter months.—Mrs. Parker, 2, Shand-terrace, Lower Walmer.

TO PARENTS RETURNING to INDIA.—The wife of an Indian officer, now in England for the health and education of her only little girl, is willing to take CHARGE of one or even two other LITTLE GIRLS under seven years of age. Terms merely to cover expenses. Apply, first by letter, to A. Z., care of Messrs. H. S. King and Co., 65, Cornhill.

OVERLOOKING BUSHY-PARK.——Added to medical attention, ONE INVALID (nervous or otherwise) can enjoy unsurpassed hygienic advantages, in a sheltered, elevated, and cheerful residence, within extensive gardens. Terms from 2 guineas.—Apply 48, Kensington-gardens-square.

HYDROPATHIC SANATORIUM, Sudbrook-park, Richmond-hill, S.W.—Physician, Dr. EDWARD LANE, M.A., M.D. Edin. Turkish baths on the premises.

HYDROPATHY.——Malvern.—Dr. RAYNER'S ESTABLISHMENT (formerly Dr. Wilson's). The dry, equable climate of Malvern renders it a most desirable residence for invalids in winter; and in numerous cases the water treatment is even more efficacious at this season than during the warmer weather. Prospectus on application.

LEAMINGTON HYDROPATHIC ESTABLISHMENT.—This establishment, especially suitable as a winter residence from its situation in a town well known as a winter resort as well as from its internal arrangements, is now OPEN for the reception of patients and visitors. Prospectuses may be obtained on application to Mr. MABERLY, M.R.C.S.

A LADY, mentally afflicted, REQUIRES a HOME, with a thoroughly practical medical gentleman.—Solon, post-office, Manchester.

MALE PATIENTS—Nervous, Hypochondriacal, Dipsomaniacal, or Strictured.—A west-end physician has VACANCIES. Judicious medical and surgical care. First-class patients only. Highest references.—Delta, Wilkinson's, chymist, Oxford-circus.

BOARD and RESIDENCE (superior), Harbro-house, 235, Brompton-road, situate opposite South Kensington Museum and close to the parks. A VACANCY for a married couple, single lady, or gentleman. Terms moderate.

BOARD and RESIDENCE (superior) near Addison-road Station.—VACANCIES for ladies or gentlemen, with comforts of a private home. Terms 35s. and 2 guineas per week. Late dinner.—Veritas, 74, Elsham road, West Kensington.

BOARD and RESIDENCE (superior), by the day or week.—22, Upper Woburn place, Tavistock-square, W.C.; close to Metropolitan and other Railway Stations, and omnibuses to all parts.

BOARD and RESIDENCE.—REQUIRED, a comfortable HOME, in a family receiving only two or three. Near South Kensington Museum preferred. Address G. L., post-office, 8, Fulham-road, S.W.

BOARD and RESIDENCE.—A lady and gentleman, having a larger house than they require, at South Kensington, wish to RECEIVE a LADY, Gentleman, or married couple, to board, or would let part of their house. Terms moderate. Address T., Messrs. Kelly's Advertising office, 23, King-street, Westminster.

BOARD and RESIDENCE (superior), in a new, spacious, and elegantly furnished house. Large rooms for married couples, &c. Hot baths. Two minutes' from Notting-hill-gate Station and Kensington-gardens.—Linden-house, 55, Linden-gardens, Bayswater, late of 56, Pembridge-villas.

BOARD, &c., in a superior house, replete with every convenience and comfort, handsomely and elegantly furnished. Appointments and table particularly good. Excellent cuisine. Strict cleanliness and individual comfort studied. Late dinner. Terms from two guineas.—Theta, Mr. Cooper's, Chemist, 80, Gloucester-road, S.W.

BRIGHTON (WEST), Ponsonby-hall, The Drive.—BOARD and RESIDENCE. Charming house, near sea and lawns. Sea-water bath.—Mr. and Mrs. Darbyshire, Proprietors.

BRIGHTON.—The Cavendish Mansion. Central, and facing the sea. Superior BOARD and RESIDENCE.—Proprietress.

BRIGHTON, 1, Cambridge-road.——BOARD and RESIDENCE, for ladies and gentlemen, by day or week. Near West-pier, Lawn Promenade. Two guineas per week. Address Proprietress.

BRIGHTON, 16, Holland-road (close to sea).—PRIVATE BOARDING ESTABLISHMENT. Home comforts. Liberal table. Inclusive terms two guineas. Special arrangements with families (not young children). Private apartments, if desired.

BRIGHTON, Lancaster-house, 47, Grand-parade, opposite the Steine Enclosures.—BOARD and RESIDENCE, for ladies and gentlemen. Billiard and bath rooms. Terms on application to the Principal.

BRIGHTON.—The RESIDENTIAL CLUB, 1, Marlborough-place, established as a residence for ladies and gentlemen visiting Brighton, combining the comforts of a home with the advantages of a club. Terms moderate. Apply to the Secretary.

BRUXELLES.——Un Ingénieur, marié, parlant plusieurs langues, possédant une instruction sérieuse, pouvant donner les plus belles références, OFFRE LOGEMENT, Pension, et Instruction à un ou deux jeunes gens de bonne famille. Ecrire L. S., No. 31, Boulevard de l'Observatoire, Bruxelles.

A WIDOW LADY and FAMILY, residing in South Kensington, would be happy to RECEIVE two or three ENGLISH GENTLEMEN in their cheerful, musical home.—Domus, Mr. Earle's, Stationer, 5, Victoria-grove, Kensington, W.

A YOUNG LADY wishes to meet with a lady, engaged in the stationery or some light business, with whom she could BOARD and RESIDE, on moderate terms, at the same time gaining an insight into the business. References exchanged.—G. B., care of Walker and Co., Advertising Agent, 7, Finch-lane, E.C.

A LADY, of small income, seeks a HOME with a lady or friendly family. Large bed rooms, south aspect required, and partial board. Country town preferred, about 20 miles from London. References exchanged. Address, full particulars, Delta, St George's-square, Upton, Essex.

A LADY of POSITION, having much larger house than she requires, in desirable situation, wishes to meet with a LADY of independent or liberal income, to SHARE her HOME. Excellent rooms, carriage entrance to the Botanical-gardens at her disposal.—M. W. G., Stent's, 15, Gledhow-terrace, South Kensington

A LADY (good linguist and musician), residing at the sea-side, wishes to RECEIVE one or two LADIES to BOARD with her. A comfortable home offered, and educational advantages for young ladies if required. Terms very moderate. Highest references. Address, in first instance, to H.R., 34, Sea-side-road, Eastbourne

A GENTLEMAN wishes to meet with a cheerful HOME, and own apartments if required, in a private and domesticated family on the South Coast. State particulars of situation and terms and inmates to H. M., May's Advertising offices, 159, Piccadilly.

A HOME OFFERED, in a lady's family, to a lady or children. Excellent education and care provided. Large house and garden. Very healthy. References to the Vicar, Great Yarmouth, medical men, and others. For terms, B., Telegraph House, Great Yarmouth.

A PROTESTANT FAMILY, having resided in England for some time, wishes to RECEIVE one or two English young ladies as BOARDERS. They would have the opportunity of taking any lessons they might require. Highly respectable references in London.—E. Z., 42, Stern Strasse, Frankfort-on-Main.

A FAMILY of POSITION, residing in Brighton will be happy to RECEIVE a YOUNG LADY, or Two Sisters, to share their refined home, with introduction to society. Address Q27, at C. H. May and Co.'s, General Advertising offices, 78, Gracechurch-street, London.

Toys, Games & Novelties

DUGWELL and SON'S GUINEA BOX of EVERLASTING AMUSEMENTS contains

THE SULTAN'S VOLCANIC FOUNTAIN. A Chymical Wonder.

FIVE BUNDLES of STICKS, and How to Use Them.

ELECTRIC SPIDERS that Resent being Trod Upon.

A SNAKE in the GRASS, the Scientific Mystery. Caution.—Not the L. S. Company's.

FAIRY INCANTATIONS, or Transformation Scene.

THE FUNNY WRESTLERS—The Lover Link—Wheel of Life—Optic Gyrator—Conjuring for Ladies—A Star to Puzzle Wise Men, &c. Most astounding guinea's worth (vide public press). Sent free on receipt of post office order payable to R. DUGWELL, toy importer, 97, New-road, Whitechapel, London, E. City depot, Stevens's model dockyard, 22, Aldgate.

THE SURPRISE.

THE SURPRISE. For Smokers and Jokers. Roars of laughter. Free seven stamps. Sold by all tobacconists, and wholesale at DUGWELL and SONS', the inventors, 97, New-road, Whitechapel, E. City depot, Stevens's model dockyard, 22, Aldgate.

IZZARD (estab. 1797), 136, Regent-street, for TOYS, games, English and foreign novelties, dolls' houses, bagatelle tables, cockamaroo, lessons in kissing, Chinese billiards, besique, Siamese, velocipedes, bicycles, &c.

NARCOTTI, the American Wizzard, from Izzard's, 136, Regent-street.—SCHOOLS and PRIVATE PARTIES ATTENDED. Engage your conjuror, then invite your friends. Entire satisfaction is invariably given.

IZZARD.——EVENING PARTIES ATTENDED with CONJURING and VENTRILOQUISM, conjuring, jugglery, marionettes, Punch and Judy, magic lantern, dissolving views and chromatrope.—136, Regent-street, W.

WHEEL of LIFE, for 5s.—The greatest wonder of the age. This marvellous optical toy, complete, with 12 strips of figures, price 5s. Carriage free for 90 stamps.—H. G. CLARKE and Co., 2, Garrick-street, Covent-garden.

THE MOST LAUGHABLE THING on EARTH.—A New Parlour Pastime, 50,000 Comical Transformations. Endless amusement for evening parties. Post free for 14 stamps.—H. G. CLARKE and Co., 2, Garrick-street, Covent-garden.

THE MAGIC SAILOR. Roars of laughter at this amusing figure, which will, when placed on the ground, immediately commence dancing in perfect time to any tune, astonishing all present, and defying detection. Post free, with full instructions, for 14 stamps.—H. G. CLARKE and Co., 2, Garrick-street, Covent-garden.

BESIQUE, at H. RODRIGUES', 42, Piccadilly. This new and fashionable game, with printed rules, marking boards, markers, and two packs of superior playing cards, in box complete, 10s. 6d., 7s 6d., and 5s., or by post for 11s. 2d., 8s. 6d., and 5s. 8d.

THE most ingenious invention ever brought before our notice (Scientific Mystery).—Cassell's Household Guide.

The results seem miraculous (Scientific Mystery).—Chymist and Druggist.

How the extraordinary results are produced will be a puzzle and a wonder to many a Christmas gathering (Scientific Mystery).—Standard.

Will prove to thousands a welcome cabinet of scientific amusement. The effects are inscrutable.—Daily News. See under.

THE "SCIENTIFIC MYSTERY" reveals hidden questions. (By Royal letters patent). 5s. ; free for 66 stamps.

IMPROVED CHAMELEON TOP. 2s. 6d. Extra discs. Free 38 stamps. Effects endless in variety and beauty.

OBEDIENT BALL. 2s. 6d ; free 38 stamps.

CORUSCATING METALLIC WHEELS. Nos. 1 and 2. 2s. ; free 30 stamps.

INVISIBLE GIFT. 1s. ; free 16 stamps.

VANISHING COIN. 1s. ; free 14 stamps.

ENCHANTED BOTTLE. 1s. ; free 14 stamps.

EXPERIMENTS for JUVENILES. 1s. ; free 14 stamps.

A PHOTOGRAPH in OPAL. 7s. 6d. Packed and sent free for 100 stamps. This most exquisite novelty is mounted on a massive cube of crystal. (See below.)

THE STEREOSCOPIC COMPANY'S GUINEA BOX includes all the above, carriage free to any railway town, for 21s. Cheques and post-office orders to SAML. CLARK, 54, Cheapside; 110 and 108, Regent-street. As the demand for these guinea boxes is enormous, purchasers are recommended, who require them promptly, to apply early.

JAQUES'S NEW CARD GAMES:—Sol, or the Signs of the Zodiac, 1s.; the Realm, 1s. ; Quits, 1s. ; Snap, 1s. ; the Wedding, 1s. 6d. ; the Counties of England, three series, 1s. 6d. each ; Illustrated Proverbs, 1s.; May Day, 1s.; The Sixteenth Century, 1s. ; Pumblechook, 1s.; the Bride, 1s.; Happy Families, 1s. (post free two extra stamps). Wholesale, Jaques and Son, 102, Hatton-garden.

JAQUES'S NEW WINTER GAMES:—Matrimonial Dominoes, 3s. 6d. ; Railway Traffic, 6s. ; Drawing-room Pyramids, 15s. ; Picture Loto, 7s. 6d. ; Table Croquet, 14s. ; Geographical Loto, 7s. 6d. ; Excelsior, 3s. 6d. ; Moorish Fort, 10s. 6d. ; Floral Loto, 7s. 6d. ; Tourist, 4s. 6d. ; Faces, 6s. 6d.; Whitworth gun, 12s. 6d.; Enfield Skittles, 17s. 6d. Wholesale, Jaques & Son, 102, Hatton-garden.

NOTICE.—AURORA'S BLUSH.—The public are respectfully informed that to meet the extraordinary and unprecedented demand for this beautiful Christmas novelty, a fresh supply is now ready. Price 1s. 6d. ; post free 1s. 8d.—G. HYETT, Haydon-house, New-cross.

CHRISTMAS PRESENTS.—2,000 MODELS of BOATS and STEAM ENGINES on view at the Model Dockyard, No. 31, Fleet-street. The boats, from the smallest size to 14 feet long, are guaranteed to sail fast. The engines, from the smallest size to 1-horse power, are warranted to work well. Send 6d. in stamps, for handy catalogue, containing 120 illustrations. Established 1774.

COX'S SCIENTIFIC AMUSEMENTS, galvanic batteries, electric bells, and telegraphs, model steam-engines, and all philosophical experiments, fully described in "Cox's Illustrated Guide of Scientific Instruments," free seven stamps.

COX'S DISSOLVING VIEWS on HIRE.—The custom of Hiring Dissolving Views having considerably increased, we are enabled to make a material reduction in the charge for their use. Our stock being one of the largest in London, and of the very best quality, we are enabled to offer advantages over any other house. List of subjects free one stamp.—Frederick J. Cox, 26, Ludgate-hill.

GAMES for WINTER EVENINGS.—BAGATELLE and BILLIARD TABLES, Chess, draughts, dominoes, Pope Joan, bezique, check, volunteers, race, drole, loto, table croquet, calabrasella, the new cabinet of games, and an unrivalled variety, at CREMER, Jun.'s game warehouse, 210, Regent-street.

DIRECT from GERMANY.—CASES of TOYS, made expressly for Messrs. CREMER, admirably adapted for school treats. Price 5s. 6d., 10s. 6d. Remittance of 5s. 3d. or 10s. 8d. must accompany country orders. To guard against imitations observe the address, Cremer, 210, Regent-street, or 27, New Bond-street.

EVENING PARTIES.—The Talking Hand and the Curious Little Old Lady.—This Entertainment, with which is included some of the most diverting experiments in modern popular magic, is arranged specially for drawing-room representation by CREMER, Junior, 210, Regent-street.

EVENING PARTIES.—JAPANESE, Chinese, and Indian NECROMANCY and JUGGLING; including the flying plates and golden balls, aerial feather, fire eating, the egg and straw, Japanese top and butterfly, and many novelties.—CREMER, 210, Regent-street.

EVENING PARTIES. —— VENTRILOQUISM, really genuine and natural; including representations of the Englishman, the Irishman, and the Scotchman; a voyage from Australia, Yankee notions, hotel accommodation, and the laughable heads. To be secured only at CREMER, Jun.'s, 210, Regent-street.

ENTERTAINMENTS for DRAWING-ROOM PARTIES.—Mr. CREMER, of 27, New Bond-street, respectfully informs the nobility that he has completed arrangements with professors of recognized talent for the representation of MAGIC, Ventriloquism, Punchinello, Marionettes, Jugglery, Dissolving Views, &c.

AMATEUR THEATRICALS and FANCY BALLS.—Caution in Address.—Messrs. JOHN SIMMONS and SONS', the eminent Court Costumiers, respectfully announce that their only address is 4, Tavistock-street, Covent-garden. Fancy and historical costumes on hire. Their celebrated portable theatres, to be had only at their establishment. Costumes made to order on hire. Country orders receive. immediate attention.—4, Tavistock-street only.

RODRIGUES' BALL PROGRAMMES and DINNER CARTES, of new designs, arranged, printed, and stamped, with arms, crest, or address in the latest fashion. A card plate engraved and 100 cards printed for 4s. 6d.—42, Piccadilly.

MAGIC LANTERNS LIT by GAS, from any chandelier. No oil—no trouble. Price 7s. 6d. This important improvement fully described in catalogue of lanterns, and 3,000 slides, four stamps; ditto including 57 lectures, splendidly illustrated, 18 stamps. MILLIKIN and LAWLEY, 161, Strand.

LECTURES for the MAGIC LANTERN:—Franco-Prussian War, Fairy Tales, Pantomime, Travels, Adventures, Christmas Carols, Hymns, Sermons, Popular Science, 57 Lectures, with catalogue of 3,000 slides, splendidly illustrated, 18 stamps. Lantern and comic slides, 7s. 6d.—MILLIKIN and LAWLEY, 161, Strand.

CONJURING and VENTRILOQUISM.—Entirely new and clever ENTERTAINMENTS, adapted for children of all ages, also for adults. To be obtained only at IZZARD'S, 136, Regent-street, W. N.B. Early application is necessary.

ENTERTAINMENTS for PARTIES, Schools, &c., in Town or Country.—CONJURING, Ventriloquism, Marionettes, Punch and Judy, with Dog Toby, magic lanterns, dissolving views, &c. Professors of the highest reputation are engaged exclusively by JAMES IZZARD, 136, Regent-street, W.

BINGHAM'S GAMES, post free two extra stamps: Stella, played like Bezique, 1s.; Parade, 42 cards, 1s.; Trousseau, 39 cards, 1s.; Sweepstakes, 36 cards, 1s.; Wants, 40 cards, 1s.; Happy Thoughts, 64 cards, 1s.; Quiz, 109 cards, 1s.; Quid Pro Quo, 78 cards, 1s.; Levée, an Heraldic Game, in a box, 1s. 6d.—R. W. Bingham, publisher, Bristol; and Evans and Sons, London.

NEW WINTER GAMES:—Picture Loto, 7s. 6d.; the Malakhoff, 10s. 6d.; Railway Traffic, 6s.; the Counties of England, 5s. 6d.; Excelsior, 3s. 6d.; Floral Loto, 7s. 6d.; Table Croquet, 5s.; Patchesi, 2s. 6d.; Faces, 6s. 6d. Also the following Shilling Card Games, beautifully coloured, post free 14 stamps:—Snap, Sovereigns of England, Quits, 16th Century, Mayday, Realm, Happy Families, Sol, Pumblechook, Illustrated Proverbs. Sold at all fancy repositories; wholesale, JAQUES and SON, 102, Hatton-garden.

LONG EVENINGS.—IN-DOOR GAMES of every kind:—Bagatelle boards, 28s. 6d., 50s., 58s. 6d., 65s., 78s. 6d., with ivory balls, cues, &c.; chessmen, Staunton do., draught men and boards, dominoes, backgammon, and cribbage boards, table croquet, loto, race games, besique, 2s. 6d., 3s. 6d., 5s.; playing cards, 8d. per pack. Price lists free. Orders over 20s., prepaid, sent carriage paid any station in England.—PARKINS and GOTTO, 27, Oxford-st., London.

THE ZOETROPE; or, Wheel of Life.——The Greatest Wonder of the Age.—This marvellous optical top, complete, with 12 strips of figures, price 5s. Carriage free for 90 stamps.—H. G. CLARKE and Co., 2, Garrick-street, Covent-garden.

THE LEARNED POODLE is a scientific, amusing, and instructive toy, which any boy or girl can easily understand and derive endless pleasure in playing with. To grown up persons it will prove equally attractive. Price 10s. 6d. ; packed for rail, 11s. 6d. Inventor and sole manufacturer, CHAPPUIS, reflector patentee, optician, &c., 69, Fleet-street. Also, the Toupie Caméléon, see advertisement below.

TOUPIE CAMELEON, the new French top, best out, 2s. 6d. ; free 3s. Amuses every one. The Pedometer, new instrument, in silver case, size of a watch, to measure distances when walking, 42s., by post 43s. Building slabs, capital games for boys, 6s. and 12s. per box. Numerous games and articles, suitable for all ages and for every taste. See catalogue for three stamps. All orders to be accompanied with remittance to CHAPPUIS, optician, reflector patentee, &c., 69, Fleet-street.

THE TOP of the PERIOD.—The Echo says :—"The CHAMELEON TOP is the name given at the Model Dockyard, No. 31, Fleet-street, to a new Christmas toy. It is a toy for all ages, and far superior to anything yet introduced." Price 2s. 6d. ; free 3s. 6d. 2,000 models on view. Catalogues, six stamps.

PRUSSIAN POP-GUNS. Rare fun. 18 post free seven stamps.—DUGWELL and SONS, toy importers, 97, New-road, E., sole agents for England. Trade supplied.

SPECIALITY.—DOLLY for the promenade, row, dinner, or ball. Above 1,000 most tastefully dressed, always to select from. Dolls in wax, china, and rag, with mechanical limbs, to walk, talk, cry, and sleep.—CREMER, Jun., 210, Regent-street.

OGILVY'S GAMES :—Playing Cards, with conundrums and bezique markers, 1s. 6d. ; Cabinet Council, 2s. 6d. ; Lions of London, 2s. 6d. ; Intellectual Dominoes, six sorts, 1s. 6d. and 2s. 6d. ; Charade Games, two sorts, 1s. 6d. ; Laughing made Easy, 1s. ; Fireside Fun, 1s. ; Victoria, 1s. ; On the Cards, 1s. By post 2s. 8d., 1s. 8d., 1s. 2d. London, D. Ogilvy, 50, Edgware-road.

DANCING NIGGER by STEAM (Patent), 2s. 6d. Selling by thousands. This ingenious and laughable contrivance is very unique ; the nigger dancer being worked by means of a novel steam engine, constructed entirely of metal, and with polished brass works, and when in motion the nigger dances in various graceful attitudes for one hour at each operation. Packed in boxes, with directions, and carriage paid, for 40 stamps. From R. F. BENHAM, manufacturer and patentee, office, 1, Gresham-buildings, Guildhall, E.C. Descriptive catalogue, embellished with illustrations of novelties, seven stamps ; wholesale at D. Hyam and Co.'s, Houndsditch, E.

WALKING DOLLS, by clockwork, 5s. 6d. ; extra size, 7s. 6d. ; strong and beautifully dressed. No little Miss can be happy without one. Only had at PEACOCK'S, 526, New Oxford-street. Forwarded on receipt of post order or stamps. A few only left.

FIREWORKS of every kind. Price list and further particulars free by post. Every article supplied to amateurs requisite for the manufacture of fireworks. Address STEANE, BROTHERS, Brixton, S.W. Balloons, &c.

FIREWORKS.—Merchants and shippers supplied on the lowest terms. BAKER and SON, 11, Squirries-street, Bethnal-green-road, late Cambridge-road. Price lists sent free. Fireworks for exhibitions and fêtes prepared to any extent.

DE LA RUE and Co.'s PLAYING CARDS.—The NEW PATTERNS for the season may now be had of all booksellers and stationers. Wholesale only, of the manufacturers, Thos. De La Rue and Co., London.

STEWARD'S MAGIC LANTERNS.——The following sent to all parts of the kingdom on receipt of P.O. order:—
Steward's No. 1 Lantern, 3ft. disc, with 40 comic pictures, 7s. 6d.
Steward's No. 2 Lantern, 4ft. disc, with 40 comic pictures, 10s. 6d.
Steward's No. 3 Lantern, 5ft. disc, with 40 comic pictures, 18s. 6d.
Steward's No. 4 Lantern, 6ft. disc, with 50 comic pictures, 25s. 0d.
Steward's No. 5 Lantern, 7ft. disc, with 50 comic pictures, 35s. 0d.
Steward's No. 6 Lantern, 8ft. disc, with 60 comic pictures, 50s. 0d.
Catalogues gratis, post free. Address J. H. Steward, 406 and 66, Strand, and 54, Cornhill, London.

MAGICAL and CONJURING REPOSITORY, exclusively for the sale of conjuring tricks and magical apparatus. The largest and most beautiful collection in Europe of all the wonders in the magic art. Extraordinary novelties for the present season. Full instructions with country orders. New Illustrated catalogues, post free, 12 stamps. Lessons given in legerdemain. Evening parties attended—J. BLAND, 478, New Oxford-st., opposite Mudie's

Scholastic

EDUCATION.—To Persons of Limited Income.—Great Educational Advantages.—BOARD and EDUCATION, in a superior ladies' school, for 30 guineas per annum; usual terms 100 guineas; including all accomplishments and all extras. Address A. Z., 12, Southampton-street, Strand.

EDUCATION.—To Parents of Troublesome Boys.—A gentleman, of great experience, tact, and patience, residing in a healthy suburb of London, undertakes to manage such BOYS and prepare them for superior situations. Apply, stating boy's age, disposition, &c., to X. Y. Z., Messrs. Baker and Co.'s, 27, Walbrook, E.C.

EDUCATION.—The best SCHOOLS RECOMMENDED in London and on the continent, and prospectuses forwarded gratis on application to Miss WILSON, 166, Regent-street. Schools for the daughters of gentlemen only, where a limited number of pupils are received, and the first masters attend.

EDUCATION (superior).—In a first-class establishment of long standing, where the number is limited to 12, TWO YOUNG LADIES can be RECEIVED. The house is beautifully situate, eminent professors attend, and highest references given. Address Miss Stokes, 34, Ladbroke-gardens, Bayswater.

EDUCATION.—ARTICLED PUPIL. English, French, music, dancing, drilling, and deportment. Lowest premium 17 guineas per annum. First-class instruction, light duty, and the kindest treatment.—B., care of Mrs. Brightwell, Market-place, Stamford-hill, N. State exact age.

EDUCATION, 28 guineas per annum.—THREE YOUNG LADIES can be RECEIVED on the above reduced terms. This sum includes English, French (constantly spoken), Latin, piano, drawing, dancing, and laundress. Masters attend for all accomplishments. Address R. R., Mr. Stanford's, 6, Charing-cross, S.W.

EDUCATION (near the Crystal Palace), 40 guineas a year, without a single extra of any kind; usual terms 60 guineas. Resident English and foreign masters. Preparation for any of the Examinations. Number limited. Single beds, Palace season ticket, best diet, and every comfort. The highest references.—M. A., Mr. Edwards', 12, Walbrook, E.C.

EDUCATION at the SEA-SIDE.—PEMBROKE-HOUSE SCHOOL, Folkestone, conducted by Mr. G. W. RUSSELL, of the London University (with well-qualified assistance). The house, built expressly for a school, is spacious and airy. Pupils enjoy the privilege of sea-bathing during the season. The ensuing term will commence January 24th.

EDUCATION (inclusive terms from 30 to 50 guineas per annum) for YOUNG LADIES, conducted under superior advantages, including English, French, German, music, singing, drawing, and dancing by eminent masters. Laundress. No holydays unless required. Address Principal, Claremont-house, St. James's-square, Notting-hill, W.

EDUCATION in PARIS.—Madame HAVET, 93, Avenue d'Eylau, Bois de Boulogne, RECEIVES TEN YOUNG LADIES, to whom she offers a comfortable home, complete education in French, and facilities for pursuing their other studies. Prospectuses on application to A. Roche, Esq., Educational Institute, Sloane-street, W., London; or to Mme. Havet's husband, Monsieur A. Havet, Director, Foreign Language Institute, Edinburgh.

EDUCATION (superior) for BOYS, 25 guineas per annum. No extras whatever. Near town. No charge for laundress or books. Extensive premises, well adapted, and most healthfully situate. Several acres of grounds, offering every facility for outdoor recreation, cricket, safe bathing, &c. Principal has been a successful tutor many years. Corporal punishment dispensed with. The best diet, and without limit. References to parents of pupils.—Alpha, No. 256, Oxford-street.

EDUCATION in GERMANY.—INTERNATIONAL COLLEGE, Godesberg, near Bonn-on-the-Rhine; Principal, Dr. A. BASKERVILLE (in connexion with the London International College, Spring-grove). Terms 80 guineas. Applications for the admission of pupils to be made to the Principal, at the College. Prospectuses may be had on application to E. F. Tremayne, Esq., Secretary to the International Education Society (Limited), Spring-grove, Middlesex, W.

EDUCATION.—Blackheath.—£30, £35, and £40 per annum.—There are a few VACANCIES in an old-established and well-conducted LADIES' SCHOOL. The course of instruction comprises all the essentials of a thorough English education. The fees of eight masters are included in the above sum, and there is no charge for laundress, hot and cold baths, stationery, or musical pieces. A liberal table is kept. Situation unrivalled. Address D.D., Post-office, Dartmouth-row, Blackheath.

EDUCATION.—A lady, residing in one of the best parts of Bedford, RECEIVES the DAUGHTERS of GENTLEMEN, to whom she gives the comforts of home and a sound and high-class education. Terms 70 guineas a year. References -H. C. Wise, Esq., M.P., Woodcote, Warwick; Miss Disbrowe, 26, Chester-square, London; Rev. Canon Hopkins, Littleport Vicarage, Ely; Miss Beale, Ladies' College, Cheltenham; his Excellency the Hon. A. Burlingame, Hotel de Rome, Berlin. For prospectuses address J. F. L., 6, The Crescent, Bedford.

EDUCATION.——There are VACANCIES for Christmas in a very superior SCHOOL for LADIES, near London. It is conducted by the sisters of a beneficed clergyman and eminent professors. The situation combines all the privileges of a country home, with the advantages of London masters. References given to many well-known clergymen, and to other friends of pupils. Inclusive terms from 60 to 100 guineas. Two sisters or the daughters of clergymen could, at the present time, be received on reduced terms. Address Meta, Carrington's library, 6, Grove-terrace, Notting-hill, W.

EDUCATION.—Brighton.—High-class LADIES' SCHOOL, of long standing, situate in one of the handsomest squares in Brighton, with large lawn and pleasure grounds immediately in front, available for the recreation of the pupils. This establishment offers peculiar advantages, and for healthiness of locality, sound educational training and domestic arrangements, is on a par with any school in Brighton. The usual eminent professors attend. For terms (varying according to age), address Delta, post-office, Western-road, Brighton. There are Vacancies

EDUCATION.—Richmond, S.W.—The COLLEGE, beautifully situate near the station, the park, and Kew-gardens, successfully PREPARES for the public schools, competitive examinations, professional and mercantile pursuits. An efficient staff of English, French, and German masters. French and German constantly spoken. Home comforts, liberal treatment, meals with the principal, separate bed rooms. Testimonials from the Ven. Archdeacon Bickersteth, D. D., Rev. J. B. Reade, M.A., F.R.S., and other clergymen.—Principal, Mr. J. E. EINGLE.

EDUCATION, 40 to 50 guineas per annum.——A desirable opportunity now offers for parents who may wish to PLACE their DAUGHTERS in a first-class school of known respectability, near London, where they may secure for them, on moderate terms, the advantages of a solid and highly finished education, combined with every domestic comfort. The best professors attend for music, French, German, drawing, dancing. The use of the globes, natural philosophy, and those higher branches of study taught in accordance with the most improved methods of modern professors, and which are calculated to enlarge the mind, cultivate the understanding, and improve the character. Resident French and German governesses. Address R. N., Mr. Horrocks', stationer, Wimbledon, Surrey.

EDUCATION.——Richmond-hill.——FRENCH and GERMAN PROTESTANT ESTABLISHMENT for GENTLEMEN'S DAUGHTERS. Six resident governesses and 12 visiting masters are permanently engaged for English, French, German, drawing, painting (daily), Italian, Latin, music, singing, dancing, scientific lectures, &c. Conversational proficiency under French and German governesses. Religious instruction by a clergyman. Inclusive terms 40 to 50 guineas. The principals devote their undivided attention to the comforts and improvement of their pupils. Parents can best appreciate the domestic arrangements, which include single beds, by inspection and reference. The house is on a healthy eminence, with five acres of land; is thoroughly ventilated, and contains 49 lofty rooms and four bath rooms.—Theta Richmond-hill, Surrey.

EDUCATION for YOUNG GENTLEMEN (old established). The instruction, by the principal and able masters, includes every branch of a first-class English education, French, German, Latin, and the preparation for examinations. 40 pupils only are received. The domestic arrangements, conducted by the wife of the principal, are those of a well-ordered family. Meals are taken with the principal. The diet is the best, and unlimited, and every attention is given to promote gentlemanly manners and conduct. The premises, the property of the principal, and specially built for a college, contain numerous rooms, baths, bed rooms for three or four boys in each, and every modern requirement. The situation is most healthy and pleasant, completely in the country, an easy distance from town, on high gravelly soil, and close to a station. Recreation grounds 20 acres. Terms 40 and 50 guineas per annum, payable per term in advance. There are no extra charges, and no bills are sent home. First-class references.—M. A., 430, Oxford-street.

EDUCATION.—Choice of 10,000 Schools (gratis) in England, France, Germany, Belgium, &c.—Parents and Guardians seeking really good SCHOOLS or TUTORS should apply to Messrs. BIVER and Co., British and foreign school agents, 46, Regent-street, W. Prospectuses and every reliable information gratis. Est. 1858.

EDUCATION.—1858 to 1869 (gratis).—It is an important matter for parents (in England or abroad) to decide upon a really good school for their children. Mr. F. S. de CARTERET BISSON, F.R.G.S., M.B.A., Editor of "Our Schools and Colleges," will send (gratis), by post or otherwise, PROSPECTUSES and reliable information, of the best CONTINENTAL and ENGLISH SCHOOLS for BOYS or GIRLS.—Berners-chambers, 70, Berners-street, W.

ARTICLED PUPIL.—REQUIRED, in a first-class ladies' school, west, an ARTICLED PUPIL. French, German, music, singing, drawing, &c., by masters of repute. Premium 25 to 30 guineas. Address Theta, Mr. Cooke's, 513, Oxford-street.

ARTICLED PUPIL REQUIRED, in a finishing ladies' school, near Hyde-park. Premium 25 guineas per annum. Great advantages for music and languages.—Cox, Mr. Hall's, 310, Edgware-road, W.

A GOVERNESS PUPIL WANTED, in a finishing school, near town. Superior advantages in French, German, Italian, music, singing and drawing, lectures, &c. Premium 25 guineas. Duties one hour daily. Address Beta, Roberts's library, Arabella-row.

A FRENCH LADY, of great musical talent, desires to PLACE her LITTLE GIRL at a good BOARDING SCHOOL, where her own instructions would be received as equivalent. Address Madame B., Hope-cottage, Kew.

A MARRIED BENEFICED CLERGYMAN, experienced in tuition, receives six pupils, under 14 years of age. THREE VACANCIES. Constant care and attention, with home comforts. Terms moderate. Address Vicar, East Halton, Ulceby Junction.

A YOUNG LADY, age 18, desires a SITUATION as GOVERNESS PUPIL in a school. She can teach French (acquired at one of the best schools in France), which she speaks fluently and with a good accent; also music to junior pupils. Terms—improvement in music and accomplishments. Address B. C., 142, Church-road, London, N.

AN OXFORD M.A., Graduate in Honours, residing in a large house surrounded by park-like grounds of several acres, within eight miles of London, RECEIVES TWELVE PUPILS to be preptred for Oxford, Cambridge, Sandhurst, &c. He is assisted by a resident Cambridge graduate, and by professors of French, German, and drawing. Terms 80 guineas and 100 guineas per annum. Address C. J. H., Mr. Stanford's, 6, Charing-cross.

A CLERGYMAN and his WIFE, who are educating their children at home, with the assistance of an accomplished governess, are willing to RECEIVE TWO LITTLE GIRLS, well connected, as companions to their daughters. The most tender home care and careful training would be combined with a sound and liberal education. References would be given to names of well-known position and standing, and the same would be required. The rectory is situate in a healthy and pleasant country village, within four miles of a railway station. Terms, inclusive of all extras, £100 a year. Address G. B., 7, Paternoster-row, London.

ALBERT MIDDLE-CLASS COLLEGE, Framlingham, Suffolk. County Middle-class School, established 1864, by Royal Charter. Is a centre for the Cambridge Local Examinations, and in December, 1868, passed 22 boys out of 25 presented. Education complete and sound, including English thoroughly, French, German, Latin, mathematics, chymistry, land surveying, bookkeeping, and drawing. Terms for board, tuition, washing, medical attendance, mending of clothes and boots, stationery, and use of school books—Suffolk boys, £10 per term (three terms in the year); out county boys, £12 per term. No school bills. Reductions for brothers and for boys under 12. References to parents in London. For reports of examiners, prospectus, and all information, address the Head Master, the Rev. A. C. Daymond, 25, Essex-street, London, W.C. (personally between 9 and 11 a.m., by letter at any time), from December 28th to January 20th.

PRIVATE TUITION for the ARMY, Sandhurst, Universities, &c.—A married rector, M.A. Oxon, late Scholar of his College, of long experience and uniform success in tuition, RECEIVES SEVEN PUPILS. He is assisted by a resident mathematical tutor, experienced in the Civil Service and Army Examinations, and by efficient masters of modern languages. Much time and individual attention bestowed upon those whose education has been neglected, or who have failed in previous examinations. Terms 105 guineas. Rectory most healthily situate in Berks, near a railway station. Address Rev. M., 35, Baker-street, W.

PRIVATE PUPILS.——Stratford Abbey, near Stroud, Glocestershire.—The Rev. WALTER BAKER, B.A. (Cantab.), late Scholar of his College, &c., RECEIVES a few PUPILS, to prepare for the public schools and examinations, or the universities. He is assisted by a resident tutor (Graduate) and first-rate modern language and other visiting masters from Cheltenham and elsewhere. Every endeavour is made to carry out the wishes of parents. Manly sports and amusements are encouraged. References allowed to parents of pupils. Terms according to age, from 60 to 120 guineas per annum.

TO GROCERS and DRAPERS.—A YOUNG LADY can be RECEIVED in a superior SCHOOL, 15 miles from London, on reciprocal terms. A resident French and German governess, and professors for music, dancing, and drawing. A Vacancy for an Article Pupil. Terms 20 guineas per annum. Address A. B., 45, Thornhill-road, Islington.

TO PARENTS.—Blackheath, in the best part of, and overlooking the heath.—PREPARATORY SCHOOL for YOUNG GENTLEMEN in this very healthy locality. The rudiments of a sound education may be secured, together with the comforts of a home. Conducted by Mrs. HOLLOWAY and Miss McPHERSON, No. 6, Grotes-place, Blackheath.

TO PARENTS and GUARDIANS and INDIAN FAMILIES.—A married clergyman, M.A., Trinity College, Cambridge, accustomed to take charge of children (especially from India and the colonies), can offer the comforts of a HOME, combined with the advantages of a liberal education. Terms according to number, age, and requirements. Address Clericus, Clyde-house, Sydenham-road north, Croydon, Surrey.

TO PARENTS and GUARDIANS.—WANTED, in a highly respectable school, in the neighbourhood of London, a young lady, as GOVERNESS PUPIL. She must be above 16, a member of the Church of England, and fairly advanced in education. She will be received on half terms, and have the advantage of lessons from professors in English literature, music, and French or German. Address G. C. S., Messrs. K. J. Ford and Son's, 179, Upper-street, Islington, N.

UNMANAGEABLE or BACKWARD BOYS, or Youths (up to 20 years), made perfectly tractable and gentlemanly in one year, by a clergyman, near town, of 30 years' experience, whose peculiarly persuasive system and high moral and religious training soon elevate children of peculiar tempers and dispositions (because not understood) to the level of others. A most liberal education, including modern languages, successful preparation for every examination and vocation in life, and every gentlemanly comfort, on moderate terms. Address Alpha, Messrs. Street's, 5, Serle-street, Lincoln's inn.

UNIVERSITE IMPERIALE de FRANCE.—INTERNATIONAL COLLEGE of DIEPPE.—This establishment, under the direction of Monsieur E. BORELY, Officer of the University and principal, is patronised by His Excellency the Minister of Public Instruction, as uniting with a complete classical education every facility for acquiring proficiency in the French language. The College has been newly and entirely refitted, and can offer every possible advantage for health, convenience, and comfort. Prospectuses to be had at the College. Terms—ordinary boarders, 40 guineas per annum, entrance fee three guineas; parlour boarders, 60 guineas per annum, entrance fee five guineas.

INDIAN TELEGRAPH, Works, Forests, Home, Civil Service, and Army.—Mr. W. M. LUPTON (Author of English History and Arithmetic), assisted by a gentleman in the War-office, PREPARES CANDIDATES for all departments. Address, 15, Beaufort-buildings, Strand.

INDIA CIVIL SERVICE or WOOLWICH.—CANDIDATES requiring much attention, and who will work well with those taking great interest in their success, can apply to Rev. Dr. Hughes, Castlebar-court, Ealing, W., who has had 18 years' experience.

ARMY.—India and Home Civil Service.—An Oxford Graduate, assisted by a Cambridge Wrangler, RECEIVES EIGHT PUPILS. Recently passed—India Civil Service, 5; Woolwich, 10; India Telegraph, 3; Sandhurst and Direct Commissions, 60. Address Oxon, 24, Alma-square, St. John's-wood.

AS MUSICAL GOVERNESS.—A young lady, teaching superior music and singing, desires a RE-ENGAGEMENT in a good school. £40.—H., Mrs. Wilson's, 39, Berners-street, W.

AS GOVERNESS for BOYS.—Family or School.—A lady, age 27, desires a RE-ENGAGEMENT. Good English, fluent French, Latin, and music. Calisthenics, dancing. £35 £40.—O., Mrs. Wilson, 39, Berners-street, W.

AS FINISHING GOVERNESS (superior).—A lady, age 38, desires a RE-ENGAGEMENT. Thorough English, fluent French, German, and Italian (in their respective countries), Latin, drawing, painting, sketching, &c., brilliant music and singing. £100-120.—A., Mrs. Wilson's, 39, Berners-street, W.

AS HEAD ENGLISH TEACHER.—A lady, age 30, desires a RE-ENGAGEMENT. Thorough English, fluent French (French extraction), and Latin. £60.—L., Mrs. Wilson's, No. 39, Berners-street, W.

A CLERGYMAN'S DAUGHTER wishes for a SITUATION, in a gentleman's family, as GOVERNESS to young children. Acquirements—English and music. Good references. Address M. A., Bessborough Library, Pimlico.

A RE-ENGAGEMENT as GOVERNESS is REQUIRED, by a lady, undertaking thorough English, fluent French, good music, singing, drawing, and rudimental Latin. Salary £30. Address Miss Peter, 37, Welbeck-street, W

GOVERNESS.—A lady, of many years' experience in tuition, who has been especially successful in training young gentlemen, desires a RE-ENGAGEMENT. Acquirements—thorough English, French (studied in Paris), Italian, Latin, music, singing, drawing in various styles, and flower painting. Unexceptionable references given. Terms £100. Address S. H., post-office, Kingswinford, Dudley.

GERMAN GOVERNESS. Family or first-class school. Thoroughly experienced. Excellent references. German, French, music, good English. Salary £40 to £50. Address Mrs. Price, 53, Davies-street, Grosvenor-square.

LADIES' SCHOOL.—A young lady desires a RE-ENGAGEMENT as ASSISTANT or JUNIOR TEACHER in a good school. Will give her services in exchange for good lessons. Address M. P., post-office, Ilford.

LADIES of NEGLECTED EDUCATION rapidly IMPROVED, in strict confidence.—A lady, who has specially adapted her system to ADULTS, RECEIVES and VISITS PUPILS for elementary and finishing English, correspondence, language, singing, piano, drawing, painting.—R. M., 24, Old Cavendish-street, W.

MUSIC GOVERNESSES.—M., 24, piano and singing, very successful, £60; C., 25, pupil of Sidney Smith, will give other assistance, £40; E. M., 20, thoroughly educated for the position, first engagement, £25; S., daily, piano and drawing, salary according to time.—Mrs. Richmond, 6, Holland-road, Kensington.

PIANO and SINGING.—A lady, certified pupil of F. B. Tewson, Professor R.A., and of Mme. Bodda (Louisa Pyne), gives LESSONS as above on moderate terms. Address Miss Morison, 103, Ladbroke-grove-road, Notting-hill, W.

RESIDENT GOVERNESS.—REQUIRED, by a lady of long experience, a RE-ENGAGEMENT. Her acquirements are English, French, and music thoroughly, with German and Italian to beginners. Salary £50. Age 35. Address A. S., Mr. Young's, Stationer, Shacklewell-green, N.

AN experienced DAILY GOVERNESS is REQUIRED, to teach two girls, age eight and 10, who speak French fluently. Salary £130. Address, stating acquirements and full particulars of previous situations, to W., post-office, Isleworth, W.

AN experienced FRENCH PROTESTANT RESIDENT GOVERNESS WANTED, by January 20, accustomed to school work and able to teach music well. Apply, with testimonials, to Miss Daniels, Sandywell-park, Andoversford, near Cheltenham.

AN ENGLISH FINISHING GOVERNESS REQUIRED, for Vienna. Good music and singing, fluent French, Italian, thorough English, drawing. Salary £60 to £70. A most comfortable home. Apply to Mrs. Price, 55, Davies-street, Grosvenor-square.

A LADY REQUIRED, immediately, as ENGLISH GOVERNESS, in a school, with good music. Liberal salary and a most comfortable home. Apply, at once, Miss Coghlan, 18a, Orchard-street, Portman-square. Interview to-day. No fee for this address.

A LADY WANTED, for a family, residing in the country, to instruct five pupils, eldest 16, youngest (a boy) eight. Thorough English, fluent French, Latin, and German, music, plain and fancy needlework. Elder pupils have masters for music and drawing. Address, with full particulars of acquirements, age, and salary, to E. D., post-office, Cosham, Hants. No agents.

A LADY REQUIRES a NURSERY GOVERNESS to take entire charge of two little girls aged 7½ and 6, and one boy age 4. Must be thoroughly able to maintain discipline, and to amuse as well as instruct her pupils. A personal interview will be required before any engagement is made. Address, stating age, qualifications, and salary required, to Mrs. L., Whitgift lodge, Wellesley-road, Croydon.

BELGIUM.—REQUIRED, immediately, for a school, an ENGLISH CATHOLIC YOUNG LADY, with music. Reciprocal terms, with advantages. Apply Mesdames Oppenheim, International Scholastic Institution, 69, Berners-street.

DAILY GOVERNESS.—WANTED, by a young lady, a RE-ENGAGEMENT to children under 12. Acquirements—thorough English, good music, and grammatical French. Highest references. Distance immaterial. Salary £30.—H. A., post-office, Hemingford-road, Barnsbury, N.

A GRADUATE in ARTS WANTED, as PROFESSOR in LATIN and MENTAL and MORAL PHILOSOPHY, for Doveton Protestant College, Madras. Salary £450 per annum, with £100 for passage and outfit. Testimonials to be forwarded, immediately, to Dr. Urquhart, 10, Union-terrace, Aberdeen. Further particulars may be had on application to any of the following gentlemen:—Dr. J. Urquhart, Aberdeen; Dr. Herdman, Melrose; T. Clarke, Esq., Tavistock, Devon; Colonel G. Rowlandson, 3, Manor-way, Blackheath-park, S.E.; the Rev. W. Gray, Nottingham.

DRAWING TAUGHT, on the method of drawing from objects, by an experienced artist and assistants. Terms moderate. Schools and families attended. Address A. B., 5, Bridge-street, Ludgate-hill, E.C.

FRENCH, by an eminent Professor, Parisian Graduate. Schools and families attended. Classes and private lessons. Terms moderate.—C. Ker, Vestry, French Protestant Church, Monmouth-road, Westbourne-grove, and 125, Regent-street.

PIANOFORTE and HARMONY.—An experienced pianoforte master and well-known composer will have a few hours DISENGAGED next term. Address Professor, care of Bertini, Seymour, and Co., 40, Poland-street, Oxford-street.

TUTORSHIP or MASTERSHIP desired, by an experienced and competent teacher, Graduate of Cambridge Would not object to take entire charge, or to go abroad.—A. M. C. No. 6, Albion-buildings, Bath.

TUTORSHIP REQUIRED, by an Oxford Graduate, in honours, musician, with long experience. References to Bishop of Dover and others. Address M. A., Rev. R. Girdlestone, Bible Society, Blackfriars.

TUTOR.—A Graduate in Honours, of long and varied experience, is open to a VISITING ENGAGEMENT. Subjects—classics, English, French (acquired abroad). Address L. V., Martin's Library, Blackheath.

TUTORSHIP WANTED, in a family, by an earnest and conscientious tutor. 20 years' experience; five with last pupils. Highest testimonials. Greek, Latin, French, and English. Terms moderate.—Alpha, 4, David's-road, Forest-hill, S.E.

TO SCHOOLS.—DRAWING, in town or country.—An artist, with first-rate references, desires a good SCHOOL. Oil painting, water-colours, model drawing, &c. Address A. A., Mr. Bell's, 11, Pickering-terrace, Bishop's-road, W.

TO LADIES' SCHOOLS and COLLEGES.—An eminent PROFESSOR of FRENCH (Parisian Graduate), now attending several first-class schools, has a few hours disengaged.—C. Ker, Vestry, French Protestant Church, Monmouth-road, Westbourne-grove, and 125, Regent-street.

VISITING TUTOR, for little boys or adults, or ladies.—A clergyman gives LESSONS in Latin, Greek, French, German, English, Hebrew, mathematics. Address S. S., 16, Church-road, Willesden, N.W.

AN ASSISTANT MASTER REQUIRED, to teach French and German, &c. Salary £60, with board and rooms. Apply to E. Turner, 3, Trinity-street, Cambridge.

REQUIRED, by the 18th inst., a TEACHER, in a school in the country, to instruct one class in English generally, and to teach class singing and the pianoforte to advanced pupils and assist with a drawing class. Address Retnart, post-office, Southend, Essex.

OXFORD and CAMBRIDGE CLERICAL and TUTORIAL AGENCY, 196, Piccadilly. Established to aid the nobility and gentry in selecting private tutors, assistant masters, &c. Qualified men only recommended.—G. GLASS (London University), Manager.

SCHOLASTIC.—TUTORS WANTED (FOREIGN and ENGLISH) 200 Vacancies. Salaries £30 to £150. Interviews arranged daily between principals and assistants at Griffiths and Smith's Agency offices (established 1833), 34, Bedford-street, Strand.

SCHOLASTIC AGENCY. —— Under Episcopal, Clerical, and Lay Patronage.—Heads of schools and families can have well-qualified MASTERS and TUTORS introduced to them through this Agency.—FRANCIS ASKIN, 9, Sackville-st., Piccadilly.

SCHOLASTIC.——WANTED, ENGLISH and FOREIGN GRADUATES, to fulfil positions in high class schools at good salaries; and non-graduates, at from £20 to £120. Send full particulars to Mair and Co., Educational Agents (established 42 years), 24, Bloomsbury-street, W.C. 80 Schools to Sell.

SCHOLASTIC.—MASTERS REQUIRED:—Head Master, £300, non-resident, and can receive boarders or introduce any if he has them; terms very advantageous. Wanted also, Classics and Mathematics, with degree, £100; Classics and Mathematics and German, £80; Under Graduate, London or Dublin, £70; German, French, and Music, £60; Juniors, £40. Apply quickly at G. W. White's offices, 10, Southampton-street, Strand, W.C. No charge for registration or correspondence; no names without direct authority.

SOCIETE PROTESTANTE FRANÇAISE de PLACEMENT pour PROFESSEURS et INSTITUTRICES: Secrétaire, Madame la Baronne CELLI, Eglise Française, Monmouth-road, Westbourne-grove, Bayswater, W. Tous les jours, de 1 à 5 heures p.m. On place également les domestiques des deux sexes. Pas de commission sur le salaire.

TUTORS (the most successful), for Woolwich, the Line, Cooper's-hill, Home and Indian Civil Service, Forests, Navy, Universities. Prospectuses, with full particulars, sent gratis by Biver, Gordon, Orellana, and Bell, 32a, George-street, Hanover-square, W.

SCHOLASTIC.—St. Clement Danes' Holborn Estate Grammar School, Houghton-street, New-inn, London. W.C.; Head Master, the Rev. W. J. Savell, M.A., late Scholar of St. John's College, Cambridge.—REQUIRED, on the 25th March, 1874, a NON-RESIDENT ASSISTANT MASTER, to teach French especially, and also to take part in the usual work of a Middle-Class Grammar School. He must be a member of the Church of England. Salary £75 per annum, rising to £95 by a yearly increase of £10, together with a capitation fee of 10s. per annum on all boys learning French—at present about 70 in number. Applications and copies only of testimonials to be sent on or before Thursday, the 12th March, addressed to the Head Master, as above.

W. RAIMONDI, Clerk and Solicitor to the Managers.

SECKFORD GRAMMAR SCHOOL, Woodbridge, Suffolk.—The HEAD MASTERSHIP of this School will be VACANT in September next, in consequence of the resignation of the Rev. Dr. Tate, the present Head Master. The Local Trustees, therefore, invite applications for the appointment.

The scheme for the management and regulation of the School (under an order of the Court of Chancery) requires that the Head Master shall be a member of the Church of England. The Trustees intend to appoint a Graduate of either Oxford or Cambridge.

There is a commodious house for the residence of the Head Master attached to the school, with accommodation for at least 25 boarders. The annual stipend of the Head Master will be £250, besides which he will be entitled to a moiety of all capitation fees, which moiety during the past year amounted to £160.

The Trustees provide the Second Master, and allot £70 a year towards an assistant master.

It is requested that no personal application be made to the Trustees.

Gentlemen disposed to become candidates for the appointment must transmit their application, accompanied by testimonials, to the Clerk, on or before the 23rd day of March next.

Upon request further particulars will be furnished to candidates.

J. R. WOOD, Clerk.

Seckford Office, Woodbridge, 25th February, 1874.

A CAMBRIDGE HONOURMAN wishes to hear of a VISITING TUTORSHIP, to prepare for University entrance, or to teach younger boys. Some experience in preparatory school work.—B. A., 13, Ladbroke-road, London, W.

A YOUNG FRENCHMAN, of respectable family, wishes to LEARN ENGLISH, in exchange for the French language. Address A. Z., 3. William-street, Albert-gate, S.W

A YOUNG ENGLISH PUBLIC SCHOOL MAN, who has for the last two years lived abroad as resident tutor, wishes for a SITUATION of the same kind to boys under 14, either in an English or foreign family. Address J. G. C., Debenham Vicarage, Suffolk.

MUSIC (Finishing, or otherwise).—Herr L., experienced Professor Pianist, has some time DISENGAGED for LESSONS in schools and families. Moderate terms. Distance no object.—15, Arlingford-road, Lower Tulse-hill, Brixton.

MR. C. STIEBLER COOK, Associate of the Royal Academy of Music, five years Music and Choir Master at Uppingham School. For PIANO and HARMONY LESSONS address 17, Keppel-street, Russell-square. W.C. Schools attended. Classes conducted.

ORGAN, Piano, Harmonium, and Singing LESSONS given by an experienced organist and choirmaster of two large West-end churches. Terms, with opportunities of practice, moderate. —A. Z., Chappell and Co.'s, 50, New Bond-street.

TO SCHOOLS.—The French and German master of a public school, B es L. (native of Paris), wishes to fill a few hours. He is just now disengaged. Address to Professor B., 29, Greenwood-road, Dalston.

TUTORSHIP.—An Oxford Graduate, age 24, wishes for an ENGAGEMENT as TUTOR, in a private family, to one or more boys Good references. Address B. A., 4, Burlington-villas, Redland, Bristol.

A RESIDENT TUTOR WANTED, for a nobleman's family. Qualifications—English, good piano, and drawing. Must be Catholic. Apply to the Secretary, International Scholastic Agency, 13, Avenue de la Grande Armée, Paris.

A Gentlemanly YOUNG MAN WANTED, to assist in a provincial middle-class boarding school. Board, lodging, laundress, and assistance in studies, but no salary. Address H. C. G., No. 7, Southerton-road, Hammersmith, W.

SCHOLASTIC.—The HEAD MASTERSHIP of a College will shortly be VACANT. There are several boarders. Commodious, large premises, in good condition. 20 acres of land and a fine garden, well stocked with fruit trees, all rent free. Applications will be considered only from gentlemen who can produce unexceptionable references as to character and ability, and who have means to purchase from the present holder the goodwill, furniture, fixtures, &c., for which from £500 to £1,000 would be necessary. Address B. 20, at C. H May and Co.'s General Advertising offices, No. 78, Gracechurch-street, London.

EDUCATION.—Germany, Heidelberg.—Dr. KLOSE'S SCHOOL. Thorough German, French, correspondence, sound education, through medium of French, German. Preparation for high examinations. English diet. Large grounds. Cricket. Highest references. Terms £13 quarterly, including holidays. Escort shortly.

EDUCATION.—DELICATE BOYS.—A Physician, retired from active practice, RECEIVES a very limited number, for whose health and education he holds himself responsible. Highest references. Address M. D., Mr. Bolton's, Chemist, Robertson-street, Hastings.

EDUCATION in GERMANY.——The INTERNATIONAL COLLEGE, Godesberg, near Bonn-on-the-Rhine, gives a first-class education, with perfect German and French. Terms 80 guineas. The Principal, Fr. Terberger, will be in London from December 27th to January 3d, and be at home every morning till 12. Address 40, Bedford-place, Bloomsbury-square, W.C.

EDUCATION in GERMANY for the SONS of ENGLISH GENTLEMEN.—Dr. B. THIEL'S Institute, Gotha, under the patronage of H.R.H. the Duke of Saxe-Coburg Gotha. Modern languages. Thorough preparation for the Army, Civil Service, and Commerce. Dr. Thiel will be in London to take back pupils, and can see parents at the Golden Cross Hotel, Strand, on and after Dec. 27.

EDUCATION.—There will be two or three VACANCIES, at Christmas, in an old-established SCHOOL for YOUNG LADIES, where no daily pupils are received, and where, in addition to a thorough English education, there are exceptional advantages for the study of music, and also for the study and practice of the French and German languages. Terms from 80 to 100 guineas per annum.—A. A., care of L. Sealy, 125, High-street, Notting-hill, W.

EDUCATION for the DAUGHTERS of GENTLEMEN.—Professors attend from the Royal Academy of Music and South Kensington. Resident English and Foreign Governesses. Lofty class rooms, private garden and recreation lawns. Liberal domestic arrangements. Inclusive terms, 80, 100, 120 guineas. Interview any morning before 12 o'clock. References exchanged.—Lady Principal, Mayfield-lodge, 93, Addison-road, Kensington west.

EDUCATION.—In a select school of long standing, a short distance from London, two or three PUPILS can be RECEIVED, on reduced terms, to fill unexpected vacancies. 45 guineas per annum would include lessons in advanced English, French, German, drawing, music, class-singing, dancing, and calisthenics. Good masters. Large house and grounds. Healthy locality.—S. T., No. 8, Pond-road, Blackheath-park, London, S.E.

EDUCATION for the DAUGHTERS of GENTLEMEN, in a healthy country town on the Great Northern, one hour and a quarter from London. Terms for boarders moderate. School conducted by the daughters of a clergyman of the Church of England, assisted by masters. A resident French governess. Vacancy after Christmas for a governess pupil; premium £25. For prospectus address Miss Lockwood, Camden-house, Biggleswade.

EDUCATION.—TAPLOW GRAMMAR SCHOOL, Maidenhead, 20 miles from London; 30 guineas, no extras, no charge for laundress or books. Extensive premises, well adapted and healthfully situate; 20 acres of ground, affording every facility for out-door recreation, cricket, bathing, &c. Pure milk and vegetables from school farm. Preparatory department. Principal has been a successful tutor many years. No corporal punishment. No quarter's notice. Best diet. References. Address the Principal.

EDUCATION.—An opportunity now offers for the DAUGHTERS of GENTLEMEN to obtain a superior and highly-finished EDUCATION on moderate terms. 45 guineas per annum, to include advanced English, French, German, music, singing, drawing, and dancing. House replete with every comfort; large garden, liberal diet, &c. Resident French and German governesses. Address B. L., Andrews and Son's Library, Epsom, Surrey. A Governess Pupil Required.

DANCING.—13, Berners-street.—American Waltzes.—The Misses CARLETON (late Woods) RECEIVE ADULT PUPILS daily, for instruction in the Rockaways, Boston Glide, Trois Temps, Lancers, &c. Four private lessons, at any hour, one guinea. Schools attended. Evening Assemblies Mondays and Fridays.

DANCING.—Mr. BLAND and DAUGHTERS, having the honour of instructing Royalty, the nobility, and gentry, give LESSONS in the new valse and all the modern dances. Four lessons one guinea. Assemblies Tuesdays and Fridays. Prospectus on application.—22, Golden-square, W.

DANCING.—To those who have never learned to dance.—Mr. and Mrs. JAQUES WYNMAN and lady assistants teach daily all the fashionable dances perfectly to any one who is without the slightest previous knowledge. Private lessons at any hour. Prospectus on application. Assemblies every Monday and Thursday, at 8 o'clock.—Academy, 74, Newman-street, Oxford-street, W.

MISS FREND (pupil of Madame Taglioni) has RESUMED YOUNG LADIES' CLASSES for fashionable DANCING and graceful EXERCISES, at her residence. Visits Brighton and high-class schools. Private lessons.—16, Pembridge-villas, Bayswater.

Medicinal & Dental

INVALID COUCHES, from £5 5s., possessing all the movements of the most expensive ones. Invalid tables from £1 5s. Bath and carrying chairs, bed-rests, in-door wheel chairs, back-boards, &c. Drawings post free.—J. CARTER, 6a, New Cavendish-street, Great Portland-street, W.

DEAFNESS. — Newly-invented ACOUSTICS to relieve every degree, for church, general conversation, &c., a variety of invisible Acoustics, Sound Magnifiers, Artificial Tympanum, Auricles, Conversational Tubes, and every other kind of Trumpet.—REIN & SON, Patentees, 108, Strand, London.

ROUND SHOULDERS, Stooping Habits, and Deformities CURED by Dr. CHANDLER'S CHEST EXPANDING BRACE. Strengthens the voice and lungs, and is recommended to children for assisting growth, promoting health, and a symmetrical figure.—66, Berners-street, W. Illustrations forwarded free.

TO MOTHERS, Nurses, and Invalids.—ELASTIC SILK ABDOMINAL SUPPORTERS, of very superior make and construction, for debility, corpulency, &c. Directions for self-measurement and prices, with illustrations, by post free. English and foreign enemas.—ELAM, 196, Oxford-street.

SEE Mr. HALSE'S PAMPHLET on GALVANISM for CURES of PARALYSIS, Rheumatism, indigestion, nervousness, debility, loss of muscular power, spinal complaints, sciatica, sleepless nights, &c. Send two stamps to Mr. Halse, 40, Addison-road, Kensington, London, for it. See Mr. Halse's Letters on Galvanism.

THREATENED PARALYSIS.—All persons having the least symptoms of threatened paralysis, now so very prevalent, particularly those whose parents have been paralysed, should send to Mr. HALSE, 40, Addison-road, Kensington, for his Pamphlet on Galvanism. See pages 10, 11, and 45 to 54.

PULVERMACHER'S, IMPROVED PATENT GALVANIC CHAIN BANDS, Belts, Batteries, and accessories, from 2s. and upwards. Reliable evidence in proof of the unrivalled efficacy of these appliances in rheumatism, gout, neuralgia, deafness, head and tooth ache, paralysis, liver complaints, cramps, spasms, nervous debility, and those functional disorders, &c., arising from various excesses, is given in the pamphlet, Nature's Chief Restorer of Impaired Vital Energy, post free, price 6d.; or Medical Electricity; its Use and Abuse, post free for three stamps. Apply at Pulvermacher's Galvanic Establishment, 194, Regent-street, London, W.

DELLAR'S CORN and BUNION PLASTERS give instant relief and cure in a short period. Can be worn between the toes. Wonderfully effective for enlarged toe joints. Boxes 1s. 1½d. and 2s. 9d. Sold by most chymists.—J. PEPPER, 237, Tottenham-court-road, London. By return of post 14 or 34 stamps.

KEATING'S COUGH LOZENGES are daily recommended for coughs, colds, asthma, &c., by the faculty. Testimonials from the most eminent may be seen. Sold in boxes, 1s. 1½d., and tins, 2s. 9d. each, by all druggists. N.B. They contain no opium or preparation thereof.

PATERNOSTER'S PILLS. Certain relief and frequent cure are attained by these inimitable and justly celebrated pills in rheumatism, pains in the head, face, and limbs, tic, lumbago, sciatica, gout, &c. Sold by all chymists, price 1s. 1½d. a box; 15 stamps a box free.—71, Old Kent-road, S.E. Established 1812.

WHEN a PERSON TAKES COLD safe and immediate relief may be obtained by the use of SPENCER'S PULMONIC ELIXIR. The best remedy for Asthma and Disorders of the Chest and Lungs. In bottles, at 1s. 1½d. and 2s. 9d. each. Sold by all Chymists.

COCKLE'S COMPOUND ANTIBILIOUS PILLS. A celebrated family aperient, in use for 73 years by all classes of society, for indigestion, bilious and liver complaints, may be had in the United Kingdom in boxes at 1s. 1½d., 2s. 9d., 4s. 6d., and 11s., as well as in India, China, New Zealand, and the Australian colonies.

TRUSSES.—SALMON, ODY, and Co., Patent Truss Makers to His late Majesty William IV. Elastic Stockings Ladies' Abdominal Belts.—292, Strand, London, W.C.

GALVANISM v. NERVOUS EXHAUSTION is most successfully and painlessly self-applied by means of PULVERMACHER'S PATENT IMPROVED VOLTA-ELECTRIC CHAIN-BANDS, Belts, and Pocket Batteries, in rheumatic neuralgic, and gouty pains, nervous debility, sleeplessness, paralysis epilepsy, indigestion, cramp, asthma, nervous deafness, functional disorders, &c. The strong guarantees to their truly marvellous efficacy, furnished in the numerous authenticated medical reports and testimonials of cures, in a recent pamphlet, sent post free, are enhanced by a test sent on loan, if required, for discerning the above genuine from the spurious electric appliances advertised by quackish impostors under various aliases. Single chains-bands, 5s. to 22s.; a set of bands specially combined for restoring impaired vital energy, 30s. to 60s.; new patent volta-electric chain batteries, £3 3s. and £4 4s. Apply to J. L. Pulvermacher, 200, Regent-street, London, W.

COCKLE'S COMPOUND ANTIBILIOUS PILLS a medicine in use during the last 69 years among all classes of society, for indigestion, sick headache, flatulency, acidity, or heart-burn, &c., may be obtained throughout the United Kingdom, in boxes at 1s. 1½d., 2s. 9d., 4s. 6d., and 11s.

DRINKING GARGLE for relaxed throat, bronchial irritation, loss of voice; hoarseness and cough arising therefrom. This drinking gargle, by its astringency, slight acidity, and tonic properties, affords immediate relief in any of the above affections.—ELAM, chymist, 196, Oxford-street. 2s. 3d. and 4s. 6d. a bottle.

BILE and INDIGESTION, Wind, Headache, Sickness, loss of appetite, torpid liver, costiveness, and debility entirely cured, without mercury, by Dr. KING'S DANDELION and QUININE LIVER PILLS. Sold by all chymists, &c., at 1s. 1½d., 2s. 6d., and 4s. 6d. a box. Established 74 years.

ASTHMA CURED by the USE of ESPIC'S CIGARETTES. The smoke of these cigarettes, inhaled into the lungs, lulls the nervous system, facilitates expectoration, and gives tone to the organs of respiration. Price 1s. 3d. per box. Depot at Mr. JOZEAU'S, French chymist, 49, Haymarket, London.

INFLUENZA and RHEUMATISM —BARCLAY'S (Dr. Bateman's) PECTORAL DROPS are held in high estimation, curing pains in the limbs, bones and joints, inducing gentle perspiration, and preventing fever. Numerous testimonials of its value can be obtained of Barclay and Sons, 95, Farringdon-street. May be had of all respectable druggists and dealers in patent medicines. In bottles, at 1s. 1½d. and 2s. 9d. each. Ask for Barclay's (Dr. Bateman's) Drops, and observe names and address (95, Farringdon-street) affixed to each bottle.

FOR COUGHS, Colds, Asthma, &c., the great remedy of the day is Dr. J. COLLIS BROWNE'S CHLORODYNE. A few doses will cure all incipient cases. Caution.—The extraordinary medical reports on the efficacy of chlorodyne renders it of vital importance that the public should obtain the genuine, which is now sold under the protection of Government, authorizing a stamp bearing the words "Dr. J. Collis Browne's Chlorodyne," without which none is genuine. See decision of Vice-Chancellor Sir W. Page Wood, The Times, July 16, 1864. Sold in bottles, 1s. 1½d., 2s. 9d., and 4s. 6d., by all chymists. Sole manufacturer, J. T. Davenport, 33, Great Russell-street, London, W.C.

HUNT'S APERIENT FAMILY PILLS, prepared by qualified medical men, and so extensively used for more than 60 years, that thousands may be appealed to for their medical efficacy. They should be taken in all cases of disordered health, and as they contain no mercury whatever, they in no way interfere with ordinary habits or avocations, and their operation is followed by an accession of tone and vigour throughout the system. Ladies find them very beneficial both before and after confinement. Prepared by Messrs. Hunt, Bath, and sold by all chymists at 1s. 1½d. the box, or 2s. 9d., which contains three boxes.

DR. DE JONGH'S LIGHT-BROWN CODLIVER OIL, prescribed by the most eminent medical men as the safest, speediest, and most effectual remedy for consumption, chronic bronchitis, coughs, and general debility. Convincingly proved by the highest medical testimony, and by the real test of practical experience during the last 20 years in all parts of the world, to be unequalled for purity, palatableness, and efficacy. Select medical opinions:—Dr. Edward Smith, F.R.S., Medical Officer to the Poor Law Board of Great Britain: "It is a great advantage that there is one kind of cod liver oil which is universally admitted to be genuine—the light brown oil supplied by Dr. de Jongh." Dr. Lankester, F.R.S., Coroner for Central Middlesex: "I deem the cod liver oil sold under Dr. de Jongh's guarantee to be preferable to any other kind as regards genuineness and medicinal efficacy." Dr. Granville, F.R.S., author of "The Spas of Germany": "Dr. de Jongh's light-brown cod liver oil does not cause the nausea and indigestion too often consequent on the administration of the pale oil." Edwin Canton, Esq., F.R.C.S., Surgeon to Charing-cross Hospital: "I find Dr. de Jongh's cod liver oil to be much more efficacious than other varieties of the same medicine." Sold only in capsuled imperial half-pints, 2s. 6d.; pints, 4s. 9d.; quarts, 9s., by all respectable chymists. Sole consignees, ANSAR, HARFORD, and Co., 77, Strand, London, W.C.

CHILBLAINS. ——— WOUND-PROTECTIVE FLUID, prevents contact and excludes air, moisture, and dirt. The effect of painting over the part with this fluid, using a camel's-hair brush, is that a thin, firmly-adhering membrane is immediately formed over the part, and all irritation at once ceases. Sold only in 1s. 6d., 2s. 6d., and 4s. 6d. bottles, labelled, by JAMES EPPS and Co., Homœopathic chymists, 112, Great Russell-street, 170, Piccadilly, 48, Threadneedle-street.

WINTER COUGHS, Colds, Asthma, and Influenza are speedily cured by the use of SPENCER'S PULMONIC ELIXIR. The two great characteristics of Spencer's Elixir are, the allaying of all irritation in the delicate and susceptible coating of the throat and chest, and the imparting of tone and vigour to the respiratory organs, whereby they are enabled to discharge their functions freely, and thus to overcome all difficulty of breathing arising from a cold, foggy, or impure atmosphere, and to throw off those insidious attacks which too often lay the ground-work of consumption.

LIVER COMPLAINTS, Bile, Wind, and Indigestion, headache, sickness, torpid liver, costiveness, giddiness, spasms, nervousness, heartburn, &c., entirely cured without mercury by Dr. KING'S DANDELION and QUININE LIVER PILLS. Sold by all Chymists, &c., at 1s. 1½d., 2s. 9d., and 4s. 6d. a box.

HEALTH, Strength, Energy. —— PEPPER'S QUININE and IRON TONIC strengthens the nerves, enriches the blood, promotes appetite, improves digestion, animates the spirits, restores health. Bottles 4s. 6d., 11s., and 22s. Carriage free 66 stamps. —Pepper, 237, Tottenham-court-road, and all chymists.

DIGESTIVE TONIC WATER.—"To persons subject to imperfect digestion the Digestive Tonic Water will be a perfect boon."—Court Circular. "It has much the same effect as a fresh sea breeze."—Press. Price 1s. 1½d. and 2s. 6d., through any Chymist, or of R. LAKE, 193, Brixton-road. Particulars may be had.

NEURALINE, the instant cure for Tic Doloureux, Neuralgia, Sciatica, Toothache, Rheumatism, Gout, and all nerve pains. Prepared by LEATH and ROSS, Homœopathic Chymists, No. 5, St. Paul's churchyard, and 9, Vere-street, W. Sold by all Chymists, in bottles, 1s. 1½d. and 2s. 9d., by post 1s. 3d. and 3s.

GLYKALINE, the new cure for all descriptions of colds, coughs arising from colds, hoarseness, loss of voice, and difficulty of breathing.—LEATH and ROSS, Homœopathic Chymists, No. 5, St. Paul's churchyard, and 9, Vere-street, W. Sold by all Chymists, in bottles, 1s. 1½d. and 2s. 9d., by post 1s. 3d. and 3s.

DINNEFORD'S PURE FLUID MAGNESIA.—The medical profession for 30 years have approved of this pure SOLUTION of MAGNESIA as the best remedy for acidity of the stomach, heartburn, headache, gout, and indigestion, and as the best mild aperient for delicate constitutions, specially adapted for ladies, children, and infants.—Dinneford and Co., chymists, 172, New Bond-street, London, and of all other chymists throughout the world.

CHILBLAINS, Rheumatism, Lumbago, &c.—Chilblains are prevented from breaking, and their tormenting itching instantly removed by WHITEHEAD'S ESSENCE of MUSTARD, so universally esteemed for its extraordinary efficacy in rheumatism, lumbago, and gouty affections. The great value of the Essence of Mustard is guaranteed by an extensive and successful experience of nearly a century. In bottles, 2s. 9d. each, of BARCLAY and SONS, 95, Farringdon-street, and all medicine vendors.

ALGONICON BALM.——CRE-FYDD'S NEW REMEDY cures Rheumatism, Neuralgia, Lumbago, Gout, Sciatica, Stiff Joints, Sprains, Bronchitis, Sore Throat, Mumps, Stiff Neck, Faceache, Cramp, Chilblains, Spasms, Earache, &c. To be had, with authentic testimonials, of the Agents, Sanger and Sons No. 150, Oxford-street; F. Newberry and Sons, 37, Newgate-street; W. Edwards, 38, Old Change; Barclay and Sons, 95, Farringdon street, London; J. Thompson, 121, New North-road, N.; and retail through all Chymists, in half-pint bottles, 4s. 6d.

DR. PARIS'S NERVOUS RESTORATIVE LOZENGES, for imparting tone and energy to the nervous system. Pleasant to the taste, and possessing highly reanimating properties, they will be found an invaluable remedy in all cases of debility, nervousness, depression of spirits, trembling of the limbs, palpitation of the heart, &c., restoring health, strength, and vigour in a few weeks. Sold in boxes at 4s. 6d., 15s., and 33s.; by post 4s. 8d., 15s. 4d., 34s. 9d. Wholesale by Cleaver, 39, Great Portland-street; and retai by Wilcox, 336, Oxford-street, and Mann, 39, Cornhill; in Manchester, by Westmacott, Market-street, and all Chymists.

HEAD, Face, and Body.—Skin eruptions are incident to childhood, and children of all ages are subject to them. The daily use of the COAL TAR SOAP (Wright's Sapo Carbonis Detergens), from its sanitary action on the skin, which it purifies and disinfects, is a certain remedy. Mothers availing themselves of it will save their children much suffering and consequent ill-health. Recommended by the Lancet, the Medical Journal, and Medical Times. By all chymists, perfumers, and first-class grocers, in tablets, 6d. and 1s.—W. V. WRIGHT and Co., Southwark-street, London. Caution.—The public should note that this is the only coal tar soap that is recommended by the medical profession.

TEETH and PAINLESS DENTISTRY.—Messrs. LEWIN MOSELY and SONS' improved ARTIFICIAL TEETH are recommended by the most eminent of the medical profession as undeniably the best substitutes for the natural organs, securing, without possibility of the slightest pain, the greatest amount of ease and comfort. They are the lightest, strongest, most economical, and durable that can be produced, and are securely retained in the mouth without springs, wires, or large and cumbersome plates. For efficacy, utility, speech, mastication, and the restoration of the original youthful appearance of the features they are unrivalled. Their resemblance to nature is so perfect as to frequently deceive the wearers themselves. Messrs. Mosely's specialité in the use of the gas enables them to guarantee a perfectly painless performance of all appertaining to dentistry with a speed ease, and comfort unattainable by any other method, pain, unpleasantry, or anger being utterly impossible. Teeth filled with imperishable liquid enamel, which, without pain, renders useful the most decayed tooth, and so exactly restores its appearance as to defy detection. Indestructible pure gold stoppings and every description of filling.—Lewin Mosely and Sons, M.D., Surgeon-Dentists to the Royal household, 30, Berners-street, Oxford-street, and No. 448, Strand, opposite Charing-cross Railway Station. The oldest established of the name. Teeth from 5s. ; sets from five guineas. Consultation and every information free.

THE NEW SYSTEM of FIXING TEETH by ATMOSPHERIC PRESSURE by Mr. ESKELL of 25, Hanover-square, and ESKELL and GREY, of 69, Strand, opposite the Adelphi Theatre. Mr. Eskell's work on the teeth, explaining his new system, sent for six stamps. The adamantine teeth never discolour or decay, and last a lifetime ; fixed without wires of any kind, are perfectly secure in the mouth. All operations painless by the use of nitrous oxide gas. Decayed teeth and stumps filled with adamantine enamel, making a stump into a sound tooth useful for mastication. In consequence of Mr. Eskell's improvements in dentistry he is enabled to lower his charges. A single tooth, 5s. ; a set, £5. Observe the address. All consultations free. Established 30 years.

DENTISTRY WITHOUT PAIN.—G. H. JONES, Doctor of Dental Surgery (by diploma), operates daily, upon an improved principle, with Nitrous-oxide Gas, for the painless extraction of teeth, at 57, Great Russell-street, immediately opposite the British Museum, where he supplies every description of Artificial Teeth extant, and being the actual maker, selects for each patient's mouth the mechanism most suitable, thereby a fit is obtained in the most difficult case, even when all other systems have failed. Sets, upper or lower, from 1 to 10 guineas. Factory, Gilbert-street, Bloomsbury. (Testimonial).—Oct. 18th, 1873. My dear Doctor,—I request you to accept my grateful thanks for your great professional assistance, which enables me to masticate my food, and to add, wherever I go I shall show your professional skill, as I think the public ought to know where such great improvements in dentistry and mechanical skill can be obtained. I am dear Doctor, yourstruly, S. G. Hutchins, by appointment, Surgeon-Dentist to the Queen.—G. H. Jones, Esq., D.D.S.

NITROUS OXIDE GAS.—Perfectly Painless Dentistry.—Established 1851. By the use of this, the most simple, speedy, and successful agent, after an experience of over 45,000 cases, Mr. B. L. Mosely, the Dentist, Member College of Dentists, England, and original introducer of this gas, guarantees entire immunity from pain in every operation pertaining to dental surgery and successful painless adaptation of artificial teeth. The daily experience of Hospital and extensive private practice demonstrates that, unlike every other anæsthetic, the Nitrous Oxide gas is innocuous and even pleasant, while want of success or any pain is simply impossible. For confirmation of this vide Lancet, British Medical Journal of January 15th, and opinions of leading members of the Faculty. Mr. B. L. MOSELY'S PATENTED ARTIFICIAL TEETH combine with all the advantages advertised in every other system the following, actually unobtainable by other specialité :—Perfectly painless manipulation, facial anatomy faithfully studied and youthful appearance restored ; elegance of appearance and naturalness combined with the utmost strength and durability ; mechanical lightness of the greatest attainable degree ; perfect security in the mouth without spring, wire, or ligature ; mastication and articulation equal to one's own natural teeth ; there is no difference whatever. Consultation and all information free. Teeth, from 5s.; sets, 5 to 30 guineas. Only addresses, 312, Regent-street (opposite the Polytechnic), and 23, Moorgate-street, City.

GOLD STOPPINGS for DECAYED TEETH.—These, the only really permanent fillings, are made a specialité in my practice. Numberless teeth ruthlessly extracted or discoloured with unsightly amalgams, may, by the judicious use of pure American gold, be retained in the mouth for 5, 10, or even 20 years ; in fact, many decayed teeth or apparently useless shells can be effectually restored to masticatory power without pain or discomfort, present or prospective.—Mr. B. L. MOSELY, the Dentist, M.C.D.E., 312, Regent-street (opposite Polytechnic), and 23, Moorgate-street, E.C. Consultation free. Only addresses.

TOOTHACHE.—Messrs. GABRIEL'S SEDADENT, infallible cure, forms a stopping for the teeth of children or adults, destroys the nerve without pain, and is easily applied. Price 1s. 1½d., of all chymists; post 1s. 3d. Note.—Messrs. Gabriels' only addresses 72, Ludgate-hill, and 56, Harley-street, Cavendish-square.

DENTOCRETE, or SOLUBLE TOOTH POWDER TABLETS, though wonderfully improving the teeth, are guaranteed not to contain acid nor injurious ingredient of any kind. 2s. 6d. per box. Of all chymists and perfumers. Wholesale, Barclay and Sons, Farringdon-street. N.B. Each box contains more than half a gross of tablets.

Situations Wanted & Vacant

BARMAID, age 21.—WANTED, a SITUATION in a restaurant or luncheon-bar. Speaks several languages. Well recommended.—R. D., 33, Brewer-street, Golden-square.

TO CONFECTIONERS, Hotelkeepers, Refreshment-bars, and others.—A highly respectable tradesman's daughter wishes for an ENGAGEMENT in any of the above situations. Competent to keep books. Will give time it required. Highest references. Address C. A., 71, St. George's-road, Peckham.

DRESSMAKING.——To Ladies.——Mrs. ELLIOT, Court Dressmaker, 310, Regent-street (established 20 years at the west-end), undertakes to make dresses (walking or evening costume) most fashionably, and elegantly fitting, at 8s. 6d. for cash. An In-door Apprentice Required.

TO LADIES of LIMITED INCOMES.——J. TOOHEY and SON manufacturers of ladies' fancy work, will SEND WORK and INSTRUCTIONS to ladies at any distance. Instructions, 10s. 6d. Apply, personally or by letter, for a prospectus, with a stamp (prospectus free), at 6, Soho-square. Importers of Berlin wool and German canvas. Established 1851.

AS COMPANION or WARDROBEKEEPER in a School. A lady, age 24. Would give three months without salary to insure a comfortable home. Good references. Address Miss Wilson, scholastic agent, 1t6, Regent-street.

A CHILD WANTED, to WET NURSE, by a highly respectable young married woman. Been confined two days. Own baby died in birth. Address E. J. C., 2, Norfolk-street, Choumert-road, Peckham.

NOBLEMEN and FAMILIES REQUIRING superior HOUSEKEEPERS. Foreign Servants (direct from continent), couriers, &c., are invited to apply to Messrs. Culliford and Mitkiewicz, English and Foreign Institute, 16. Beaufort-buildings, Strand.

COOK.—WANTED, a good PLAIN COOK, not more than 30 years of age. Wages, £14 a year, and all found. Apply, personally, between 10 and 4, at Belgrave-house, 402, Camden-road, Holloway, N.

COOK WANTED, in a private family, where only two servants are kept. Boy to clean boots and knives. Apply at 18, Queen-square, St. James's-park.

COOK (£30) and KITCHENMAID WANTED; also an Upper Housemaid. Apply to Mrs. Howard, 153, Great Portland-street, Oxford-street.

COOK WANTED, in a small family. Good references essential. Apply, between 9.30 and 1 o'clock, at 4, Victoria-road, Finchley-road, N.W.

COOK WANTED (good PLAIN). Age not more than 35 years. Apply 64, Oxford-street, at private door in Wells-street.

A COOK and HOUSEKEEPER WANTED, to a gentleman. Good wages will be given to a suitable person. It is requested that none but those of undeniable respectability and able to give references will apply. Age not to exceed 30. For particulars apply at Mr. Preston's, chymist, 100, Fulham-road, S.W.

A Thorough COOK and PARLOURMAID REQUIRED, from the country. Good wages. 12 months' characters from gentlemen's families. Ages 30.—M. A. B., Loader's, Sheldon-street, Westbourne-terrace.

A Thorough COOK WANTED, in a gentleman's family in the country. A kitchenmaid is kept. A steady, respectable person required. Must be able to bake bread, cure hams, and make good butter, as there is a small dairy. Address, stating wages required, where and with whom she has lived, and her age, to F. R., Messrs. C. and E. Layton's, 150, Fleet-street, London, E.C.

PARLOURMAID WANTED, in a gentleman's family, a few miles from town. Must be a thorough servant and good needlewoman, with not less than 12 months' personal character. Salary from £16 to £18. Apply at 95, High Holborn, W.C.

A PARLOURMAID WANTED, in a family near London. Must thoroughly understand her work, and have a good character from a similar situation. Apply, by letter, to Y. Z., No. 38, Wigmore-street, W.

A PARLOURMAID WANTED, who thoroughly understands her duties. Wages £16, and all found. Also a German Under Nurse. Personal characters indispensable. Address E. B., The Glebe, Lee, Kent, S.E.

A Thorough PARLOURMAID (English or Foreign) WANTED, immediately, in a gentleman's small family, in the country. She must be a good needlewoman, able to wait on a lady and to get up fine things, of active habits, and of neat, genteel appearance. Apply, between the hours of 10 and 12 o'clock, at Messrs. Rastall and Son's, stationers, Eccleston-street, Pimlico.

HOUSEMAID WANTED. Must be neat and obliging. Cook kept. Family of two only. Apply, before 11 a.m. or after 5 p.m., at 11, Clarence-terrace, Seven Sisters'-road, N.

HOUSEMAID WANTED. A respectable young person, not under 21 years, for a family, a few miles from town. She must be neat in her dress and appearance, and willing to oblige. Three servants are kept. No washing. Apply at 155, Regent-street, St. James's, W.

HEAD HOUSEMAID WANTED, for a large, country house, in a midland county. Must have filled a similar situation for some time with ability, and be in every respect a desirable servant, and not under 30 years of age. Apply, by letter only, prepaid, to H., 5, Albemarle-street, W.

AN UNDER HOUSEMAID and KITCHEN-MAID WANTED, age not under 25. Must have at least two years' good personal character. Apply, personally, at Harland's, butterman, 24, High-street, Kensington.

AN UPPER HOUSEMAID WANTED, in a gentleman's family, at Sheerness. Age about 36. Wages £18, beer money, and all found. Address Mrs. Warren, Admiralty-house, Sheerness, Kent.

A SITUATION as UPPER HOUSEMAID WANTED, by a highly respectable young person. Can be highly recommended. Wages £18, and all found. Age 29.—H. F., at Mrs. Grieve's, 10, Devonshire-terrace, Notting-hill.

A HOUSEMAID WANTED. Apply, this day and the next, between 12 and 2 p.m., at 20, Upper Glocester-place, Dorset-square, W.

A Good HOUSEMAID WANTED, for a gentleman's family, near town. Must wait well at table. Apply, by letter only, to M. D., 3, Chancery-lane, Fleet-street end.

A Good HOUSEMAID WANTED. Two in family. None but an experienced servant, with a good personal character, need apply. Wages £12 to £14.—Mrs. Watson, 388, Camden-road, Holloway.

TWO respectable GIRLS WANT PLACES as UNDER HOUSE or NURSE MAID and KITCHENMAID. Address Rev. T. H. Hickens, Speldhurst, Tunbridge-wells.

GENERAL SERVANT WANTED, at Kingston-on-Thames. Must be a good plain cook. Address M. S. D., at Deacon's, Leadenhall-street, stating particulars of age, wages, &c.

A Respectable GENERAL SERVANT, above 16, WANTED, for a family of three. Apply, between 11 and 1 o'clock, at 11, St. Mark's-crescent, Notting-hill.

A GENERAL SERVANT WANTED, where a nursemaid is kept. Good character indispensable. Apply at No. 6, Percy-terrace, Nunhead-lane, Peckham-rye, S.E.

THOROUGH GENERAL SERVANT WANTED, plain cook. Good personal character. Age 20 to 30. Private family. Wages, £12 to £14; all found.—8, St. Augustine's-road, Camden-town.

TWO respectable YOUNG WOMEN WANTED, immediately, in a private family—one as thorough General Servant (must be a good cook); the other, as Housemaid (be able to wait at table). Good characters, early rising, cleanliness, and steadiness required from both. Liberal wages will be given to suitable persons. Apply, to-morrow, at Mr. Robins's, baker, 76, Richmond-road, Westbourne-grove, Bayswater.

MRS. PAGE'S SERVANTS' INSTITUTION has REMOVED from 57, Great Portland-street, to Gothic-house, No. 22a, Mortimer-street, Cavendish-square.

ONE HUNDRED SERVANTS WANTED, at Miss MAUD HAMILTON'S, 28, Southampton-row, Holborn; No. 25, Norfolk-terrace, Westbourne-grove; 3, Manor-rise, Brixton. For men-servants, 6, Piccadilly.

TO NOBLEMEN and GENTLEMEN who, from failing health or sight, require the assistance of a RESIDENT READER and SECRETARY.—A gentleman, of good birth and education, 29 years of age, offers himself. A good, practical knowledge of the French language might render him a useful travelling companion. The best references can be given. Address P. C. R., care of Messrs. Hatchard, 187, Piccadilly.

A GENTLEMAN, qualified to take the entire charge of the editorial department, WANTED, for a weekly agricultural newspaper. Only those who have had experience in the work of an agricultural journal need apply. Address N. E. F., care of Mr. G. Street, 30, Cornhill, London, E.C.

A SITUATION of TRUST, or Partnership, to go out to India, WANTED. Highest references and security. Address Mr. Albert, Box A 65, post-office, Leeds.

A GENTLEMAN wishes EMPLOYMENT in a commission or agency business, with the view of partnership if mutually agreeable.—Bona Fide, Bull's library, Surbiton, S.W.

A Respectable YOUTH, about 14 or 15, WANTED, as APPRENTICE to the drapery. Apply to Fredk. Gorringe, 55, 57, and 59, Buckingham Palace-road, Pimlico.

A Good CARPETMAKER. Good at loose covers; old mattresses made equal to new. Reasonable charges. Ten years' good reference.—E. Burnop, 23, Brown-street, Edgware-road, Bryanston-square.

A GENTLEMAN WANTED, of first-class address, to call on wine merchants and hotelkeepers in the country. Apply, between 10 and 2 o'clock, at 8, Martin's-lane, New Cannon-street.

AN AGENT in London WANTED, by a Manchester shipping house, having a good connexion, and who can influence business with houses shipping to India, China, Brazil, &c. Address Box P. 52, post-office, Manchester.

AN APPRENTICE WANTED, by a chymist and druggist, in a family, dispensing, and country trade. For particulars apply to C. R., care of Messrs. Barron and Co., wholesale druggists, Giltspur-street, London.

A GENTLEMAN, who resides in the country, a short distance from town, is in WANT of a good BUTLER, and one that has been accustomed to the routine of a country house, where there has been much company kept. Direct H. K., Oakmere, Potter's-bar, N.

AN intelligent YOUTH, of 16 or 17 years, WANTED, as APPRENTICE in an accountant's office. A premium will be required. None but parents or guardians treated with, and the applicant must have suitable qualifications.—T. H. C., 7, St. Philip's-terrace, Kensington.

ANY YOUNG GENTLEMAN desirous of obtaining a practical knowledge and experience of FARMING BUSINESS in its several details, will find an opening, with board, lodging, and attendance, by applying to W. J., post-office, Leigh, near Tunbridge, Kent.

A HEAD WORKING GARDENER WANTED. Must be married, without children. Wife will have to take charge of a lodge, and must be a good laundress. Apply, by letter, with full particulars of recent employment, to N., care of Messrs. Charles Barker and Sons, 8, Birchin-lane, E.C.

A LADY wishes to RECOMMEND a married man as BUTLER or IN-DOOR SERVANT, who is leaving her through the family going abroad. Steady, sober, honest, and efficient in all his duties. Address A. B., at Moreau's, stationer, 95, Queen's-road, Bayswater.

AN OPENING occurs for a YOUNG MAN, to conduct a branch of a manufacturing and wholesale business in London, of the highest respectability, on liberal terms. Would be required to hold an interest in same to the extent of £300 to £700. Principals or their solicitors only treated with. Address W. O., care of Mr. Steel, Spring-gardens, S.W.

A GENTLEMAN, of considerable experience in manufacturing and mercantile pursuits, both in England and India, who is also a first-class correspondent, desires an APPOINTMENT in any capacity where business habits, integrity, and good address are essential. Could draw up reports or fulfil the duties of secretary to a private or public company. Salary not so much an object as permanent occupation, with prospect of improvement. First-class testimonials can be given. Apply, by letter, to M. B., 82, Long-acre, London.

A SITUATION WANTED, as BOOKKEEPER, Assistant Bookkeeper, or General Clerk. Five years' experience in an accountant's office. First-class references. Address Y. X., post-office, Throgmorton-street, E.C.

ACCOUNTANT or MANAGER.—An Englishman, educated in France, for 17 years with first-class foreign firms in London, Liverpool, and abroad, desires a RE-ENGAGEMENT. Acquainted with the Mediterranean, Russian, American, and Brazilian trades; also with Italian and modern Greek. Guarantee to any amount. Address Mr. Amsden, 20, Church-road, De Beauvoir-town.

MANUFACTURERS.—A SITUATION as JUNIOR CLERK WANTED, by a youth of 17. Writes a legible and expeditious hand, and is a good correspondent. Salary 15s., or less, if prospect of advancement. Address Wm. Oliver, 8, Martin's-terrace, Greenwich-road.

SPANISH CLERK.—WANTED, a YOUTH (English), possessing a good knowledge of Spanish, to assist as invoice, account sale clerk, &c. Address H. S. C., care of Hopcraft, No. 1, Mincing-lane, E.C.

SHORTHAND WRITER and COPYING CLERK WANTED, immediately, in an auctioneer's office. Must be able to write a good hand, transcribe fluently, and willing to make himself generally useful. Address, in own handwriting, to F. H. S., care of Mr. Wallis, stationer, 147, Fenchurch-street, E.C.

TO MERCHANTS and others.—WANTED, by the advertiser (age 20), a SITUATION as JUNIOR CLERK in a merchant's warehouse or wholesale house of business. Excellent references. Address X., 34, Brooksby-street, Barnsbury, N.

TO BROKERS, Merchants, &c.—WANTED, by advertiser, age 24, a SITUATION as CLERK. Thoroughly acquainted with dock, Custom-house, and shipping business. Understands bookkeeping, quick at figures. Unexceptionable references. Salary expected about £80 per annum. Address N. D., 150, Leadenhall-street, E.C.

THE LEATHER TRADE.—WANTED, an INVOICE CLERK, who writes a good hand and is quick at figures. One with a knowledge of shipping and clearing preferred. Good character and references required. Address, post-paid, with full particulars, to Y. Z., Messrs. Brook and Roberts', stationers, Tooley-street, S.E.

TO LEDGER CLERKS.—WANTED, a CLERK, accustomed to keep the ledgers and make up the ledger balances. None but those who have filled this position in a wholesale city house, and having good characters for carefulness and accuracy, need apply, by letter only, addressed to A. Z., care of Joseph Morley, Esq., public accountant, 27, Leadenhall-street, city.

WRITING or COPYING to any amount, by a gentleman having plenty of spare time and wanting employment. Address H. A., post-office, Exeter.

BAILIFF.—The son of a farmer, of good education, and of several years' experience in farming pursuits, is desirous of obtaining a SITUATION as FARM BAILIFF or MANAGER. He is a good judge of stock, has had the entire management of a prize flock, and understands agriculture in all its branches. Age 27. First-class references. Salary not so much an object as a respectable engagement. Address Mr. F. Matthews, The Taft, Wolseley-bridge, Stafford.

COMMISSION.—A gentleman, representing a London house through Kent, Sussex, and Hants, calling upon grocers, oilmen, and ironmongers, is open to a good COMMISSION. Address A. B., 20, Wansey-street, Walworth-road.

CASHIER and BOOKKEEPER.—A young lady desires a RE-ENGAGEMENT, or as Housekeeper, and to assist with the books, having just concluded an engagement of four years. Address F. A. C., Warren's library, Kensington, W.

COACHMAN WANTED. One well used to horses and driving, and oiling up carriages. No objection to one from the country. Apply at 31, Cambridge-place, near Praed-st., Paddington.

CHIEF CELLARMAN. A practical and thoroughly efficient man, not over 35, capable of managing all wines and controlling a cellar and men. Long reference required. Address T. B., Messrs. Fuller and Co.'s, stationers, St. Martin's-court, Leicester-sq.

COURIERS and TRAVELLING SERVANTS' SOCIETY, composed of respectable men of different nations (established 1851, and enrolled according to Act of Parliament).—The nobility and gentry are informed that trustworthy persons may be obtained by applying to the Secretary, 12, Bury-street, St. James's.

COURIERS and TRAVELLING SERVANTS.—The nobility and gentry are informed that only men with first class characters and testimonials have been admitted, and can be engaged by applying to Mr. Ponsford, Secretary, United Couriers and Travelling Servants' Society, 58, Mount-street, Grosvenor-square.

EMPLOYMENT (according to his capacity) WANTED, by a respectable man, speaking and writing grammatically and fluently German, French, and some Spanish. Residing 20 years in town, and knowing town and the commercial business in town well.—A. B. C., post-office, 227, Walworth-road.

QUEENSLAND.—A large sheep station-holder of Queensland is prepared to take a gentlemanly YOUNG MAN, of character, to learn COLONIAL SHEEP FARMING. A premium will be expected. Particulars of A. B., 30, Great St. Helen's.

REQUIRED, a young gentleman, in a merchant's office, as an APPRENTICE for three years. Premium 250 guineas. Apply, in own handwriting, to China, Jerusalem Subscription Rooms, Cornhill, E.C.

A YOUNG MAN, married, age 26, with 12 years' experience in a leather and fancy goods house, now traveller in the north and midland, is open for an ENGAGEMENT as TRAVELLER, or to take the management of a department in a wholesale house, either in town or country. Will be at liberty on the 1st February next. Address to J. C., Guildhall Hotel, Bristol.

TO PARENTS and GUARDIANS.—WANTED, in an architect and surveyor's office at the seaside, a well-educated youth, having a taste for drawing, as PUPIL. Premium required. Address J. S., post-office, St. Leonard's-on-Sea.

TO PARENTS and GUARDIANS.—A manufacturing stationer and envelope maker has a VACANCY for a respectable youth, with a premium. Apply, by letter, to H. J., care of Messrs. Carter and Bromley, 23, Royal Exchange, E.C.

TO PARENTS and GUARDIANS.—A gentlemanly youth REQUIRED, in an old-established estate agent's office at the west end, as an ARTICLED CLERK. Moderate premium. A. Z. B., Mr. Knowles', stationer, Celbridge-place, W.

TO PARENTS and GUARDIANS.—An opening occurs for the placing of a gentlemanly YOUTH in the offices of a well-established, west-end auctioneer and estate agent. Premium moderate. Address A. Z., care of Mr. Charles Pool, 34, Bouverie-street, Fleet-street, E.C.

TO PARENTS and GUARDIANS.—An opportunity offers of PLACING a well-educated YOUTH in a first-class office connected with the shipping trade, in the city of London. Address Messrs. Deere and Bourne, solicitors, 18, King's Arms-yard, Moorgate-street.

TO PARENTS and GUARDIANS.—A YOUTH, leaving school, can find EMPLOYMENT in the office of an old-established auctioneer and estate agent. No salary at first. Address, with handwriting, Agent, Wakeham's printing offices, Bedford-terrace, Campden-hill, Kensington, W.

TO PARENTS and GUARDIANS.—A young gentleman can be received by a land surveyor and valuer as RESIDENT PUPIL, who would also have the opportunity of learning practical farming. For terms address X. X., Surveyor, post-office, Cheltenham.

TO PARENTS and GUARDIANS.—A firm of accountants, auditors, and arbitrators are willing to accept a young gentleman as ARTICLED PUPIL. Premium 200 guineas. Salary after first three years, with view to ultimate partnership. For particulars apply to Mr. Harcourt Sawyer, financial agent, 7, George-yard, Lombard-street.

TO PARENTS and GUARDIANS.—An architect and surveyor, of established reputation and good general practice, having several large works in hand, has a VACANCY in his office for an ARTICLED PUPIL. A good education and a decided taste for the profession indispensable. Premium moderate, and salary after the first year. Address Zeta, Cole's newspaper-office, 2, Queen-street, Cheapside.

TO SOLICITORS.—PUPIL.—An architect and surveyor, of established reputation, and having a good general practice, has a VACANCY in his office for the above. A solicitor who could introduce business would find this a desirable opportunity of articling his son on advantageous terms. Address M. J. B. A., De Knock's library, Clifton-gardens, Maida-hill.

LAW.—An experienced BILL CLERK, who has been engaged several years in offices of large business, desires a RE-ENGAGEMENT in an office of respectability. References, &c.—C. D., 74, Pratt-street, Camden-town.

LAW.—Articled Clerk.—There is a VACANCY for an ARTICLED CLERK, in an old-established practice in a healthy market town, in one of the home counties. Premium required 300 guineas. Apply, by letter, to P. H. F., care of Messrs. Waterlow and Sons, 24, Birchin-lane, Cornhill, London.

LAW.—WANTED, in an office in South Wales, a thoroughly competent and trustworthy CLERK (unadmitted), well up in common law and bankruptcy, and able to see and advise with clients. Salary to commence £120 a year, and prospective advantages. Good references essential.—Box 151, post-office, Bristol.

LAW.—The advertiser, 22 years of age, six years in the profession, and under articles for 3½, wishes for an ENGAGEMENT as GENERAL MANAGING CLERK, with an assignment of articles and a moderate salary. Address Lex, 13, Bernard-street, Russell-square, W.C.

LAW.—WANTED, a CONVEYANCING CLERKSHIP, in an office of good practice, by an admitted gentleman, holder of a certificate of merit, who has, since his examination, been engaged in a large London office. Highest references. A liberal salary required. Address R. A., 59, Carey-street, Lincoln's-inn.

LAW.—WANTED, by a respectable youth, age 16, a SITUATION in a solicitor's office. Knows the public offices, can write expeditiously, and has a good knowledge of shorthand. Satisfactory references can be given. Salary required 15s. per week. Address X. Y., at Messrs. Hatchett's, stationers, Moorgate-street.

A HOUSE and PARLOUR MAID (combined) WANTED, in a gentleman's small family, at Upper Norwood. Personal character required. Wages £18 and all found. Address L. L., Highland-villa, Central-hill, Upper Norwood.

HOUSE and PARLOUR MAID (tall) WANTED, who is a clever waitress. Apply, by letter, A. B., Mr. Ruffe's, Stationer, North-end, Croydon.

HOUSE and PARLOUR MAID WANTED, in a gentleman's family, five miles from Hyde-park-corner. Good personal character indispensable. An English Roman Catholic would be preferred. Apply at Subiaco-lodge, Roehampton-lane, seven minutes' walk from Barnes Station. Expenses will be paid.

HOUSEMAID WANTED, in a gentleman's family (small). Must be respectable, steady, and a good needlewoman. Five others kept. Wages £14, and all found. Apply, between 11 and 2, at Criswell-lodge, West Brompton, W.

A GENERAL SERVANT WANTED. Must be a good plain cook. Wages £16. Not a lodging-house. Address P. L., 1, Chesham-road, Brighton.

A GENERAL SERVANT WANTED. Three in family, one child of five, for whom a nurse is kept. Must have a good character and be able to do plain cooking. Apply, between 10 and 12, at 11, St. Leonard's-terrace, opposite Chelsea Hospital.

FEMALE SERVANTS.—Owing to the excessive demand for respectable plain cooks and house and parlour maids in London, clergymen and ministers are urged to make this want known. Information will be given to applicants by letters and respectable homes named.—Agency, Soho Bazaar.

A YOUNG MAN, 22 years, WANTS a SITUATION in a private family or hotel. Well acquainted with service at table. Good reference. Speaks French and little English. Apply T. B. F., 32, Langham-street.

IN-DOOR SERVANT (thorough), single-handed, WANTED, in a small family. Must be a good valet, clean plate well, and be generally useful. Wages £40. Apply, by letter only, real name and address, Porter, Junior Carlton Club, Pall-mall.

INDOOR SERVANT WANTED, by a family, in Monmouthshire—a thorough in-door servant, single-handed. Must have a good character from his last place. Boy cleans knives and boots. Apply, with particulars as to age, wages, &c., to A. B., care of Mr. Mullock, Stationer, Newport, Monmouthshire.

A Good IN-DOOR SERVANT WANTED (single-handed), in a gentleman's family, at Hampstead—a respectable, active man, with good personal character. Liberal wages given. Apply, personally, from 3 to 6, or by letter, to M. H., Belmont, Hampstead, corner of Belsize-avenue.

THOROUGH IN-DOOR SERVANT, out of livery, WANTED, in a small family, residing 12 miles from London. He must be perfectly sober, honest, and industrious; wait well at table, clean plate well. A good character required. Apply, by letter, stating wages and length of character from last place, age, &c., to H., post-office, Bickley, Kent.

REQUIRED, in the house of a tutor for Eton and Harrow, a thorough IN-DOOR SERVANT, active, and not afraid of work. No other man-servant kept. About 40 in family, including pupils. Wages £45, all found. Personal character required. Address The Beacon, Sevenoaks.

A GENTLEMAN wishes to RECOMMEND his FOOTMAN for under a butler, or Single-handed. Three years' good character. Age 22 years. Height 5ft. 7in. Apply to W. V. Paley, Esq., Great Barton, Bury St. Edmunds.

A PAGE WANTED, in a gentleman's family. Age from 12 to 14. Must be highly respectable. Address C. D., Key's Library, 7, Bishop's-road, W.

A PAGE and TWO HOUSEMAIDS WANTED, for a boys' school, at Blackheath. Apply, by letter, to Harris, Confectioner, Dartmouth-row, Blackheath, S.E.

LITERARY.—A London clergyman, an experienced writer, seeks EMPLOYMENT as CONTRIBUTOR to a newspaper, magazine, or other publication, or as Editor. Address Sigma, Cook's, 9, Desboro'-place, Harrow-road, W.

A GERMAN GENTLEMAN, with a thorough knowledge of English and French WANTS an ENGAGEMENT as CORRESPONDENT, Bookkeeper, &c., in a stock-exchange firm, bank, or merchant's office. He understands thoroughly the stock-exchange business, foreign exchanges, arbitrage, export, &c., and is a first-rate arithmetician.—B., post-office, 1, King's College-road, Adelaide-road, N.W.

CORRESPONDENT WANTED—one who has had charge of the corresponding department in a large private firm or public office preferred. State age, experience, and if conversant with shorthand and any Continental language. A good salary to a really competent man. Apply, by letter, to Correspondent, 38, New Bridge-street, Blackfriars.

A CLERKSHIP WANTED, by a youth, over 15. Good writer, ready reckoner. Knows French. One year's experience at office work.—B., 105, Hatton-garden.

A YOUNG LADY WANTED, to take the entire management of the made-up lace department. Must be accustomed to a first-class trade, and fully competent.—2, King Edward-street, Newgate-street, E.C.

TO DRAPERS and SILKMERCERS.—WANTED, by a young lady, who has recently finished her apprenticeship in a large house of business, a SITUATION in the drapery department. Unexceptional references given. Address A. B., care of Mr. Potter, Newsvendor, 53, Piccadilly.

TWO YOUNG LADIES WANTED, one in-door and out-door, to learn the photographic business, show room duties one and colouring included. Premium required and salary given. Apply at the Photo Company, 352, Strand.

A YOUNG LADY, age 19, sharp, active, wishes for a SITUATION in a pastrycook's or confectioner's. Can give first-class references, &c. Address Z., post-office, corner Ball's-pond, Islington.

A SITUATION WANTED, by an experienced person, in a first-class family and commercial hotel in London, as HEAD BARMAID, and to assist with books if necessary. Address H. E., Carrington's, Notting-hill.

LEISURE EMPLOYMENT for EITHER SEX, highly remunerative and respectable. Sample, &c., 12 stamps (returned if desired). Address Evans, Watts, and Co., Merchants, The Exchange, Birmingham.

NEEDLEWOMAN WANTED—a superior servant, neat plain worker. Knowledge of Wheeler and Wilson's machine desirable, but not essential. Wages £18, and all found. Apply this day and to-morrow, 12, Winchester-road, Swiss-cottage Station, St. John's-wood.

USEFUL MAID WANTED, not under 35 years of age. She must understand hairdressing, and be well experienced in all her duties. As the place is one of trust, none need apply who have not lived in well regulated families. She will have to assist the lady in her housekeeping. Address J. S. M., Lord's Library, Gloucester-road, South Kensington.

CHILDREN'S MAID REQUIRED, in a gentleman's family. One who has been in the nursery preferred. Must be dressmaker and thorough plain needlewoman. Would have to wait on the lady. No housework. Apply on Thursday, January 8th, between 12 and 3 o'clock, at 37, Throgmorton-street, City, near the Bank. Ring housekeeper's bell.

A YOUNG PERSON (ENGLISH) wishes a SITUATION, to take charge of one or two children in France. Good references. Address E. H., post-office, Barking, Essex.

A MAH or AYAH WANTED, by a lady and gentleman, returning to China towards the end of February, to take charge of a young child during the voyage. Address H. B., post-office, Oxton, Birkenhead.

NURSE WANTED, experienced with children and a good needlewoman. Not under 25. Apply, to-day and to-morrow, from 11 till 4, at 34, Belsize-park, N.W., near the Swiss-cottage.

NURSE WANTED, clergyman's family, Sussex. Experienced, trustworthy, good personal character. Under nurse kept.—F. G., Mr. Jenkinson's, Chymist, Lindfield, Sussex.

NURSE and HOUSEMAID WANTED. The former to take charge of five children. She must be not over 30 years, and have at the least 12 months' personal character. The housemaid will have to wait on nursery and dining room. Address, stating references, age, &c., to M. P., Fern-lodge, Streatham-common.

NURSE WANTED, to reside in Paris, to take entire charge of two children, aged five years and six months. Must be a good needlewoman, able to iron fine things, and willing to make herself useful. Wages £18. Good personal character required. Apply, this day and to-morrow, between 11 and 1 o'clock, at 25, Craven-hill-gardens, W.

A NURSE WANTED, immediately. Must be a good needlewoman. Age about 25. An under nurse kept. Apply at 10, Greville-road, St. John's-wood.

A Thorough good NURSE WANTED, for a little girl 16 months old. Must be a good needlewoman and fond of children, and have two years' personal character. Apply at 80, Queen's-gate, S.W.

A Steady, respectable PERSON WANTED, age about 30, to give a little attendance in the early part of the night to an invalid gentleman, and to make herself useful in the nursery by day, where there is one child, who has a wet nurse. She will be required to go to the South of France immediately. Apply to Mrs. G. T., post-office, Spring-grove, Isleworth.

LADY MATRON, well educated, and of pleasing address (widow without encumbrance preferred), WANTED, immediately, for a superior ladies' school, west London. Indispensable qualifications. Church views moderate. Kind conciliating disposition. Experienced domesticity, energy, and tact. Apply, by letter, giving all possible particulars, to Veritas, 103, Cornwall-road, Bayswater.

SECRETARY WANTED. Salary £150, rising to £250. Security required £250, for which 5 per cent. will be given. Facile correspondence essential. Duties light and gentlemanly. Write Treasurer F521. Address and Inquiry office, The Times Office, E.C.

TO MERCHANTS or others.—A young Englishman, age 17, who writes and speaks French and German as well as his own native tongue, REQUIRES a SITUATION as CORRESPONDENT or otherwise. Moderate salary expected. Apply to B., 29, Greenwood-road, Dalston.

MERCHANTS, Manufacturers, and others REQUIRING occasional FOREIGN CORRESPONDENCE in any language, carried on efficiently, promptly, and confidentially, whether technical, legal, or general, should address C., the Secretary, Academic Institution, Liverpool.

BOOKS, Balance-sheets.—An experienced accountant, holding a Government certificate, regularly POSTS BOOKS, Audits Accounts, &c., for 5s. weekly.—Primus, F527, Address and Inquiry office, The Times Office, E.C.

TO CITY FIRMS,—SMALL SETS of BOOKS KEPT, or quickly Investigated, and Balance-sheets Prepared, by an accountant's experienced clerk (30). Attendance as required. Address N. C., Messrs Dawson and Sons', Cannon-street.

CLERK and BOOKKEEPER WANTED, immediately. Must write a clear hand, and be quick at figures. Age about 30. References and security required. Salary £130 to commence. Apply to C. R. Crossley and Co., 38, Poultry, E.C.

CLERKSHIP WANTED, by a young man, age 26. Good knowledge of shorthand. Excellent references. Address O. R., 53, Burgoyne-road, Stockwell, S.W.

AN experienced CLERK seeks EMPLOYMENT in a good firm. First-class references. Address R.W., 1, Arthur-road, Holloway.

A YOUNG MAN, as CLERK, age 25. Six years' experience in the corn trade; three years' in a Colonial office. Can have excellent characters from both employers. Salary not so much an object as a prospect of advancement. Address J. N., Mr. Neale's, Grocer, Milton-road, Walthamstow.

SITUATION of some kind urgently REQUIRED, by a gentleman, steady and trustworthy, who has had many years' experience in City and Borough firms, as MANAGING CLERK, Cashier, Salesman, and Traveller. Excellent references. Address E., 1, Elgin-terrace, Catford.

A CLERK WANTED, in a merchant's office, to keep books and make himself generally useful. Salary £80 to £120, according to qualifications. Unquestionable references required. Address, in handwriting of applicant, F523, Address and Inquiry office, The Times Office, E.C.

JUNIOR CLERK WANTED. Good writing indispensable. One with a knowledge of bookkeeping preferred. Salary moderate. Apply, by letter, to J. T., 117 and 118, Leadenhall-street, E.C.

JUNIOR CLERK REQUIRED, in a City wholesale house. Must be a good and expeditious writer. One accustomed to Dundee manufactures preferred. Address, stating age, previous engagements, and salary expected, to F522, Address and Inquiry office, The Times Office, E.C.

A JUNIOR CLERK WANTED, by a Fire and Life Insurance Company. Good writing indispensable. Commencing salary £30 per annum. Apply, by letter only, to Alpha, care of J. W. Vickers, General Advertising offices, 5, Nicholas-lane, Lombard-street, E.C.

AS GENERAL AGENT for GERMANY.—The undersigned respectfully OFFERS his SERVICES for the sale of all articles. Highest references.—Wilhelm Jaeger, Magdeburg.

AGENCIES WANTED, for Germany, by a well experienced Berlin merchant, with highest references. Address to I 3,322, care of Rudolf Mosse, Berlin.

AN established STOCKBROKER, with offices in a leading City thoroughfare, is desirous of meeting with a YOUNG GENTLEMAN, with connexion and small capital.—A. Z., 21, Porchester-road, W.

AGENTS WANTED, on good commission, by a large firm of wine merchants, whose products are well known, and for which they received prize medals. Address, stating references and particulars, to Mr. Abel, 91, Rue Notre Dame, Bordeaux.

AGENTS WANTED, wholesale and retail, throughout the United Kingdom and the Continent. Marvellous discovery, Royal Alexandra Tooth Powder, 6d., 1s., and 2s. 6d. boxes. Income from 10 to 300 per annum, large profits, great demand. Cash only.—Alexandra-house, Lewes, Sussex.

Musical Instruments

BROADWOOD 7-octave PATENT COTTAGE PIANO, in elegant rosewood, nearly new, price 45 gs. ; a Cottage, by Collard, in plain case, 25 gs. ; a 7-octave rosewood Console Oblique, by Pape, 30 gs. ; and a fine walnut truss cottage, 25 gs.—J. COOPER and SON, 35 and 36, Berners-street, Oxford-street.

BOOSEY and Co.'s PIANETTES, 19 and 26 guineas. Foreign grandiobliques, from 50 guineas. Erard, Collard, and Broadwood oblique and cottage pianos, which have been hired, many of them nearly new, at greatly reduced prices.—24, Holles-street, W.

A BARGAIN.—Collard's 7-octave Cottage Piano.—Mr. Day, organist of the Bishop of London's Church, 52, Glocester-street, Belgravia, is instructed to DISPOSE OF, at a great sacrifice, TWO superb COTTAGE PIANOS ; cost £121 15s. These costly instruments are guaranteed genuine, and new within four months, presenting an opportunity seldom offered through an advertisement.

SIXTY PIANOFORTES, by Broadwood, Collard, Kirkman, Allison, Cadby, 10 Harmoniums by Cesarini, &c., eight stop finger Organ by England, four Harps by Erard, together with a quantity of violins, violoncellos, concertinas, musical boxes, sheet music, &c., will be included in the SALE by AUCTION, at M. Charles-street, Berners-street, Oxford-street, on Wednesday, January 5th, at 1 o'clock precisely.

BREWER and Co.'s MODEL PIANETTE, 24 guineas.—This unique instrument, in elegant walnut case, handsome fretwork door, check action, with all the latest improvements, thoroughly sound and good, and admirably adapted for extreme climates, may be had of the manufacturers, Nos. 16, 17, and 18, Castle-street, Finsbury, where may be seen a stock of first-class pianos, at 25, 30, 35, 40, and 50 guineas each. Orders received at the music publishing department, 23, Bishopsgate-street within.

KEITH, PROWSE, and Co.'s MUSICAL INSTRUMENTS.

PRESENTS for CHRISTMAS and the NEW YEAR.—Every variety of MUSICAL GIFTS, including Albums, New Music, Batons, &c., and the following Instruments :—

ALEXANDRE'S gold prize-medal HARMONIUMS may be seen in all varieties, for church, drawing-room, and cottage, from 5 to 100 guineas, new and second-hand, at the city agency. Folding harmoniums, 8, 12, 14, and 18 guineas.—48, Cheapside.

THE ORGAN ACCORDION has two rows of vibrators, organ keyboard, three octaves, and is as easily played as the accordion. Any pianist can perform upon it without study. Price, four and five guineas. Book of airs, 2s. 8d.—At KEITH and Co.'s.

MUSICAL BOXES by NICOLE, FRERES.—KEITH, PROWSE, and Co., direct importers, offer parties seeking really fine, well-tuned instruments a selection of more than 200 BOXES, with all the recently-introduced improvements, from four guineas. The new boxes, with accompaniment of flutes, bells, and drum, should be heard to be appreciated, as the expressive effects upon the ear are exceedingly novel and beautiful. Album boxes.

CONCERTINAS, Guitars, Zittars, and Flutinas, for India, from two guineas upwards. Barrel Pianofortes, playing a variety of dance music, &c., from 14 guineas.—At KEITH and Co.'s.

FLUTES.—The NEW MODEL FLUTE (old fingering), for beauty and volume of tone unsurpassed, 3½ guineas and seven guineas. Also, Rudall and Co.'s Prize Medal Flutes, new and second-hand. A great variety of second-hand flutes of all fingerings. Just published, third edition, "Hints to Flute Players," price 6d.

SECOND-HAND HARPS, TWO GRECIAN, equal to new, 35 and 40 guineas ; self-acting Barrel Pianoforte, £30 ; pianofortes (five), by Broadwood and Collard, 14 to 40 guineas.

PIANOFORTES.—OETZMANN, 27, Baker-street. —PIANOFORTES for HIRE, 14s. per month, 7-octaves.

PIANOS for HIRE, from 12s. per month, first-class. —PEACHEY, maker, show rooms, 72 and 73, Bishopsgate within. The largest assortment of pianofortes in London from 20 guineas. Pianofortes, Three Years' System, from two guineas per quarter.

PIANOFORTES for HIRE and for SALE, from 25 guineas upwards.—JOHN BROADWOOD and SONS, 33, Great Pulteney-street, Golden-square, W.; Manufactory, 45, Horseferry-road, Westminster.

PIANOFORTES (SECOND-HAND) by Collard and Collard and Erard. The instrument by Collard is a 7-octave cottage in walnut wood. The Erard is a 7-octave oblique in walnut. To be SOLD great bargains.—P. Holcombe, 43, Berners-street, W.

PIANO, a bargain.—A gentleman OFFERS his superb and brilliant-toned walnut COTTAGE PIANO, by one of the first makers, new within three months, and every modern improvement, worth 50 guineas, to an immediate purchaser for 25 guineas. Maker's warranty.—83, Seymour-street, Portman-square.

PIANOS.—The NEW SHORT IRON GRAND, by KAPS, of Dresden, is the very best and cheapest instrument ever made. May be purchased, or hired, at C. E. FLAVELL'S, 26, North Audley-street, Grosvenor-square. Sole importer, C. Russell, same address. Cottage pianos by the best British and foreign makers.

BROADWOOD TRICHORD, 7 octaves, nearly new, to be SOLD, at a low price for cash, owner going abroad. An opportunity seldom to be met with. Apply, between 11 and 4, to C. M., 77, Southampton-row, Russell-square, W.C.

TWO BROADWOOD GRAND PIANOFORTES —a 7-octave drawing room, and a superb walnut boudoir—both full trichord, and perfect. Half-price for cash, or for hire; or hire system on very easy terms.—34, Finchley-road, near Eyre Arms, St John's-wood.

GRAND PIANOFORTES. — R. WORNUM and SONS, Store-street, W.C., beg to announce that four sizes of their new patented instruments are manufactured, varying in length from 5 feet 6 inches to 8 feet 6 inches, and respectively priced from 56 to 96 guineas. Illustrated price lists upon application.

MOORE and MOORE'S superior PIANOFORTES for SALE, Hire, or on the three years' system, from 2½ and 3 guineas per quarter. Warerooms, 104 and 105, Bishopsgate-street within, E.C.

MOORE and MOORE have PIANOFORTES returned from hire, for SALE, at low prices. Pianofortes from 16 guineas.

MOORE and MOORE apply their THREE YEARS' SYSTEM to HARMONIUMS, from 2 and 2½ guineas per quarter.

MOORE and MOORE extend their THREE YEARS' SYSTEM to all parts of Great Britain. Illustrated lists post free.

CRAMER'S NEW CITY WAREROOMS, 43, 44, 45, 46, Moorgate street.—A stock of New Grand, Oblique, and Cottage PIANOS, by Broadwood, Collard, Cramer, Erard, and Kirkman, such as has not hitherto been shown in London, for SALE, Hire, and on Cramer's Three Years' System. Also a variety of first-class instruments used, but in the best possible condition, at greatly reduced prices.

CRAMER'S HARMONIUMS and AMERICAN ORGANS, in great variety, for SALE, Hire, and on Cramer's Three Years' System. Prices for cash from seven guineas upwards. —43, 44, 45, 46, Moorgate-street. Harmoniums and Pianos for India.

ERARD'S PIANOFORTES.——Sole City Depot, 43, Moorgate-street, E.C. Every size sold, hired, or sent out on the three years' system.

ERARD'S PATENT FULL GRAND PIANOFORTE, seven octaves, metal bracings, and all the last improvements; also a ditto, by Steinway, New York. Both these very fine instruments are in as perfect condition as new, and will now be SOLD at greatly reduced prices for cash. May be seen at J. B. CRAMER and Co.'s, 43, Moorgate-street, City.

DULCIANA ORGAN HARMONIUM, by Alexandre. This new instrument is especially adapted to the drawing room. It has the sweetest tone possible, resembling the soft dulciana stop of the best organs, and by a new patent air chest is free from the slightest harshness. Price, three stops, oak, 12 guineas; mahogany, 13 guineas; rosewood, 14 guineas.—CHAPPELL and Co., 50, New Bond-street.

ORGANS.—AMERICAN ORGANS, Organ Harmoniums, and Alexandre Harmoniums, may be compared together, for purchase or hire, on the three years' system, at CHAPPELL'S, 50, New Bond-street.

CHAPPELL and Co. have on view PIANOFORTES, by all the great makers; Alexandre Harmoniums, greatly improved; and Organ Harmoniums. Any of these instruments can be hired for three years, and provided each quarterly instalment shall have been regularly paid in advance, the instrument becomes the property of the hirer at the expiration of the third year.—50, New Bond-street, W

THE GREATEST of all PIANOFORTES.—Descriptive Catalogues of the STEINWAY PIANOFORTES—Grand, Upright and Square—in English, French, German, or Spanish, can be obtained on application.—Steinway-hall (London), Lower Seymour-street, Portman-square, W.

SHORT IRON GRAND PIANOFORTES, by Kaps, of Dresden.—These celebrated instruments have lately been much improved, and for quantity and quality of tone and perfection of touch are superior to most large and expensive Pianos. Upright Grands, Obliques, and ordinary Cottages, new and second-hand, by the best British and foreign makers, for Sale or Hire, at C. E. FLAVELL'S, 26, North Audley-street, W.

EAVESTAFF'S (WILLIAM G.) PIANOFORTES are well known for their good qualities of tone, touch, standing well in tune, and general durability. The obliques, with his patent vertical repeater check action, are unsurpassed by any, either English or foreign. Prices from 24 guineas; lent on three years' system. Established 1823. Removed from Great Russell-street and Sloane-street to 14, Berners-street, Oxford-street. N.B.—No other address.

MOORE and MOORE.—PIANOFORTES for SALE, Hire, or on the Three Years' System. Prices from 24 guineas; second-hand from 14 guineas. Harmoniums and American Organs. Illustrated price lists post free.—104 and 105, Bishopsgate-street within, London, E.C.

HOPKINSON'S PIANOS, awarded highest honours, London, 1862; Paris, 1855 and 1878, for SALE, from 25 guineas, or Hire, 10s. per month. Lists free.—235, Regent-street, W.

PIANOS, £10, £15, £20.—GREAT SALE of PIANOS.—In consequence of the serious depression in commerce, the whole of the stock of Second-hand Pianos are now offered at such prices as will ensure immediate sale. For cash only.—THOMAS OETZMANN and Co., 27, Baker-street, Portman-square. No other address.

SECOND-HAND BROADWOOD, Collard, and Erard PIANOS, full compass, and in perfect condition, having been but little used, are now on SALE, at greatly reduced prices, for cash only.—At OETZMANN'S, 27, Baker-street (exactly opposite Madame Tussaud's).

BROADWOOD PIANO, 25 guineas.—Full-compass PIANOFORTE, in rosewood case, good condition, fine tone, at above moderate price, for cash only.—At OETZMANN'S, 27, Baker-street (exactly opposite Madame Tussaud's).

COLLARD PIANO, 30 guineas.—Full-compass COTTAGE PIANOFORTE, fine, full, rich tone, perfect condition. May be seen at OETZMANN'S, 27, Baker-street (exactly opposite Madame Tussaud's).

PIANO, £35 (Civil Service cash price), Trichord drawing-room model, repetition action, grand, rich, full tone, in handsome Italian walnutwood case, elaborately carved and fretwork front and cabriole truss legs. The usual price charged for this instrument is 50 guineas. Drawings of this beautiful piano sent post free.—THOMAS OETZMANN and Co., 27, Baker-street, Portman-square.

COLLARD'S IRON BOUDOIR GRAND, 70 guineas.—ONE of these charming and unique SHORT GRANDS, very nearly new, and of sweet tone, is for SALE, at above low price for immediate cash.—At OETZMANN'S, 27, Baker-street (exactly opposite Madame Tussaud's).

ERARD PIANO, 45 guineas, fullest compass of seven octaves.—Trichord COTTAGE PIANOFORTE, in handsome ebonized and gilt case, fine, full, powerful tone. Cash only. N.B.—Guaranteed to be a genuine instrument, manufactured by Messrs. Erard, of Great Marlborough-street, London, and new within three months.—OETZMANN'S, 27, Baker-street, Portman-square exactly opposite Madame Tussaud's).

ERARD'S PIANOS.—Messrs. ERARD, of 18, Great Marlborough-street, London, and 13, Rue du Mail, Paris, Makers to Her Majesty and the Prince and Princess of Wales, caution the public that pianofortes are being sold, bearing the name of Erard, which are not of their manufacture. For information as to authenticity apply at 18, Great Marlborough-street, where new pianos can be obtained at 50 guineas and upwards.

ERARD'S PIANOS.—Cottages, from 50 guineas.

ERARD'S PIANOS.—Oblique Grands, from 85 guineas.

ERARD'S PIANOS.—Horizontal Grands, from 125 guineas.

GRAND PIANOFORTES of all the three sizes that have been in use, but are in excellent condition, may be had of J. B. CRAMER and Co., at very moderate rates. Purchasers have the advantage of every instrument being guaranteed by the firm as the genuine manufacture of the maker whose name it bears, as good in quality of tone and as being durable. The best are those by Broadwood, Collard, Erard, Kirkman, and Cramer. They are sent out either for cash, or on Cramer's Three Years' System of Hire from 2½ guineas per quarter.—46, Moorgate-street, and 209, Regent-street.

NEW GRAND TRICHORD PIANOFORTES, compass seven octaves, repetition action, and additional metal bracings for extreme climates. The tone full and rich, articulation rapid and distinct. They embrace every important advantage secured by grand pianofortes costing nearly double the prices quoted and, they are guaranteed of the greatest durability and excellence. The Boudoir Grand, 7ft. 6in. by 4ft. 7in., 60 and 65 guineas; the Drawing-room Grand, 8ft. by 4ft. 7in., 80 and 85 guineas.—48, Cheapside.

CORNET-A-PISTONS.—The NEW MODEL CIRCULAR POCKET CORNET, electro-plated (with case complete), £5 5s., is most beautiful in appearance, and extremely easy to play; also the New Long Model Cornet, electro-plated, £7 7s., in case complete. Ordinary models from £2 2s.—At KEITH, PROWSE, and Co.'s.

CITY ROYAL MUSICAL REPOSITORY, 48, Cheapside.

ORGAN, CC.—The powerful, temporary ORGAN, now in the Catholic pro-Cathedral, Kensington, will be SOLD, on liberal terms, if purchased before the second week in January. Great, 10 stops; swell, six stops; pedal open, CCC to E; 29 notes.—BRYCESON and Co., Stanhope-street, Euston-road, N.W.

MUSICAL BOX DEPOT for NICOLE, FRERES celebrated INSTRUMENTS. Boxes of exquisite tone, in rosewood cases, playing four airs, £4 4s. Also a choice assortment of boxes playing selections from the works of the great masters. Lists of tunes and prices gratis and post free.—11 and 12, Cornhill, London, E.C.

EAVESTAFF'S (WILLIAM G.) PIANOFORTES are well known for their good qualities of tone, touch, standing well in tune, and general durability. The obliques, with his patent vertical repeater check action, are unsurpassed by any, either English or foreign. Prices from 24 guineas; lent on three years' system. Established 1823. Removed from Great Russell-street and Sloane-street to 14, Berners-street, Oxford-street. N.B.—No other address.

SHORT IRON GRAND PIANOFORTES, by Kaps, of Dresden.—These celebrated instruments have lately been much improved, and for quantity and quality of tone and perfection of touch are superior to most large and expensive Pianos. Upright Grands, Obliques, and ordinary Cottages, new and second-hand, by the best British and foreign makers, for Sale or Hire, at C. E. FLAVELL'S, 26, North Audley-street, W.

CRAMER'S extensive CITY WAREROOMS, 40 to 46, Moorgate-street.—NEW GRAND and COTTAGE PIANOFORTES, also Pianettes, in great variety, by Broadwood, Collard, Erard, and Cramer, for SALE, Hire, and on Cramer's three years' system. A number of superior second-hand cottage and grand pianofortes, in perfect condition, at very moderate prices.

MOORE and MOORE.—PIANOFORTES for SALE, Hire, or on the Three Years' System. Prices from 20 guineas; second-hand from 14 guineas. Harmoniums and American Organs. Illustrated price lists post free.—104 and 105, Bishopsgate-street within, London, E.C.

GRAND PIANO, by Broadwood—the Boudoir. This superb piano was new last year, and has had very little use. It is seven octaves, full trichord, and has all recent improvements. Price 65 guineas, a genuine bargain. Apply to Mr. Fieldwick, Organist of St. John's, Putney, near railway.

PLEYEL, WOLFF, and Co.'s PIANOS.—The agents in London beg to announce that where there is any difficulty experienced in procuring these pianos in the country, purchasers can have the instruments sent, free of carriage, if the order be sent direct to London, to 170, New Bond-street, W.

THE GREATEST of all PIANOFORTES.—Descriptive Catalogues of the STEINWAY PIANOFORTES—Grand, Upright and Square—in English, French, German, or Spanish, can be obtained on application.—Steinway-hall (London), Lower Seymour-street, Portman-square, W.

J. and J. HOPKINSON'S PIANOFORTES for SALE, Hire, or on the Three Years' System. Prices from 25 guineas, for hire from 10s. per month. Awarded highest honours, London, 1862; Paris, 1855 and 1878. Lists free.—235, Regent-street, London, W.

PEACHEY'S PIANOS for HIRE or SALE, or on the three years' system of purchase, from two guineas per quarter. Manufactory and extensive show rooms. Established 50 years. Peachey, Maker to the Queen, 73, Bishopsgate-street within, E.C.

MR. J. S. GROGAN, Selector of Harps and Pianofortes. 40 years practically engaged in the eminent firms of Messrs. Broadwoods, Erards, and Collards, 1a, Selwood-terrace, Fulham-road, S.W. Notice.—The public, generally, are not aware that the limited few practical men engaged in the final completion of instruments, after 30 to 40 years' experience, are diffident in making a selection, hence the difficulty of securing a perfect instrument. N.B.—Touch, tone, and perfect construction only a practical man can discriminate. Instruments taken in exchange from five to 10 guineas warranted. The full amount deducted at any time for a superior instrument.

MUSICAL BOX DEPOTS, 22, Ludgate-hill, and 56, Cheapside, for the SALE of NICOLE'S celebrated MUSICAL BOXES and CABINETS. Prices from £4 to £260. Snuffboxes from 18s. to 60s. Choicest music and largest stock in London. Catalogues of tunes, sizes, and prices gratis on application to Wales and McCulloch, as above.

Business Opportunities

PARTNER WANTED, in the public line, in a promising business. £200 to £300 required. Preference given to a professed cook, an experienced waiter, or a barman. Address G. H., post-office, King-street, Covent-garden.

PARTNER.—A respectable young man, with good connexions and moderate capital, will be received into a bona fide business. Address Q. P. V., care of Mr. J. W. Vickers, 2, Cowper's-court, Cornhill, E.C.

PARTNERSHIP.—To Millers.—A gentleman, with £5,000, would JOIN a miller having a good business and wishful to extend it. Address, with full particulars, in strict confidence, to S. C. M., 1, Mincing-lane, London. No agents.

PARTNERSHIP, or otherwise.—A gentleman is open to INVEST £1,000 in any bona-fide established BUSINESS. The highest references given and required. Address, stating full particulars, to J. O. G., post-office, Bilston, Staffordshire.

PARTNERSHIP.—To Firms Requiring Capital.—Mr. LILWALL has clients (one with £10,000) open to JOIN a bona fide business, where capital can be safely and profitably employed. Communications confidential. Address Mr. J. Lilwall, 14, Walbrook, E.C.

PARTNERSHIP or otherwise.—A gentleman in the wine trade REQUIRES from £500 to £1,000, to enable him to extend his business, which is well established, and entirely a ready-money one, and without risk a good income may be derived. Address Alpha, care of Housekeeper, 57, Gracechurch-street, E.C.

PARTNERSHIP.—WANTED, a GENTLEMAN, with £1,500 or £2,000, to join a firm of metal agents and contractors, or to invest money in their business, taking a share of profits under "The Act to Amend the Law of Partnership." Only principals or their solicitors treated with. Apply to Messrs. Dixon and Tempany, solicitors, 10, Bedford-row, W.C.

PARTNERSHIP.—There is an excellent opening for any gentleman with capital and wishing for active employment, to JOIN the advertiser in extending a most important city BUSINESS. A small amount only required in the first instance, although any amount could be employed without the least risk. Address K. W., post-office, Cannon-street, E.C.

PARTNERSHIP.-WANTED, an Acting or a Sleeping PARTNER, with not less than £3000 cash, to join a party working an old-established business on the Thames, without risk. In coming partner can have 15 per cent. guaranteed, also the security of the working plant and the services and securities of two acting partners, endorsed by first-class city references. Address Thames, care of Thos. Hunter and Co., 1, Gresham-chambers, E.C.

PARTNERSHIP.-WANTED, an ACTIVE PARTNER, with about £3,000 capital, in a well-established mechanical business. Manufactures very lucrative, fully protected under letters patent, and confined to one staple article. The concern is in full operation and mainly engaged upon execution of Government contracts. Incomer must be prepared to give entire attention and can have full control of the finances and general supervision. Address N. R. and Co., care of J. Harper, Esq., 18, Coleman-street, E.C.

A YOUNG MAN, with from £300 to £500, wishes to ENTER a good wholesale JEWELLER'S BUSINESS. For particulars apply to Mr. Harcourt Sawyer, financial agent, 7, George-yard, Lombard-street, E.C.

SCHOLASTIC PARTNERSHIP.—The principal of a first-class and flourishing school (sea-side), desires to receive a gentleman (clergyman preferred), as PARTNER. Premium moderate. Address Partnership, Mr. Watkins's, 5, Bold-street, Liverpool.

CAPITAL.—WANTED, an ACTIVE PARTNER, with capital of £1,500 to £2,000, in a lucrative extensive manufactory, with city offices. Quarterly repayments and salary. Address R., St. John's-wood Parsonage, St. John's-wood.

INVESTMENT.—CAPITAL REQUIRED, to extend an old-established business at the west end. Partner or otherwise, with from £200 to £500. Address Q., Mr. Hunt's, stationer, Duke-street, W.

THE ADVERTISER, who has a good wholesale business in London, and not being in a position to meet the demands of an excellent connexion, seeks the co-operation of an active, business-like young man with about £600, as PARTNER. Strict investigation solicited. Address Beta, Deacon's, Leadenhall-st

TO CAPITALISTS.—Two or three GENTLEMEN are invited to JOIN a newspaper enterprise. Address, in first instance, Rex, at Wolpert's advertising office, 7, St. Swithin's-lane, city.

TO CAPITALISTS.—WANTED, £1,500, for a one-third share in a valuable le d mine in Portugal, on which upwards of £500 has been already spent. Half the amount required would be expended in working the mine. None but principals or their solicitors treated with. Apply to Messrs. Farrar and Farrar, solicitors, 12, Godliman-street, Doctors'-commons.

TO CAPITALISTS, Wine Merchants, and others.—WANTED, £1,000, to complete the fitting-up of a tavern and restaurant, in the best situation in the city. £2,000 have already been expended on it. The lease for 21 years and a life policy for the amount will be deposited as security. Liberal interest will be given. Principals or their solicitors address A. B. G., at Deacon's, Leadenhall-street.

NOTICE to CAPITALISTS.—WANTED, £20,000 to £25,000, in amounts from £5,000 to £6,000, for two or three years, secured by mortgage bond bearing 6 per cent. interest, and com, mission to be hereafter settled. For particulars apply, by letter only, to A. L., care of Davies and Co., advertising agents, Finch-lane Cornhill.

INTEGRITY.—WANTED, £500, for 12 months Personal security by bill. 6 per cent. Any generous person can reply, with name and address, to A. P. G., post-office, Vigo-street.

HELP, OH!—A young gentleman WANTS to BORROW PASSAGE MONEY to AMERICA upon ample literary security. References exchanged. No loan office treated with Apply, first by letter only, Scotia, 42, John-street, Cambridge-ter., W

A YOUNG LADY (householder) desires to BORROW, from a private source, £50, on her promissory note only; or could arrange to Let handsomely Furnished Apartments. Address Honey, care of Mr. Smith, 72, New Church-street, N.W.

MORTGAGE of £4,000 REQUIRED, on freehold building land of ample value, at £5 per cent. Address J. Anderson, Esq., 51, Mortimer-street, Cavendish-square, W.

MORTGAGES immediately EFFECTED, at 5 per cent. interest, on leasehold or freehold house property. Send particulars of security to Messrs. Candy and Luckin, surveyors, 4, Upper-terrace, Upper-street, Islington.

DRYSALTERS.—Any gentleman who can INTRODUCE a few good SHIPPING HOUSES to the owner of a proprietary article will be liberally dealt with. Address A. B., 26, Shirley-grove, Lavender-hill, Wandsworth-road, S.W.

DIRECTOR.—A GENTLEMAN of position and influence is REQUIRED, to complete the board of an insurance company; also a Manager. Will require to invest in shares to a moderate extent. Apply, by letter, Marine, Messrs. Dawson and Sons', Advertising Agents, Cannon-street, E.C.

DISTRICT SUPERINTENDENTS WANTED, by a Life Assurance Society. Terms, salary and commission. If otherwise suitable, preference given to gentlemen who can influence capital. Address Manager, care of Mr. Edwards, 109, Bishopsgate-street, E.C., London.

DRUG TRADE.——There is a VACANCY in a wholesale house for an ASSISTANT competent to take either wet or dry counter, and who understands the duties of warehouseman. Liberal salary will be given, but in accordance with ability and merit. None but first-class men need apply. State age and where last engaged. Address J. B., care of J. H. Schrader, Stationer, St. Mary-axe.

PERMANENT EMPLOYMENT.—Active, intelligent men can earn £3 to £5 weekly in taking orders. Something new; bought by all. Rare opportunity. No previous knowledge required.—W. Bacon and Co., 127, Strand.

PARIS.—A French business man, thoroughly posted in the Paris trade, both buying and selling, is desirous of finding either an AGENCY for the sale of Leeds or Bradford goods to the French market, or an arrangement with a first-rate English firm for all its purchases. All references and guarantees will be furnished. English spoken and written. Address initials P. O., poste-restante, Paris.

PARTNERSHIP or otherwise. About £5,000 or £8,000 to invest by a successful man of business. It must be genuine concern, and capable of the strictest accountant's investigation. —A. Z., Mr. Shaw's, 256, Oxford-street, W.

PARTNERSHIP.—Drapery.—WANTED, a GENTLEMAN, who thoroughly understands the fancy departments as PARTNER, in a first-class business. Capital required £1,000 to £1,500. Apply, by letter, to A. B., Messrs. Peckham's, Great Knight-rider-street, E.C.

PARTNERSHIP.—A gentleman, of great experience in a profitable profession, is desirous of MEETING with an energetic GENTLEMAN, having a taste for the fine arts, with £500 at his disposal. Address Bona Fide, post-office, Ladbroke-grove-road, Notting-hill, W.

PARTNERSHIP (about £1,500).——A WORKING PARTNER is desired in a sound and increasing wholesale City business. No special knowledge required. Principals or their solicitors only address L., care of Messrs. Philpott, Brothers, 65, King William-street, E.C.

PARTNERSHIP.—An Auctioneer, whose premises are situate in one of the very best positions at the West end, and where a capital business can be done, wishes to meet with a GENTLEMAN to JOIN him, with say not less than £1,000. Previous knowledge is not actually necessary. For full particulars address X. Y., Mr. Terry's, Accountant, 17, Abchurch-lane, E.C.

PARTNERSHIP.—A gentleman, who has had the management of foreign agencies, and whose connexions with shippers and wholesale houses enable him to do a large import business, REQUIRES an ACTIVE PARTNER, with capital. References of the highest class will be given and required.—J. P., care of Pottle and Son, 14, Royal Exchange, E.C.

PARTNERSHIP.—The advertiser would be glad to hear of a gentleman as ACTIVE PARTNER in his business, which would suit a retired officer. Amount required £1,800, being the three years' purchase on last year's net profits. Unexceptional references required. Address A. B. C., Wilson's Library, High-street, St. John's-wood.

PARTNERSHIP.—WANTED, a GENTLEMAN, with capital, to join a thoroughly experienced manufacturer in a wholesale and well-established business, replete with every convenience and capable of considerable expansion. No previous knowledge necessary, but a gentleman is desired who would personally undertake the management of the counting-house. This is believed to be an excellent opportunity for a young gentleman desirous of starting in business. None but principals or their solicitors treated with. Apply, by letter, to Keene and Marsland, Solicitors, 77, Lower Thames-street, London, E.C.

PARTNER WANTED, with about £1,500, in a manufacturing business in London, capable of great extension, having large premises, with steam appliances, now doing a good trade at excellent profits. Principals only address C., 9, Liverpool-road, N.

PARTNER WANTED, in a first-class old-established engineering business. Profits good. Any gentleman with £1,200 would find this a safe investment. Address A. B., post-office, No. 628, Bow-road, E.

TO DENTISTS.—A gentleman, of education and thorough practical experience, is desirous of obtaining, by purchase or otherwise, a PARTNERSHIP, in a first-class dental practice. Apply to Mr. Bowen May, Solicitor, 67, Russell-square.

SCHOLASTIC.—A PARTNERSHIP, with prospect of succession, in an old-established school, is OFFERED to a gentleman. A graduate preferred, having some capital at command, Address X. Y. Z., Messrs. Field's Bible Warehouse, 65, Regent-street.

BREWERY PARTNERSHIP.—A clergyman, who has recently placed his son in a brewery, in consequence of the increase of business desires to meet with a PARTNER for him who can command from £1,000 to £2,000. Address Rev. H. Meeres, Haddenham Vicarage, Thame, Oxon.

ONE THOUSAND POUNDS.—PARTNER REQUIRED, Sleeping or Active; artistic bronzes, wholesale, retail, and export. Special manufacturing facilities. Extensive profits. Security. Address E. W. E., care of Messrs. Deacon, Leadenhall-street.

A GENTLEMAN, with command of capital and some experience in business, would like to hear of some established house in the Colonial or East Indian Trade, wishing a PARTNER. Would prefer to serve as clerk for some time, with ultimate view to partnership. Address L. M., Mr. Parnell's, Stationer, 63, Southampton-row, W.C.

WHOLESALE and RETAIL GROCERY, Provisions, &c.—A PARTNER REQUIRED, in an excellent old-established concern, under 30 miles from town, returning £20,000, to take the place of one retiring. The premises are most complete and extensive. Capital required £3,000. Highest references given and required. Acquaintance with the trade is not essential. Particulars of Copeman, Everett, and Whibley, 17, St. Swithin's-lane, E.C.

PARTNERSHIP.—An active gentleman, with £1,500, can secure a SHARE in an old-established CITY FIRM (manufacturing perfumers and importers of fancy goods). Large country connexion. Retiring partner going out through ill-health.—F. B., No. 10, Hamsell-street, Falcon-square, E.C.

PARTNERSHIP.—From £2,000 to £4,000 required, to purchase ONE-THIRD SHARE in an established BUSINESS. A gentleman competent to undertake the counting-house duties preferred. Full particulars on application to Cates and Son, Accountants, 23, Budge-row, E.C.

PARTNERSHIP.—An equal SHARE in an established WINE BUSINESS (connexion good, brand well known) can be had for £1,000. Partner, sleeping or active. Books open to inspection. Address J. R. Macarthur, Solicitor, 30, John-street, Bedford-row, W.C.

PARTNERSHIP.—WANTED, a PARTNER, with about £2,000, in an established manufacturing business in London, to take the place of a retiring partner. Satisfactory references given. Principals only treated with. Address L. W. A., 111, Cheapside, E.C.

PARTNERSHIP.—A SHARE in an old-established BREWERY is OFFERED to a gentleman having from £5,000 to £10,000 at command. No special knowledge required beyond that of ordinary business. Good returns. Address Messrs. G. Field and Co., 120, Salisbury-square, E.C.

PARTNERSHIP.—Wholesale Continental Produce and Commission Business.—A favourable opportunity offers for securing an equal share in the above business, confined to a staple article of consumption, by investing £1,500 to £2,000. Returns exceed £25,000 per annum, with large profits. Books can be seen, and every facility for investigation offered. Principals or their solicitors apply, in first instance, to Mr. John Hart Bridges, 20, Hart-street, Bloomsbury-square, W.C.

PARTNER WANTED (Sleeping or Active), in a first-class London hotel. Capital required about £1,500. A good going concern. Address F507, Address and Inquiry office, The Times Office, E.C.

PARTNER WANTED, in a thoroughly sound merchant's business. Must command £6,000 to £8,000. Principals only treated with. Apply to Saxelby and Faulkner, Solicitors, Nos. 7 and 8, Ironmonger-lane, London, E.C.

PARTNER.—£1,000 to £1,500.—In consequence of ill health, Half Share of old-established West-end Builder's and Decorator's, with first-class connexion. Technical knowledge preferable, but not absolutely necessary. Share worth £500 per annum. Apply to Sharratt and Cree, 9, Coleman-street, E.C.

PARTNER WANTED (Sleeping or Active), in a thriving, old-established manufacturing business. The articles manufactured are secured by patents and in constant demand. Capital required £3,000. For particulars apply by letter to F288, Messrs. Deacon's, 154, Leadenhall-street, E.C.

PARTNER.—A gentleman, with £1,500, can have HALF-SHARE of a SPECIALITY, established more than two years ago. It is a scientific preparation, recommended by the leading members of the medical profession and the élite of society. Only letters from principals will be noticed. Address H., care of Messrs. Barclay and Sons, Farringdon-street, London.

ALEPPO.—A merchant firm in London, having business connexions in Syria, wishes to meet with a gentleman, with capital or good connexions, willing to proceed to the above city, with a view to ESTABLISH a BRANCH HOUSE there. Address A. Z. A., Messrs. Deacon's, Leadenhall-street, E.C.

A GENTLEMAN WANTED, with £800 to £1,000, either to join the advertiser or to purchase the entirety of a first-class profitable going concern, the product of which is daily used. The machinery and plant worth more than the purchase-money. Address E. Jones, 3, Denmark-street, Barnsbury-road, London, N.

TWENTY per CENT. and COUNTY SOCIETY.—A PARTNER REQUIRED, in a property worth £14,000 per annum. Would be established in the best society in England. Address F520. Address and Inquiry office, The Times Office, E.C.

TO PUBLISHERS.—WANTED, one or two PARTNERS, with from £2,000 to £5,000 each at command, to join an established and profitable business. Liability limited. Parties may take an active part in the business or not, as preferred. Address, with reference, U. J. 21, Messrs. Deacon's, 154, Leadenhall-street.

THE CO-OPERATION of a GENTLEMAN WANTED, with a capital of about £1,000, to complete a syndicate for purchasing and extending a valuable wholesale manufacturing business, showing large profits. No risks. Previous knowledge not necessary. Principals address to E. B. B. George, Accountant, 174, Regent-street, W.

Apartments & Offices

APARTMENTS, Furnished, at 22, Jermyn-street, St. James's—drawing-room suites, two guineas per week, or 90 guineas per annum; three rooms on second floor, 70 guineas per annum. Extra bed rooms.

APARTMENTS, Furnished—a handsome drawing-room, with good bed rooms; suitable for gentlemen engaged during the day. Terms moderate.—7, Russell-gardens, West Kensington.

APARTMENTS, Furnished, Cambridge-street, Eccleston-square—drawing-room floor. No other lodgers. Gas and every comfort. Terms inclusive to a gentleman engaged during the day, 15s. per week. For cards Alpha, 50, Cambridge-street, S.W.

APARTMENTS.—The proprietor of STEVENS'S FAMILY HOTEL, Clifford-street and Bond-street, begs to state that he has enlarged his hotel, and makes the most economical charges, with every comfort. Arrangements made by the day or week. Best situation in London.

FURNISHED APARTMENTS, 47, Conduit-street, Bond-street—sitting, bed, and dressing room en suite, newly decorated. An extra bed room if required.

FURNISHED DRAWING or DINING ROOM APARTMENTS (superior)—sitting room and bed room en suite. Gas and piano; convenient, central position, and within 15 minutes' of Lincoln's-inn.—80, Newman-street, Oxford-street.

FURNISHED DRAWING-ROOM FLOOR, comfortable in every respect, and healthily situate, to be LET, in a superior private residence.—Chichester-house, Upper Westbourne-terrace, W.

FURNISHED APARTMENTS (superior), looking on to Portland-place—a first and second floor, to be LET, together or seperate. Gentlemen preferred. No children or other lodgers. For terms, &c., apply to Y. Z., care of Mrs. King, 12, Duke-street, Portland-place, W.

FURNISHED APARTMENTS.—A married couple (no children), who live quietly, WANT APARTMENTS, Furnished, with a view rather to convenience than show, for some time, in a private house. Dressing room desirable. Rent about 1½ guineas. S.W. district preferred. Address to X. E., at Alexander's, No. 24, Old Cavendish-street, W.

UNFURNISHED, a DINING ROOM, 14ft. by 16ft., 12ft. high, communicating with drawing room, 28ft. by 15ft., four bed rooms on second floor, china closet, and kitchens.—39, George-street, Portman-square.

UNFURNISHED APARTMENTS WANTED, in the west-end, by a single gentleman, for private occupation and a permanency; consisting of three rooms on first floor, with plain cooking and attendance. The gentleman is a great part of his time out of town. References given and required. Address, stating terms and particulars, to Y. Z., 7, Conduit-street, Regent-street.

A BARRISTER'S WIDOW wishes to LET PART of her HOUSE. Apply at 8, Upper Woburn-place, W.C.

A Comfortable BED and DRESSING ROOM WANTED, for two or three months, Furnished, within 10 minutes' walk of Albemarle-street. Reply, with particulars, to A. B., Mr. Fisher's, stationer, Angel-court, Throgmorton-street, E.C.

BROOK-STREET.—To be LET, the entire UPPER PART and BASEMENT of a spacious HOUSE, comprising two good drawing rooms, seven bed rooms, and usual offices. Apply to Messrs. White and Druce, 20, Brook-street, New Bond-street.

FIRST FLOOR, unfurnished, to be LET, in the best part of Sloane-street, suitable to professionals—lawyers, accountants, dentists, photographers, artists, &c. Apply at Louis Lichtenstein's repository of Swiss wood carvings, 13 Sloane-street, Belgravia.

GRANVILLE-MANSION.—THREE SUITES of APARTMENTS VACANT—six rooms, including kitchen, four and seven with or without kitchen, all with or without attendance. Apply to the Manager, 2a, Granville-place, Portman-square, W.

HANDSOMELY FURNISHED DRAWING ROOM, with bed room communicating, to be LET, near Westbourne-terrace, embracing the comforts and privacy of a quiet home. The rooms are spacious, with south aspect. Address or apply to Mrs. Bruce, 30, Blomfield-terrace, Westbourne-terrace, W.

MADDOX-STREET, Bond-street.—The principal PART of a desirable HOUSE to be LET, unfurnished; containing six rooms, kitchen, &c.; suited for a dressmaker, dentist, or private family.—Agent, Mr. S. G. Taylor, 3, Grosvenor-street, W.

PART of a good HOUSE, in St. John's-wood, REQUIRED, by a lady, her son, and daughter; or desirable unfurnished Apartments (five or six rooms), with or without attendance. Address, stating terms, to M. M., Chapman's library, Abbey-rd., N.W.

SUPERIOR FURNISHED APARTMENTS—drawing-room suite, with dressing room; folding doors. House large and lofty. Rail and omnibus to city and west every two minutes. Inclusive terms £1 2s. weekly. Gas. No extras.—K., 2, Arthur-road, Holloway.

TO be LET, comfortably Furnished, a DOUBLE-DRAWING ROOM and TWO good BED ROOMS, with excellent attendance. Situate in the best part of Sloane-street, Belgravia. Apply at Mrs. Turrell's 15, Sloane-street, S.W.

TO be LET, in Morpeth-terrace and Carlisle-place, near the Victoria Station, Pimlico, some desirable SUITES of APARTMENTS. For particulars apply to Messrs. Norris and Sons', No. 2, Bedford-row, W.C.; or to Mr. H. Bond, 18, Upper Tachbrook-street, Pimlico, S.W.

TO PHYSICIANS, Surgeons, and Oculists.—To be LET, on the ground floor, near the Moorgate-street Station, a CONSULTING ROOM, with part use of waiting room. Apply to Mr. Marvin, house agent, 11, Finsbury-pavement.

CHAMBERS. —— Two gentlemen REQUIRE CHAMBERS for residence. Address Omicron, care of Mr. G. Street, 30, Cornhill, E.C.

CHAMBERS to be LET, the Albion-chambers, 11, Adam-street, Adelphi, first house from the Strand. Four Rooms adjoining on the third floor. Every convenience. Suitable for a resident tenant. Rent £45. Apply to the housekeeper.

CHAMBERS.—To Noblemen, Gentlemen, and Public Societies.—THREE handsome and spacious first-floor ROOMS to be LET, unfurnished, in a recently constructed edifice, upon the site of the late Lord Braybrook's mansion, in the immediate vicinity of most of the clubs, the Royal Society, &c.; in a quiet neighbourhood, but 10 doors from Regent-street. Every convenience, en suite. None but principals or their accredited agents treated with. Rent £200 per annum, or on lease. Apply at Messrs. Cremer's, 22, Conduit-street, or upon the premises, 21, Savile-row, corner of New Burlington-street, Regent-street.

CLUB CHAMBERS, 15, Regent-street, Waterloo-place.—ROOMS may now be had at moderate rents, which include all charges for use of public rooms, attendance, &c. Apply to the Manager.

QUADRANT CHAMBERS, 52, Regent-street, facing Waterloo-place.—To be LET, SUITES of CHAMBERS, for offices or dwellings, at moderate rents. Also an excellent position for a photographic studio.

APARTMENTS, handsomely Furnished, for a gentleman, consisting of dining and bed room, with good cooking and attendance. Close to Bishop's-road Station.—26, Westbourne-terrace-road, W.

APARTMENTS, Furnished, consisting of parlour-floor, sitting room, and two bed rooms en suite. Well suited for one or two gentlemen. Good attendance.—26, Bryanston-street, Great Cumberland-place, Marble Arch.

APARTMENTS, unfurnished, with attendance, REQUIRED, in the neighbourhood of Notting-hill—a drawing room, two bed rooms, and box room, for two single ladies. Write, stating terms, with all particulars. Address M. E. B., 108, High-street, Clapham.

APARTMENTS, 17, St. James's-place, St. James's, S.W.—suite of rooms, suitable for noblemen and their families, gentlemen, members of Parliament and of clubs—to be LET, by the week, month, or year; also bed rooms for single gentlemen, with the use of a sitting room. Good cooking and attendance.

APARTMENTS, handsomely Furnished, first-class house, Bayswater—noble double drawing rooms, large bed rooms, bath room, hot supply. Gas throughout. Suitable for three or four gentlemen, or family requiring superior residence. Good cooking. Every comfort. Moderate terms.—Z., 1, Elgin-road, Kensington-park, W.

FURNISHED APARTMENTS WANTED—sitting, bed, and extra room, by a City gentleman (German). Terms 20s. to 25s. Convenient for rail. No other lodgers. Address C. H. L., No. 22, Mincing-lane, E.C.

FURNISHED APARTMENTS, for gentlemen, three minutes' from Victoria Station—drawing room and bed room communicating. Extra bed room. Every comfort and attention. Moderate terms.—67, Warwick street, Belgrave-road, S.W.

FURNISHED APARTMENTS (superior)—spacious dining and drawing rooms, large, airy bed rooms; gas and piano; bath, with hot and cold water; close to omnibus and rail. Apply on the premises, 34, Upper Park-road, Haverstock-hill, Hampstead.

FURNISHED APARTMENTS, pleasantly situate—double drawing room and two bed rooms, large and well furnished. 2½ guineas per week. Gas, bath room, &c.—Mrs. H., No. 37, Westmoreland-place, Westbourne-grove, Bayswater, W.

UNFURNISHED APARTMENTS WANTED, by two City gentlemen—two bed rooms and one sitting room, in the West-end. Address, stating terms, to C., Housekeeper, 2, Alderman's-walk, E.C.

UNFURNISHED APARTMENTS, near Notting-hill Station, to be LET—a drawing room, three bed rooms, with use of bath room, and attendance. No children or other inmates. References exchanged.—M. D., Martin's, Stationer, 19, Ladbroke-grove-road, Notting-hill, W.

UNFURNISHED APARTMENTS, for a gentleman, in Baker-street, Portman square, where only gentlemen are resident—a noble and lofty suite of three drawing rooms, with dressing room, containing water-closet, and man-servant's kitchen below; stone staircase and entrance-hall. Apply to Mr. Maddox, No. 21, Baker-street.

BRIGHTON.—Superior FURNISHED APARTMENTS to be LET, on very moderate terms, few doors from the sea. No children or other lodgers. Address Pier, 24, Southwark-street, S.E.

TO GENTLEMEN.—A DRAWING ROOM and TWO BED ROOMS (Furnished) above to be LET. Invalids not objected to. No children or lodgers. Terms 14s. a week. For address apply to Mrs. Roberts, 219, Liverpool-road, N.

TO PHYSICIANS.—The entire UPPER PART of ONE of the largest and best HOUSES in Finsbury-square to be LET, on LEASE; or a First Floor, comprising spacious waiting room communicating with a large consulting room. For full particulars apply to Mr. W. Paterson Kerr, Surveyor and Valuer, 9, South-place, Finsbury, E.C. (1,982.)

TO MEDICAL MEN.—CONSULTING ROOM and WAITING ROOM, in Finsbury-square, to be LET, Furnished. Ill-health cause of present tenant leaving. The rooms are on the ground floor, and have been in the occupation of medical men for 25 years. Apply to Mr. W. Paterson Kerr, Auctioneer, 9, South-place, Finsbury, E.C. (1,983.)

PROFESSORS or GENTLEMEN of BUSINESS can have the USE of an excellent, large, well FURNISHED ROOM, on moderate terms, according to arrangements.—Messrs. De la Motte, 15, Beaufort-buildings, Strand.

CHAMBERS, for Residence, 8, Duke-street, St. James's—first floor. Rent £70.

CHAMBERS, for Residence (rent £40), Berkeley-chambers, 13, Bruton-street, Berkeley-square; and Adelphi-chambers, 6 and 7, John-street, Adelphi (rent £25).

OFFICE of two rooms WANTED, with partial use of a clerk. Lombard-street or immediate locality. Address X. E., care of Davies and Co., Advertising Agents, Finch-lane, Cornhill.

OFFICES, Lyons-inn-chambers, 303, Strand—suite of four or six rooms, second floor. Rent moderate. Two rooms, rent £35. Immediate entry. Apply to Messrs. Cox and King, Spring-gardens, or Mr. Giblett, 172, Strand.

OFFICES to be LET, at No. 9, Strand, most convenient and in best position, consisting of one large and two small rooms on ground floor, with basement under; suitable for a public company, wine merchant, or solicitor. Address O., 49, Leicester-square, W.C.

NEWGATE-STREET.—To be LET, LARGE, light ROOMS; also a roomy, light Basement, suitable for offices, warehouse, or printing establishment; or will be Let for Residential Purposes, together or separate. Apply on ground floor, No. 97, Newgate-street; or to Mr. Stapleton, 62, Bishopsgate-street-without, E.C.

STRAND.—OFFICES to be LET; the best position of the Strand; new building, with strong rooms, lavatory, &c.; rents very moderate, from 15s. to 20s. per week; no taxes.—Savoy-house, 115, Strand.

TO PUBLIC COMPANIES.—OFFICE ACCOMMODATION provided and secretarial duties undertaken for a moderate sum. Address F. M., care of Davies and Co., Advertising Agents, Finch-lane, Cornhill.

DWELLINGS in FLATS—a few to be LET, in Artillery-buildings, Artillery-row, Victoria-street, S.W. Apply at once to the Porter, at No. 11.

HANDSOMELY FURNISHED SUITE of ROOMS to be LET, consisting of drawing room and one or two bed rooms. For terms and particulars apply to Housekeeper, 14, Piccadilly.

LOWER SEYMOUR-STREET, Portman-square.—To be LET, handsomely Furnished, DRAWING-ROOM SUITE of THREE ROOMS, comprising sitting room, bed and dressing room, and closet, with attendance; in the house of a professional man. Apply for terms to Messrs. Elliott and Son, 6, Vere-street, W.

REIGATE, Surrey.—To be LET, FURNISHED DRAWING ROOM and THREE BED ROOMS, three minutes' walk from station. Address Miss Mathews, London-road.

REQUIRED, in the neighbourhood of South Kensington, the use of a LARGE ROOM, once or twice a week, for a class of young ladies.—A. B. C. D., Nash and Teuten, Savile-passage, Savile-row, Regent-street.

ST. JAMES'S-STREET, No. 20.—FIRST FLOOR, well Furnished, comprising sitting room, bed, and dressing room, with water-closet en suite; also a Third Floor, equally well furnished, with same number of rooms, for £100 per annum. Good cooking and attendance.

TO be LET, a spacious GROUND FLOOR, suitable for a medical man. Address W., 9a, Gloucester-place, Portman-square.

TO be LET, in Euston-square, the UPPER PART of a HOUSE, with four or six rooms, suitable for a lady and servant. References given and required. No lodgers. Apply, in the first place, to A. T. A., 3, Seymour-street, N.W.

TO be LET, together or separate, the whole of UPPER PART of large HOUSE; light and lofty rooms; good entrance hall. Suitable for professional or business purposes. Apply on premises, 33, Soho-square, W.

TO CITY GENTLEMEN.—APARTMENTS—dining and two large bed rooms, well furnished, in a newly-decorated house, near Notting-hill Station. City omnibuses pass the door. References exchanged.—19, Elgin-crescent, Notting-hill, W.

TO CLUB GENTLEMEN.—To be LET, in a large house in Grosvenor-street, a well FURNISHED DINING and BED ROOM, for a gentleman of quiet habits wishing for a good address at a moderate rent.—Agents, Messrs. White and Druce, 20, Brook-street, Grosvenor-square.

WINTER APARTMENTS, at Tunbridge-wells—well furnished sitting and one or two bed rooms—in most cheerful and convenient situation, suitable for City gentlemen or others to whom careful attention to comfort would be an object.—R. E., 1, Broadway, Tunbridge-wells.

CHAMBERS, overlooking St. James's-park—large bed room and splendid sitting room, with bow windows to each, and small ante-room. Rent, including attendance and sole use of garden in Bird-cage-walk, £120 a year, Furnished, or £75 a year, unfurnished, in which latter case the present Furniture must be taken at a valuation. Apply to Mr. Millar, Estate Agent, 14, Grafton-street, Bond-street, W.

Odds & Ends

CAUTION.—HOWARD and SON'S PATENT PARQUET FLOORING, No. 1,548.—All persons are CAUTIONED against infringing this patent.—26 and 27, Berners-street, Oxford-street, and Cleveland Works.

CAUTION.-HARRIS'S SPECTACLES.-THOMAS HARRIS and SON CAUTION the public against persons using their name. Their business, established 1780, is solely conducted at 52, Great Russell-street, opposite the British Museum-gate, where only can be had their celebrated spectacles, opera and field glasses. No travellers.

CAUTION.—BETTS'S CAPSULE PATENTS are being infringed by importation of capsules made in contravention of his rights, which necessarily are numerous, Betts being the original inventor and sole maker in the United Kingdom.—1, Wharf-road, City-road, London ; and Bordeaux, France.— April 8, 1869.

CAUTION.—PILLISCHER'S QUEEN'S READING and MICROSCOPE LAMPS, as supplied by him to Her Majesty and the Royal Family.—The public are CAUTIONED against inferior imitations, M. Pillischer, optician, 88, New Bond-street, being the sole inventor and manufacturer of these celebrated lamps. Drawings and prices post free. No agents.

CAUTION.—The THREE-GUINEA GOLD BRIDESMAID'S LOCKET, of best workmanship, gold opening back to contain two miniatures and any initials, in fine pearls, turquoises, coral, or coloured enamels, can only be obtained of the registered designers and inventors, Messrs. HOWELL, JAMES, and Co., jewellers to the Royal Family, 5, 7, 9, Regent-street, Pall-mall. Five per cent. discount allowed for cash.

CAUTION.—LLOYD'S EUXESIS, for Shaving without Soap or Water.—The public are hereby informed that, in pursuance of a decretal order of the Court of Chancery, made in a suit for the administration of the estate of the late Andrew Solomon Lloyd, we have purchased of the executrix the business carried on by the late A. S. Lloyd as a perfumer, together with the exclusive right to and interest in the article known as "Lloyd's Euxesis." We, therefore, caution the public that the genuine Lloyd's Euxesis bears only the original signature and address, namely, "A. S. Lloyd, No. 27, Glasshouse-street," where it can be obtained as formerly.

R. HOVENDEN and SONS, 27, Glasshouse-street, Regent-street, London, W.

CAUTION.-SQUIRE'S MURIATE of AMMONIA LOZENGES and ASTRINGENT LOZENGES, prepared from the red gum of the "Eucalyptus Rostrata" of Western Australia. These celebrated lozenges, for the relief of bronchitis and relaxed throats, may now be ordered and obtained through any chymist, but the undersigned have particularly to request purchasers will see that each lozenge is stamped with their name (Squire) and that their label is affixed to every bottle, signed at both ends P. Squire, and bearing in the centre the words following, viz. – " Peter Squire, Oxford-street, London, chymist in ordinary to the Queen, H.R.H. the Prince of Wales, and the Royol Family."

(Signed) P. and P. W. SQUIRE, 277, Oxford-street, London.
November, 1869.

THE public are CAUTIONED against IMITATIONS of the NEW VELLUM WOVE CLUB-HOUSE NOTE. This paper has been manufactured to meet the universally-experienced want—i.e., a paper which shall in itself combine a perfectly smooth surface with total freedom from grease. It is made from the best linen rags only, possesses great tenacity and durability, and is equally well adapted for quill or steel pen. Sample packet post free for 18 stamps.

(Signed) PARTRIDGE and COOPER, sole manufacturers and vendors, 192, Fleet-street, E.C.

NOTICE.- HOWARD and SONS beg to notify to their patrons and the public that their EASY CHAIR and SOFA SHOW ROOMS, as well as the General Cabinet Warehouse, CLOSE at TWO p.m. on SATURDAYS.—26 and 27, Berners-st., W.

POLLAKY'S PRIVATE INQUIRY OFFICE.—Confidential INQUIRIES with secrecy and despatch in divorce cases, &c., by Mr. Pollaky, 13, Paddington-green.

MONOGRAMS.——The STATIONERY COMPANY'S CATALOGUE and SPECIMENS of MONOGRAMS and cheap STATIONERY, post free.—British and Foreign Stationery Company, 8, 10, and 12, Garrick-street, Covent-garden, London.

MONOGRAMS (MOURNING STATIONERY), at HENRY RODRIGUES', 42, Piccadilly.—Black-bordered note paper and envelopes, every width of border, stamped in black relief. Memorial cards and return thanks of the newest patterns.

MONOGRAMS.—RODRIGUES' MONOGRAMS. Arms, crests, and addresses designed, and steel dies engraved as gems. Notepaper and envelopes stamped in colour relief, and brilliantly illuminated in the highest style of art. Rustic and eccentric monograms designed for any combination of letters.—42, Piccadilly.

MONOGRAMS, by CULLETON.—Quarter ream of paper and 125 high-flap envelopes, stamped in four colours with monogram, 5s., postage 8d. No charge for die. All orders executed by return of post.—T. Culleton, seal engraver 25, Cranbourne-street, corner of St. Martin's-lane.

MONOGRAMS (a pretty present).—Five quires of thick note and 100 thick envelopes, stamped in four rich colours, any two or three initials, for 5s. No charge for die. Specimens of the initials required one stamp.—J. MACMICHAEL, heraldic stationer to the Queen, 207, King's-road, London, S.W.

WHAT ARE YOUR CREST and MOTTO?—Send name and county to CULLETON'S Heraldic office. Plain sketch, 3s. 6d.; in heraldic colours, 7s. The arms of man and wife blended. The heraldic colours for servants' livery, 10s. Crest engraved on seals, rings, book plates, and steel dies, 7s. 6d. A neat gold seal, with crest, 20s. Solid gold ring, 18-carat, hall-marked, engraved with crest, 42s. Manual of Heraldry, 400 engravings, 3s. 9d. All post-free. —T. Culleton, engraver to the Queen, 25, Cranbourn-street (corner of St. Martin's-lane).

RIMMEL'S NEW YEAR'S PRESENTS in immense variety, from 6d. List on application. Floral crackers, for balls and parties, 5s. 6d. per doz.; costume crackers, 3s. 6d.; rose water crackers, 2s. Rimmel's Perfumed Illuminated Almanac (Heroines of English Poets), 6d.; by post for seven stamps. N.B. Premiums to retail purchasers above 5s.—96, Strand; 128, Regent-street; 24, Cornhill.

GENERAL NURSING INSTITUTE, 5, Henrietta-street, Covent-garden, W.C.
Medical Director—ALFRED EBSWORTH, F.R.C.S.
Resident skilled medical, surgical, and monthly nurses are supplied at a moment's notice from this Institute; also fever nurses, male attendants, and wet nurses. Applications to be addressed to the Secretary or Lady Superintendent.

FUNERAL COMPANY, 82, Baker-street, W.
Funerals conducted in the best style.
Superior funeral equipages and appointments.
Exclusive proprietors of the improved open hearse.
Chief office, 28, New Bridge-street, Blackfriars, E.C.

FUNERAL UNDERTAKING ESTABLISHMENT, 31, Cambridge-place, Norfolk-square, Paddington. Funerals conducted with economy and respectability to meet the wants of all classes. See prospectus.—W. H. STOCKWELL.

SHILLIBEER'S ECONOMIC FUNERAL ESTABLISHMENTS are 53, City-road, Finsbury-square, London, and North-street-quadrant, Brighton. All needless cost avoided.

MEMORIAL BRASSES.—FRANK SMITH and Co.

CHRISTMAS CHURCH DECORATIONS.
Priced list on application.

CHRISTMAS OFFERINGS for the CHURCH and CLERGY.—A LIST of appropriate GIFTS forwarded upon application. A variety of objects may be inspected at the warehouse.

FRANK SMITH and Co.'s CATALOGUE of CHURCH FITTINGS, &c., forwarded upon receipt of six stamps. —Ecclesiastical Warehouse, 13, Southampton-street, Strand, London, W.C.

MONUMENTS, Tombs, and Tablets, in Granite, Marble, or Stone.—Designs and estimates forwarded on application to W. H. BURKE and Co., Warwick-house, 142, Regent-street, and 17, Newman-street, London.

MONUMENTAL SCULPTURE.—GRANITE, MARBLE, and STONE TOMBS ON VIEW. The largest manufactured stock in the kingdom.—GAFFIN, the Carrara Marble Works, 63, Regent-quadrant, London, W.

MONUMENTAL SCULPTURE, Monuments, Tablets, Marble and Granite Tombs, Crosses and Memorial Brasses; IMPERISHABLE LETTERS in SOLID LEAD.—GAFFIN, the Carrara Marble Works, 63, Regent-quadrant, London W.

CLAIRVOYANCE, Somnambule Extralucide.—Mme. FONTENELLE, 41, Baker-street. Séance tous les jours de 2 h. à 4 h. Prix, une guinée; luncheon and evening parties, 20 guineas.

TO AMERICAN BUYERS.—T. Bicque and E. Durresoir, 19, Gresham-street (corner of Wood-street), and No. 108, rue Faubourg St. Denis, fancy feather manufacturers, have a STOCK of GOODS, and can take any orders.

IRON RAILINGS for STAIRCASE.—To be DISPOSED OF, a quantity of very handsome RAILS and NEWELS, cast in iron and brass by Barbedienne, of Paris. To be seen at the Fine Art Gallery, 67, Berners-street, Oxford-street.

IRON PARK and CATTLE FENCING of every description. Hurdles, plain and ornamental gates, galvanized netting, tree guards, &c.—CHARLES GLANVILL (late John Boyd and Co.), 48, Cannon-street, London, E.C. Lists and testimonials free.

R. W. THOMSON'S PATENT ROAD STEAMERS, with indiarubber tires, for the conveyance of passenger and goods traffic in this or foreign countries, and now manufactured (under license from the patentee) by ROBEY and COMPANY (Limited), engineers, Lincoln. Full particulars and prices sent on application.

THE public are CAUTIONED against IMITATIONS of the NEW VELLUM-WOVE CLUB-HOUSE NOTE. This paper has been manufactured to meet the universally-experienced want—i.e., a paper which shall in itself combine a perfectly smooth surface with total freedom from grease. It is made from the best linen rags only, possesses great tenacity and durability, and is equally well adapted for quill or steel pens.

(Signed) PARTRIDGE and COOPER, Sole Manufacturers and Vendors, 192, Fleet-street, E.C.

CAUTION.—RADLEY'S HOTEL, SOUTHAMPTON.—Mr. Radley finds it necessary to state he has no connexion with any other hotel in the town.

CAUTION.—HARVEY'S SAUCE.—Each bottle of this celebrated sauce, prepared by E. LAZENBY and SON, bears the label, used so many years, signed "Elizabeth Lazenby."

CAUTION.—Ladies are informed that the only bona fide improvements in LADIES' SADDLES for hunting, India, and colonies have been made and registered by Messrs. LANGDON, Duke-street, Manchester-square, London. No agents.

CAUTION.—The new colour, Amy Robsart, can only be procured in IRISH POPLINS, at INGLIS and TRINKLER'S exclusive Irish poplin establishment, 167, Regent-street, London, W. Patterns post free.

CAUTION.—WILLS'S best BIRDSEYE is sold only in packets bearing the facsimile of their signature and prize medal, 1862, and the paper of each wrapper is in addition water-marked with the name and trade mark of the firm—W. D. and H. O. Wills, Bristol and London.

CAUTION to PURCHASERS of EASY CHAIRS and COUCHES.—Label.—Messrs. T. H. FILMER and SON upholsterers and decorators, beg to inform the public that all chairs and sofas of their manufacture bear a brass label, with their name and address, 28, 31, and 32, Berners-street, Oxford-street, London, W., this label being the only guarantee of their manufacture and quality.

CAUTION.—Cholera, Diarrhœa, and Fevers are mainly produced by impure water, which is the state of all water in cisterns. This is entirely remedied by using the CISTERN FILTERS supplied by the LONDON and GENERAL WATER PURIFYING COMPANY (Limited), requiring no attention (and which in London can be rented if preferred). For prospectuses, &c., apply to the Secretary, 157, Strand, W.C., four doors from Somerset-house.

CAUTION.—Savory and Moore's PANCREATIC EMULSION and PANCREATINE.—The undersigned request purchasers will observe that every bottle is labelled "Prepared by Savory and Moore," and surrounded by published reports of the experience of medical men. The label also bears their trade mark and the words Savory and Moore, chymists to the Queen, H.R.H. the Prince of Wales, &c. (Signed), SAVORY and MOORE, 143, New Bond-street, London.

CLOTHING and SHIRTS.—Notice.—Infringement of Trade Mark.—"Axe Brand Best Value for Money."—Wholesale buyers are CAUTIONED that goods of this registered brand can only be obtained from FAVELL and Co., 12, St. Mary-axe.

NOTICE.—Condensed Milk.—The undersigned beg to inform the trade that they are the SOLE WHOLESALE AGENTS for NEWNHAM'S CONDENSED MILK, prepared at Mallow, county of Cork.—CROSSE and BLACKWELL, Soho-square, London, Aug., 1870.

NOTICE.—The IRISH FRIEZES and TWEEDS, also the New Ulster Overcoat, exhibited in the Workmen's International Exhibition, have gained the Gold Medal, and can only be had of SAMUEL, BROTHERS, 50, Ludgate-hill, London. These goods are stamped every two yards "Samuel, Brothers, Irish Manufacture, warranted."—No. 50, Ludgate-hill, E.C.

THE IRON CROSS.—A charming arrangement, the form and size of the Iron Cross, of all the best PHOTOGRAPHS of the GERMAN CELEBRITIES. By post 12 stamps. Fine Art Gallery, 43, Piccadilly.—VERNON HEATH, Manager.

MINIATURES.—One, two, and three guineas for LOCKET, Bracelet, or Brooch, from Photographs taken here or elsewhere.—H. DAVIS, photographer and miniature painter, No. 36, Bruton-street, Berkeley-square.

PHOTOGRAPHS MOUNTED and BOUND, albums and scrap books arranged. Amateurs' negatives printed. Frames for paintings, drawings, chromos, and photographs of the newest designs and patterns.—Fine Art Gallery, 43, Piccadilly.—VERNON HEATH, Manager.

FOR CHRISTMAS PRESENTS, obtain a LIST of the NEW OLEOGRAPHS, facsimile copies of both old and modern masters, now ready, at Low, Son, and Marston's, 188, Fleet-street. Sent post free on receipt of postage stamp. A large assortment of these justly celebrated oil paintings, in handsome frames, may be viewed on the premises.

TWELVE CARTES de VISITE, 2s. 8d.; six, 1s. 8d. Carte enlarged to 10 inches, 5s.; cabinet size, 2s. Send carte with stamps, perfect copies returned free.—London Photographic Company, 304, Regent-street, W.—F. S. D. PHILLIPS, Manager.

COPIES of PORTRAITS, 12 for 2s. 8d.; six, 1s. 8d.; carte enlarged to 10 inches, 5s.; two copies, 7s. 6d.; do. cabinet, 2s. Send carte and stamps for perfect copies.—CITY PHOTO COPYING COMPANY, 15, Queen-street, Cheapside. Removed from No. 2.

CHROMO-LITHOGRAPHS, Oleographs, and Engravings, most suitable for wedding and other presents.—600 of these choice WORKS of ART after celebrated artists, comprising all the most charming and favourite subjects, including views in Italy, Switzerland, Germany, the Rhine, Lake Districts, and figure subjects, at wholesale prices. Parcels forwarded for approbation.—WILLIAMS and Co., 27, Gresham-street, near the Bank of England.

PAINTINGS (Modern) and WATER-COLOUR DRAWINGS.—A choice and varied collection by rising artists of repute, purchased direct from the studios, always ON VIEW. Purchasers should visit this establishment and compare prices. Shippers liberally dealt with.—WILLIAMS and Co., 27, Gresham-street, City.

OLEOGRAPHS and ENGRAVINGS. A large selection, from all the best masters, at reduced prices; also a large assortment of beautiful Pictures, framed complete, from one guinea each.—GEO. REES, 41, 42, 43, Russell-street, Covent-garden opposite Drury-lane Theatre.

PORTRAIT ALBUMS, at RODRIGUES', of the new make, with patent leather guards, four portraits on a page, interleaved for vignette and cabinet portraits, from 10s. 6d. to £10. Regimental and Presentation Albums.—42, Piccadilly, W.

TO GERMANS.—The DIELMANN ALBUM, price 15s., a collection of 12 Chromolithographs after Jacob Dielmann, with cover in cloth. Can be had direct, or through any bookseller and stationer, from Carl Kruthoffer, Frankfort-on-Maine. Agents Wanted.

STATUES and IDEAL BUSTS, executed by the late Hiram Powers, on view at the Studio, in Florence. Particulars, with prices, on application to LONGWORTH POWERS, Porta Romana, Florence. 17 photographs of same also forwarded for 6s., English stamps.

ART POTTERY.—A choice collection of original WORKS by Coleman, Ludovici, Solon, Mussell, &c., is now ON VIEW at Messrs. Goode's New Gallery, 19, South Audley-street, Grosvenor-square.

ART POTTERY.—A collection of original PAINTINGS on POTTERY, by W. S. Coleman, Ludovici, Solon-Miles, Lessore, Bouquet, and others, now ON VIEW for a short time at T. McLEAN'S New Gallery, 7, Haymarket. Admission on presentation of address card.

CAUTION.—The Potato Disease.—The potato that best resists the potato murrain is CARTER'S IMPROVED RED-SKIN FLOURBALL, which should be obtained direct from Messrs. Carter and Co., High Holborn, London, there being a great number of worthless varieties of potatoes sold as red-skin flourballs. J. C. and Co. will be happy to correspond with noblemen or gentlemen who are about planting potatoes, giving them the result of many years' experience as to the best sorts of potatoes suited to various soils and localities.—James Carter and Co., the Royal Seedsmen, Nos. 237 and 238, High Holborn, London.

VASES. WANTED, several SECOND-HAND ITALIAN MARBLE VASES, of the usual pattern, 1ft. 4½in. high by 2ft. wide. Apply, by letter, stating price, to A. B., Pike's Stationer, Chapel-street west, Mayfair.

VASES, 300 varieties, adapted to every style of building. Warranted to hold the earth during winter. At prices from 10s. to £30 each.—AUSTIN and SEELEY, 369 to 375, Euston-road. Also dial pillars and balustrading.

DISSOLVING VIEWS.—NEWTON and Co.'s LANTERNS and SLIDES, from 7s. 6d.; Newton's celebrated and greatly improved phantasmagoria lanterns, as supplied to Government, complete in cases, £3 3s. The slides are painted on the premises by first-rate artists. Any subject to order. Descriptive lectures for many of the sets. Illustrated price lists for four stamps.—Newton, Manufacturing Optician to the Queen, 3, Fleet-street, Temple-bar.

NEWTON'S CHEAP ASTRONOMICAL TELESCOPE, 4 feet long, 3-in. achromatic glass, day and night powers, on tripod stand. Will show Saturn's ring, the principal double stars, and read a church clock at 10 miles, £5. Brass body, rack focus, £6 10s. Tourists' telescopes, 10s. to £3; opera glasses, 21s. to £6.—3, Fleet-street.

THE Misses COST have the honour to announce that their CLASSES for their CALLANTHROPIC and CALISTHENIC EXERCISES, Deportment, and Dancing, are held at their residence, 65a, Baker-street, W. Special classes for the exercises. Private lessons and lessons at schools.

CALISTHENICS (superior instruction), privately or in educational establishments, by Captain T. KESSI, principally on Dr. Schreber's celebrated method, which is held in the highest repute on the continent. All exercises without any apparatus or instruments. 18 years of experience and the highest references.. Terms 10s. 6d. per lesson, to any number of pupils.—50, St. John's-wood-terrace, N.W.

CAPTAIN CHIOSSO'S BAYSWATER GYMNASIUM and FENCING SCHOOL, 48, Norfolk-terrace, Westbourne-grove. Open from 9 a.m. to 10 p.m. Single lessons and classes every hour of the day. Mme. Chiosso holds calisthenic and gymnastic classes for ladies; also attends schools and private families.

CAPTAIN CHIOSSO'S LONDON GYMNASIUM and FENCING SCHOOL, 123, Oxford-street, Regent-circus. Open from 9 a.m. to 10 p.m. Single lessons and classes every hour of the day. Ladies' classes for drilling and deportment at 12, on Tuesday, Thursday, and Saturday, superintended by Mme. Chiosso.

GRIFFITHS' NEW WEST LONDON GYMNASIUM, 21, Soho-square.—Mr. T. GRIFFITHS (16 years manager to the late Captain Chiosso) gives LESSONS in FENCING, gymnastics, single stick, the gloves, &c., 9 a.m. to 10 p.m. Ladies' Calisthenic and Drilling Class, Mondays, Wednesdays, and Saturdays, at 12 o'clock.

FENCING, Sabre, Boxing, Drilling.—Mr. WAITE, Professor of Fencing, late 2d Life Guards and Pupil of M. Prevost, with Assistants. Classes 4 to 7 daily, and 7 to 9 Wednesday and Friday. Private Lessons at any hour.—22, Golden-square, W.

NOTICE.—BAILEY'S IMPROVED BELTS, Elastic Stockings, &c., can only be obtained at their new address, No. 16, Oxford-street, London, W. (late of 418, directly opposite).

NOTICE.—FISHER'S GLADSTONE BAG.—We have no agents for the sale of this bag. Buyers are requested to notice that the genuine Gladstone Travelling Bag is stamped in gold in a garter.—Fisher, 188, Strand.

NOTICE.—MINTON'S CHINA.—Messrs. GOODE'S only depots are at 15, South-street, 16, South-street, 18, South Audley-street, 19, South Audley-street. The goods entrance is at No. 15, South-street, and the carriage entrance is at 19, South Audley-street, Grosvenor-square.

NOTICE of REMOVAL.—The PALL-MALL.—This RESTAURANT is now REMOVED to more spacious and commodious premises, 14, Regent-street, Waterloo-place (embracing the late Gallery of Illustrations). Entrance to private rooms in Carlton-street adjacent.

LOST DOGS.—A large number waiting to be owned at the HOME for LOST DOGS, Lower Wandsworth-road, Battersea (York-road Station). Apply between 10 and 4, except Sunday.

PREFERMENT.—The Patron of a Benefice, situate in a good midland county, with railway station in parish, net income £250, and very good residence, desires to SELL the ADVOWSON, and, in favour of a suitable clergyman, would accept of a moderate price. Immediate legal possession. Address Mr. W. Emery Stark, 27, Bedford-street, Strand, W.C.

SHOOTING WANTED, in Surrey.—WANTED, within reach of Dorking by road or rail, good MIXED SHOOTING over 1,000 acres and upwards. Apply to White and Sons, Estate Agents, Dorking, Surrey.

EIGHTEEN HUNDRED and SEVENTY FOUR.—Chymists and Medicine Vendors requiring useful and attractive BUSINESS CIRCULARS, with their names and addresses attached, can have a supply gratis, by sending instructions as to enclosure, &c., to T. ROBERTS and Co., 8, Crane-court, Fleet-street, E.C.

RARE POSTAGE STAMPS:—Corrientes (issued in 1856), Argentine Republic 1862, and Buenos Ayres 1859-62. Several unused. 45 in all. For terms apply to Bates, Hendy, and Co., 4, Old Jewry, E.C.

TO be SOLD, for £32 (cost £60 a short time ago), a GENTLEMAN'S superb DIAMOND RING, single brilliant, of great lustre and purity, set in 22 carat gold. May be seen at 22, Ludgate-hill.

VALUABLE SOUVENIR.—For SALE, the SNUFF-BOX (Tabatière) which has been in personal use by the great composer MICHAEL HAYDN. Address D 5532, care of Mr. Rudolf Mosse, Munich, Bavaria.

NORWICH and COLCHESTER.—ANTIQUES, Curiosities, Rare Porcelains, &c. SAMUEL, 2, Timber-hill, Norwich, and 73, High-street, Colchester, has frequently specimens of interest to collectors and connoisseurs.

A Valuable COLLECTION of AUTOGRAPHS to be SOLD, comprising those of Her Majesty the Queen, King George I., King George III., Duke of Wellington, Lord Palmerston, Lord Brougham, and other of the most noted members of the past generation of politicians, beside many Archbishops, Dukes, Marquises, &c., numbering in all over 300 signatures. Apply to Gadsden, Ellis, and Co., Auctioneers, 18, Old Broad-street.

THERMOSCOPIC SPECTACLES—a new invention.—NEGRETTI and ZAMBRA.

NEGRETTI and ZAMBRA'S THERMOSCOPIC SPECTACLES—a new invention, which they can confidently recommend to wearers of spectacles as superior in every respect to all at present in use. Description post free.

OPERA and FIELD GLASSES, Telescopes, &c.—NEGRETTI and ZAMBRA.

NEGRETTI and ZAMBRA'S NEW ENCYCLOPÆDIC CATALOGUE of PHILOSOPHICAL, Mathematical, and Meteorological APPARATUS, &c., now ready. 1,100 engravings and numerous tables of reference. Price 5s. 6d.—Holborn-viaduct; No. 45, Cornhill; and 122, Regent-street.

JOHN WHITEHOUSE'S SPECTACLES are the best. They suit the sight, fit the face, and do not fatigue the eyes. In elastic steel frames, 3s. 6d.; with pebbles, from 10s. 6d. —John Whitehouse, Practical Optician, 8, Coventry-street, near the top of the Haymarket. No other address.

OLD AGE or ACCIDENT, not Disease, should end our days.—Pamphlet on Use of the Portable Turkish Bath, for Curing Diseases, four stamps, by C. Hunter, of Calcutta. Rheumatism, gout, sluggish liver, &c., cured by HUNTER'S newly-invented PORTABLE TURKISH, Vapour, and Hot-air BATHS. Price, complete, 21s. and 42s. Sole agent, T. HAWKSLEY, 4, Blenheim-street, Bond-street, W. Vide leader in Daily Telegraph, Feb. 7, 1870.

CAUTION.——Eau de Cologne.——Mr. JOHANN MARIA FARINA, opposite the Julich's Place, Cologne, sole Purveyor to Her Majesty Queen Victoria and their Royal Highnesses the Prince and Princess of Wales, begs to caution the public against spurious imitations of his Eau de Cologne. His label, which has never been altered, bears his name and address as below, without the addition of any number, in black letters on a plain white ground—Johann Maria Farina, gegenuber dem Julich's Platz. It can be obtained of all respectable firms daling in perfumery.—Cologne, February, 1873.

DUCHESS of EDINBURGH. —— PIESSE and LUBIN, with consummate skill, have produced a new and exquisite BOUQUET PERFUME in honour of the Duchess of Edinburgh. "Woods and groves are of thy dressing, hill and dale doth boast thy blessing; thus we salute thee with our early song, and welcome thee and wish thee long." Sold in bottles, 2s. 6d. to 21s. each, in all parts of the globe.—Piesse and Lubin, Royal Perfumers, 2, New Bond-street, London, W.

COLD CREAM of ROSES.—PIESSE and LUBIN prepare this exquisite cosmetic with the greatest care, fresh daily, in jars, 1s. Cold cream soap, free from alkali, 2s. per lb. Sold by all fashionable druggists and perfumers. Be sure to ask for Piesse and Lubin's manufactures, to prevent disappointment.—Laboratory of Flowers, 2, New Bond-street.

FRAGRANT SOAP.—The celebrated UNITED SERVICE TABLET is famed for its delightful fragrance and beneficial effect on the skin. Manufactured by J. C. and J. FIELD, patentees of the self-fitting candles. Sold by chymists, oil and Italian warehousemen, and others. Use no other. See name on each tablet.

WHITE HANDS.—Use MARRIS'S ALMOND TABLET regularly after washing, and the hands will become white, soft, and smooth. Invaluable after sea bathing. 6d. and 1s., by post seven or 14 stamps.—Marris, 37, Berners-street, Oxford-street, W.; Staircase, Soho Bazaar; and all chymists. It is not a soap.

FURROWS in the SKIN, also indentations and flabbiness of flesh, quickly removed by the use of ALEX. ROSS'S SKIN TONIC, which is such an astringent and tightening liquid as to make all faces young in look. 3s. 6d. Sent for stamps.—Alex. Ross, No. 248, High Holborn, London, opposite Day and Martin's.

HAIR DYE. —— BATCHELOR'S INSTANTANEOUS COLUMBIAN, the best in the world, black or brown. The only one that remedies the evil effects of bad dyes. 4s. 6d., 7s., and 14s., of all perfumers and chymists. Wholesale, R. HOVENDEN and SONS, 5, Great Marlborough-street, W., and 93 and 95 City-road, E.C.

DOES YOUR HAIR TURN GRAY? Then use HERRING'S PATENT MAGNETIC BRUSHES and COMBS. Brushes, 10s. and 15s. each; combs, 2s. 6d., 5s., 7s. 6d., 10s., 15s., 20s. each. Pamphlets on application. Depots, 5, Great Marlborough-street, W., 93 and 95, City-road, E.C.; and all perfumers.

GOLDEN HAIR.—ROBARE'S AUREOLINE produces, by two or three applications, the beautiful golden colour so much admired. Warranted not to destroy the hair. Price 5s. 6d. and 10s. 6d., of all perfumers and chymists. Wholesale, R. Hovenden and Sons, 5, Great Marlborough-street, W., and 93 and 95, City-road, E.C., London; Pinaud and Meyer, Boul. de Strasbourg 37, Paris; 31, Graben, Vienna; 44, Rue de Longs Charlots, Brussels; Caswell, Hazard, and Co., Fifth Avenue, Broadway, New York.

PROFESSOR BROWNE'S WIGS and SCALPS from 30s.

PROFESSOR BROWNE'S LADIES' HEAD-DRESSES.

PROFESSOR BROWNE'S CHIGNONS, of every design, suitable for the present fashion.

PROFESSOR BROWNE'S FRONTS, Bands, Plaits, Curls, and Curls on Combs.

PROFESSOR BROWNE has the largest **STOCK** of ORNAMENTAL HAIR in the world, always on view at his establishment, 47, Fenchurch-street, London.

PROFESSOR BROWNE'S PILO-CHROMATIC, for restoring Gray or White Hair to its natural shade. Price 5s., 7s. 6d., or 15s.

PROFESSOR BROWNE'S TONIC LOTION, for ladies; used for thickening the hair at the roots, near the partings: also for re-producing the hair on bald places. By the application of this lotion eyebrows have been restored.—47, Fenchurch-st., E.C.

PROFESSOR BROWNE'S HAIR-DYE.—This unequalled LIQUID HAIR-DYE is the only one extant that will produce a natural black or brown without injury to the skin, and is also free from smell. Prices 3s. 6d., 5s. 6d., and 10s. 6d. per case. Forwarded on receipt of stamps. F. Browne, 47, Fenchurch-street, London. Private rooms for hair-dyeing. Hair brushed by machinery.

CHRISTMAS CARDS at CHAPMAN'S, from the most eminent publishers, De la Rue, Marcus Ward, Goodall, Prang's American, Eyre and Spottiswoode, Rothe, and Hildesheimer.—T. Chapman, Stationer, 54, Leicester-square, W.C.

CHRISTMAS CARDS at CHAPMAN'S.—Special Notice.—All Proof Copies, vastly superior to those advertised at trade price or sold by cheap drapers.—T. Chapman, Stationer, No. 54, Leicester-square.

CHRISTMAS CARDS.—PARKINS and GOTTO'S.

ALL CHRISTMAS CARDS TRADE PRICE.—
10,000 CHRISTMAS PRESENTS.

1d. Cards, 8d. per dozen	6d. Cards, 4d. each
2d. Cards, 1s. 4d. per dozen	9d. Cards, 6d. each
4d. Cards, 3d. each	1s. Cards, 8d. each, and so on.

The largest and most varied stock in London.—25, Oxford-street, W.

PARKINS and GOTTO'S CHRISTMAS CARDS.

CHRISTMAS PRESENTS (TEN THOUSAND).—
PARKINS and GOTTO'S.

Portrait Albums	7s.	Purses	1s.	Dressing Bags	21s.
Scrap Books ..	5s.	Card Cases ..	2s.	Dressing Cases	21s.
Hand Bags ..	7s.	Cigar Cases ..	5s.	Despatch Boxes	21s.
Work Boxes ..	6s.	Cigar Cabinets ..	21s.	Writing Cases ..	5s.
Work Baskets ..	6s.	Match Boxes	2s.6d.	Inkstands ..	6s.
Jewel Cases ..	21s.	Card Trays	10s.6d.	Envelope Cases, Blotting Books	20s.
Brush Cases ..	21s.	Chess	3s.	Tea Caddies	6s.6d.
Reticules ..	5s.	Draughts ..	2s.	Music Cases	6s.6d.
Glove Boxes ..	6s.	Backgammon ..	5s.	Portfolios ..	3s.
Scent Cases ..	21s.	Magic Lanterns	7s.6d.	Papeteries ..	3s.
Opera Glasses ..	14s.	Dominoes ..	3s.	Flasks	2s.
Smelling Bottles	5s.	Bagatelle ..	28s.6d.	Paint Boxes ..	1s.
Musical Boxes ..	21s.	Bésique	2s.	Paper Knives ..	2s.
Desks ..	5s.6d.	Coursing Games	21s.	Ivory Brushes ..	13s.
Stationery Cabinets ..	25s.	Boxes of Games	21s.	Liqueur Cases	31s.6d.
		Card Boxes	10s.6d.	Letter Boxes ..	15s.
Ivory Pencils ..	3s.	Watches, silver ..	45s.	Letter Cases	1s.6d.
Gold	20s.	Clocks	21s.	Elegant Fans ..	5s.
Silver	7s.	Silver Jewellery	4s.6d.	Postage Scales	6s.6d.
Aluminium ..	1s.	Bracelets, Necklets	10s.	Portrait Frames	1s.
Graphoscopes ..	35s.			Tool Boxes ..	2s.
Stereoscopes ..	4s.	Brooches, Earrings ..	4s. 6d.	Pocket Books ..	1s.
Scissor Cases ..	18s.				
Bookslides ..	21s.	Jet Jewellery ..	3s.9d.		

Children's Gift Books of all kinds; Bibles, Prayer Books, and Church Services; Ornamental Articles for Mantel-shelf and Writing Table; In-door Games of every kind. The largest stock in Europe of the above goods.—Parkins and Gotto, 27 and 28, Oxford-street. By special appointment to H.R.H. the Princess of Wales and H.I.H. the Crown Princess of Germany.